ADOLESCENT SELF-INJURY

AMELIO A. D'ONOFRIO, PHD, is clinical professor and director of the Psychological Services Institute in the Graduate School of Education at Fordham University. He holds degrees from Georgetown University (BS, 1985), The University of Chicago (MA, 1987), and Fordham University (PhD, 1995). Since 1994, he has served on the faculty of the Graduate School of Education at Fordham University, where he teaches and provides clinical supervision to students in the doctoral program in counseling psychology. His teaching and clinical interests include developmental psychopathology, interpersonal and existential approaches to psychotherapy, the neuropsychobiology of affect regulation, and clinical supervision.

DR. D'ONOFRIO is also a consulting psychologist at Loyola School, a private Jesuit high school in New York City, where he provides direct services to students and advises faculty, administrators, and parents on adolescent development and on matters affecting student life.

His professional experience includes serving in a number of leadership capacities for the U. S. Department of Veterans Affairs (VA) Medical Centers in the New York metropolitan area as well as serving on national committees responsible for developing VA-wide treatment protocols and establishing best practices in clinical services. He was chief of domiciliary care (psychosocial rehabilitation) for homeless veterans at the New York Harbor VA Health Care System and managed the clinical education and leadership development programs at the Hudson Valley VA Health Care System.

DR. D'ONOFRIO lectures widely to mental health professionals on a variety of topics in psychopathology, human development, and psychotherapy process issues. He maintains a private practice in adolescent and adult psychotherapy in New York City and can be contacted through his Web site at http://drdonofrio.com.

Adolescent Self-Injury

A Comprehensive Guide for Counselors and Health Care Professionals

Amelio A. D'Onofrio, PhD

SPRINGER PUBLISHING COMPANY

New York

Copyright © 2007 Springer Publishing Company, LLC.

Springer Publishing Company, LLC
11 West 42nd Street
New York, NY 10036
www.springerpub.com

Acquisitions Editor: Philip Laughlin
Production Editor: Carol Cain
Cover design by Joanne E. Honigman
Typeset by Apex Publishing, LLC

07 08 09 10/ 5 4 3 2

Library of Congress Cataloging-in-Publication Data

D'Onofrio, Amelio A.
  Adolescent self-injury : a comprehensive guide for counselors and health care professionals / Amelio A. D'Onofrio.
      p. cm.
  Includes bibliographical references and index.
  ISBN-13: 978-0-8261-0278-2 (alk. paper)
  ISBN-10: 0-8261-0278-6 (alk. paper)
  1. Self-destructive behavior in adolescence. I. Title.
  [DNLM: 1. Adolescent Behavior. 2. Self-Injurious Behavior. 3. Adolescent. WS 463 D687a 2007]

RJ506.S39D66 2007
616.85'8200835--dc22

2006036614

Printed in the United States of America by Edwards Brothers.

For
Albina, Clemente, Pietro, and Alfredo

Contents

Preface

Self-injury—the intentional cutting, burning, or otherwise wounding of the body without the intent to die—once a behavior found primarily among the severely mentally ill, has, in recent years, grown to almost epidemic proportions in the general adolescent population. Counselors, health care professionals, and adolescents themselves tell stories of how cutting or other acts of self-mutilation have become pervasive in contemporary youth culture. These ubiquitous behaviors now compete for increased clinical attention and, as such, are beginning to take their rightful place in the pantheon of the more common, better understood, and perhaps more "acceptable" forms of self-destructive acts typical of the adolescent years.

Those of us who work with adolescents have become all too familiar with (and perhaps even somewhat immune to) the destructiveness of the more typical acting-out behaviors of the young people in our charge—binge drinking, drug use, unsafe sexual practices, and disordered eating, as well as the other high-risk behaviors that invariably compromise their safety and well-being. In fact, within some adolescent subcultures, behaviors such as these have come to be considered rights of passage or badges of honor required for group membership. The prevailing attitudes seem to suggest that if one doesn't drink to the point of passing out, one is clearly not part of the fun in-crowd; or, if someone isn't sexually active, there must be something seriously wrong with him or her. In turn, we professionals have become so familiar with some of these commonplace forms of negative self-expression that many of us feel desensitized to the shock value and, perhaps, even to the actual dangerousness of some of these behaviors.

Educators and mental health professionals in the school or college setting have accordingly come to expect that adolescents will drink to excess, act out sexually, develop disordered eating patterns, and engage in other high-risk behaviors. We have come to understand these *indirect* forms of self-harm to be "normal" ways adolescents struggle to find their place in the world and deal with their problems. Many numb, medicate, or otherwise distance themselves from the difficult-to-tolerate feelings they may have about their emerging adulthood, problems at home, or difficulties in their peer relationships. As we have come to better understand how their distress is voiced through these *indirect* yet self-destructive ways, we have also learned how to more accurately conceptualize what those behaviors may represent and have, accordingly, developed effective approaches to respond, assess, and intervene.

More elusive, however, has been our understanding of the more *direct* form of adolescent self-destructiveness that, in recent years, has come to be embodied through the phenomenon of self-injury. Intentional self-injury refers to the deliberate, nonsuicidal disfigurement or destruction of bodily tissue, usually accomplished by cutting, scratching, or burning the skin, picking at wounds, inserting objects into the body, or banging one's head. While self-injury is not a new phenomenon and has been an accepted form of self-expression in some cultures and traditions (Favazza, 1996), its current manifestation in the adolescent population is clearly disturbing and represents a socially unacceptable form of self-expression (Walsh, 2006; Walsh & Rosen, 1988). Until recently, self-injury has rarely been examined as a phenomenon in itself but has been associated with other forms of psychopathology, most notably with depression and suicidality and with borderline personality disorder (Favazza, 1998; Hodgson, 2004). It had predominantly been thought of as a behavioral characteristic associated with severely disturbed adolescents found on inpatient psychiatric units or in residential treatment programs. But, to the shock and dismay of many, self-injury has now become significantly more pervasive in the general adolescent population and is often seen in nonclinical settings such as schools (Muehlenkamp, 2005) and college campuses (Whitlock, Eckenrode, & Silverman, 2006). As a result, school counselors, teachers, coaches, nurses, social workers, psychologists, and student life personnel working in these settings have now become the frontline responders who are usually the first to identify individuals who engage in self-injury and who are, therefore, the first compelled to intervene.

Consequently, the educational environment has emerged as the primary place in which adolescents who engage in self-injury first come to the attention of others and, therefore, as the place where the provision of care can often begin. Typical scenarios include situations in which students who may be concerned about a friend may confide in a trusted teacher or counselor about the friend who is cutting or burning herself. Students may approach an RA or other student life staff member on the college campus about a roommate who cuts. Or, school personnel—coaches, nurses, and administrators—may inadvertently come across signs of scarring or other evidence of bodily injury and are then faced with the task of addressing what they have noticed. What characteristically follows is that these individuals (the untrained frontline responders) often become overwhelmed by the mysteriousness, irrationality, and seeming deviancy of the self-injurious behaviors they encounter and are usually at a loss as how to take action and be of help to the student in need.

The very thought of having to respond to someone who cuts and scars herself can evoke terrifying and disturbing emotions in helpers. They may feel horror and disgust, on one hand, and, on the other, may experience a profound sense of sadness and powerlessness. They may feel helpless at their inability to come to terms with the seeming senselessness of the behavior and may become anxious about not knowing how to best intervene. As a result of these powerful reactions, the quality of their responses can vary dramatically, and the care administered can be compromised. Some helpers, who may feel shocked, overwhelmed, or angered by the behavior, may trivialize or ignore it, attributing it to the manipulative, attention-seeking maneuvers of the adolescent. Others may misidentify it as a suicide attempt and then mobilize accordingly (Favazza, 1998). Unfortunately, neither approach is well suited to effectively facilitate either the immediate assessment needs of the situation or the longer-term treatment of the individual engaging in the self-injury.

THE INTENT OF THIS BOOK

This book is written with the intention of assisting frontline professionals in developing a thorough working understanding of the nature, meaning, and function of adolescent self-injurious behavior. In doing so, it draws together seemingly disparate but, in fact, converging perspectives from the research literature in psychology, psychiatry, nursing, sociology, and feminist studies in order to paint a textured landscape of the issues involved and of the individuals who engage in the behavior. Where appropriate, the words of self-injurers themselves will be used to tell their stories. Their words are particularly poignant as they come from individuals who generally experience themselves as silenced and voiceless. Self-injury, as presented in this book, is conceptualized as *symptom*. It is a symptom of a more complex phenomenon. It is a physical manifestation of profound psychological wounding that is often inaccessible to the sufferer and, as such, represents a kind of psychological pain that is literally *unspeakable*. Self-injurers speak their pain through their acts of self-harm.

The book begins by exploring the current proliferation of adolescent self-injury, examining its nature and complexity, and identifying the challenges frontline professionals face in addressing this new epidemic. The lack of understanding of the phenomenon has helped create, in the eyes of the uninformed, a new subculture of seeming deviants who cut and mutilate themselves and have come to be seen as "fringe" characters who are mysterious, bizarre, and, perhaps, also dangerous. Even counselors and health care professionals who have little experience working with these individuals are frequently hesitant to engage these clients and, when they do, do so with trepidation and fear. Because of their lack of training and understanding, many professionals report feeling ill prepared to respond effectively to these individuals. They lack confidence in their ability to help and, therefore, are less willing to more fully invest themselves in the service of these clients (McAllister, 2003; Rayner, Allen, & Johnson, 2005; Roberts-Dobie, 2005). The purpose of the first part of the book is to provide frontline professionals with a comprehensive understanding of the etiology, dynamics, and phenomenology of self-injury so that they can more clearly see and make contact with the person behind the behavior. With greater awareness and knowledge about the phenomenon (and the person), one can more readily experience empathy and bridge the psychological distance between the injurer and the helper. Understanding can powerfully transform revulsion and fear and can more authentically bring to the fore the humanity of the individual who presents him- or herself to us for help.

Following the examination of the core phenomenological issues related to self-injury, the focus of the book shifts to the integration of understanding with practice. The steps for engaging and assessing self-injurers are reviewed, and guidelines are provided that escort the helper through the process. The guidelines are written with the school or college professional in mind, as they are often the first to respond to distressed adolescents who intentionally wound their bodies. These frontline personnel are frequently in the best position to conduct initial assessments and mobilize the appropriate resources to best effect referral and initiate treatment (American Academy of Pediatrics, 2004; American School Counselor Association, 2004; Roberts-Dobie, 2005). The assessment, triage, and referral protocols provided herein will, in essence, walk the counselor step by step through the process, from the point of initial contact with the self-injuring student, to developing a working alliance, to treatment, to exploring posttreatment follow-up considerations.

The final section of this book explores the role of the frontline responder in working with parents, teachers, administrators, student life personnel, and other stakeholders. It offers suggestions for creating both effective pathways to care and establishing support networks that will facilitate the recovery and reintegration of the self-injurer into the school or college setting.

The reader will note that individuals who engage in self-injurious behavior are referred to in this book as "self-injurers." The label "self-injurer" is used descriptively and for literary convenience. It does not imply that self-injury is the defining characteristic of who these individuals are. These are individuals *who* self-injure. The label should by no means diminish the complexity and depth of their humanity. They are much more than their self-destructive behaviors.

It should also be noted that in cases in which actual clients are quoted, names and other identifying characteristics have been changed. Additionally, the feminine pronoun is used more frequently in most third-person references. Although the rate of self-injury among men is on the rise, to date the preponderance of self-injurers who have come to the attention of clinicians and who have presented for treatment have been overwhelmingly female.

ORGANIZATION OF THE BOOK

In order to accomplish these goals, the book is divided into three parts. Part I, *The Nature and Paradox of Self-Injury* (Chapters 1–5), provides a working overview of the central descriptive and classification issues of the phenomenon. Chapter 1 identifies the overarching challenges counselors and health care professionals on the frontlines face in responding to adolescent self-injury. Chapter 2 focuses on defining, categorizing, and situating self-injury in historical and psychiatric context. Chapter 3 explores the environmental and developmental conditions that may predispose an individual to self-injury. The hypothesis that early relational trauma serves as a foundational condition for the developmental of self-injurious behaviors is examined, and a tentative profile of self-injuring adolescents is offered. Chapter 4 presents the specific developmental effects of trauma by illustrating parallels between the trauma outcome literature and characteristics identified in self-injurers. Chapter 5 concludes Part I of the book with an explication of the adolescent's phenomenological experience of the behavior itself and the role and function the behavior plays in maintaining the individual's psychological equilibrium.

Part II, *Engagement, Assessment, and Treatment* (Chapters 6–8), constitutes the clinical core of the text. Chapter 6 outlines the difficulties of engaging self-injurers and advocates a firm yet empathic and compassionate approach in meeting the person behind the self-destructive behavior. Specific assessment guidelines are then presented in Chapter 7. This chapter outlines the necessary steps to be taken in regards to assessment, triage, and referral facilitation. Part II concludes with an overview of the longer-term treatment process and outlines interventions targeted to redress deficiencies in specific psychosocial domains of functioning.

Finally, Part III, *Creating Pathways to Care* (Chapters 9–10), addresses some of the important ancillary considerations vital to the intervention process. Chapter 9 explores mechanisms for creating an environment of care for the adolescent in the school environment and on the college campus. It outlines how the counselor can play a consultative role by coordinating communication among teachers, administrators, student life personnel, and parents and offers practical suggestions on developing institutional policies and protocols for the effective management of students in distress like self-injurers. Chapter 9 also examines dispositional issues appropriate to the school and college campus setting, respectively, and provides guidelines for the prevention of contagion of self-injury in those settings. Finally, personal and professional challenges that responders face in working with this population are discussed in Chapter 10. Suggestions for self-care to help mitigate burnout are proposed, and strategies for maintaining hope in spite of the difficulty of the work are offered.

Acknowledgments

There are many people who shared in the shaping of this book. Some have contributed indirectly through the influence they have had on the development of my clinical philosophy, which serves as the backdrop for what I offer in the pages that follow. Others have helped more directly with this project through their willingness to help me refine my thinking about self-injury through our many conversations that have spanned months, if not years. Others still have contributed to this work through their encouragement, ongoing support, and good humor. To all these friends and colleagues, I am grateful.

More specifically, I want to thank Dr. Paul Greene and Dr. Linda Larkin, two of my postdoctoral clinical supervisors, who had a profound impact on my therapeutic understanding at the formative stages of my professional development. I learned from them, in different ways, the centrality of therapeutic presence in the healing we offer our patients and experienced firsthand from them the possibilities for growth that emerge when "held" well. What I learned from them remains foundational for my current work as a psychotherapist.

I want to thank Dr. James J. Hennessy, Dean of the Graduate School of Education at Fordham University and my doctoral adviser. I am grateful for his continuous support over the years and for the confidence he has demonstrated in me by the many professional opportunities he has steered my way. In particular, I thank him for his encouragement in pursuing this project and for supporting me through its execution.

I thank my colleagues and friends who have provided helpful feedback on parts of the manuscript, who allowed me to use them as sounding boards for my ideas, or who simply provided the intellectual clearing that allow me to engage more deeply in the life of the mind. Specifically, I thank Dr. Vincent Alfonso, Dr. Matt Bolton, Dr. Seamus Carey, Augusta Habeck, MSEd, Thomas Hanley, MSEd, Mara Kushner, MSW, and Dr. Stephen O'Sullivan. I also thank Ryan Androsiglio, Allison Burnett Ventura, and Julie Balzano, my graduate assistants, for their interest in the project and for being willing to help make it come to fruition.

I thank Dr. Joseph Ponterotto for his steadfast support throughout the writing of this book. His practical insights into the process of transforming ideas into words on the page were incredibly helpful. I especially appreciate his enthusiastic encouragement in those moments when the ideas failed to flow easily and when the writing process seemed to stall. His suggestions reignited my imagination.

Most of all, however, I want to thank Dr. Ingrid Grieger for her immeasurable assistance on this book. In our nearly 20 years of friendship and frequent professional collaboration, Dr. Grieger's expert professional practice has been a model for my own growth as a clinician. Many of the ideas presented in this book first emerged out of our many conversations about our respective work with our patients. Her clinical wisdom and insights have added depth and texture to the pages that follow. Her meticulous reading of early drafts of each chapter, along with her astute editorial comments, has enhanced the quality of this book significantly and given it a clarity that it would otherwise not have had. For her help on this project and for her friendship, I am deeply grateful.

I am grateful to Alfredo, Elissa, Massimo, and Albina for the many ways they demonstrate their love and understanding. For all their patience and support, I offer them my most heartfelt gratitude with admiration, respect, and all my love.

Finally, I want to thank two very special groups of people who continuously challenge and inspire me in my work. First, I thank my students in the Counseling Psychology Doctoral Program at Fordham University for their indulgence and trust. It is with them that I often "float" my yet-unformed ideas, and it is the intellectual risks that they take with me that allow those ideas to achieve greater maturity. For their willingness to be open to the unknown and to come along for the ride, I thank them. Second, and perhaps most important of all, I thank my many patients who, over the years, have allowed me to participate in their journeys and, in doing so, have enriched my life tremendously. For the honor of being their witness and for all they have taught me about the courage to strive to love well in spite of our suffering, I offer my most profound gratitude.

PART I

The Nature and Paradox of Self-Injury

The body is the guardian of the truth, our truth, because it carries the experience of a lifetime and ensures that we can live with the truth of our organism.

Alice Miller, *The Body Never Lies*

In so far as the mind is stronger than the body, so are the ills contracted by the mind more severe than those contracted by the body.

Marcus Cicero, *The Phillipics*

Scars have the strange power to remind us that the past is real.

Cormac McCarthy, *All the Pretty Horses*

CHAPTER 1

Introduction: Self-Injury
on the Frontlines

I want someone who I can talk to, who treats me like a real person and makes me feel that I'm cared about. I want help to understand myself and feel in control of my life. I want to stop hurting myself, to learn other ways of coping. I don't want to be made to feel ashamed of myself anymore, ashamed of what I do to mentally survive.

Lucy (in Smith, Cox, & Saradjian, 1999, p. 72)

At the final bell announcing the end of the school day, you notice Jessica and Abby hesitantly standing near the door of the guidance office. In a reticent, barely audible voice, Abby asks if they can come in and talk with you. You invite them in and close the door, and after a few awkward seconds of silence—with Jessica and Abby exchanging glances as if to see who will speak first—Jessica cautiously offers that they have something important to tell you. She explains that they are "really worried" about their friend Beth. They go on to report that in the past several months Beth's home life has deteriorated. Her father's drinking problems are causing havoc in the family, and her parents are on the verge of divorce. Beth finds herself in constant arguments with her mother and seems always sad, and her own drinking on weekends has gotten out of control. They then add that this past summer Beth confided to them that she occasionally cuts herself with a razor on her arms and legs. They've tried to be supportive by being with her as much as possible in the hope that she wouldn't cut herself, but that hasn't worked. To the contrary, Beth is cutting more frequently now, and they're "really scared." They don't know what to do, and they want you to help.

You are a psychologist at the college counseling center and receive a call from the Director of Residential Life informing you that the previous night, a female resident who was extremely intoxicated engaged in self-injury sufficient to result in admission to the emergency room at the local hospital. The student had inflicted deep cuts on her arms, resulting in significant bleeding, which was subsequently observed by her roommates, who were, understandably, very distressed about the incident. The student who self-injured was about to be released from the hospital after having her wounds treated, and she wanted to immediately return to her room in the residence hall. Her roommates do not want her to return because they believe she will do this again. The Director of Residential Life is calling you for help in deciding whether the student should be allowed to return to her room and is asking you to help address the roommates' concerns.

Christine checks into the nurse's office and asks to see you because she is not feeling well. As you finish with another student, you see Christine in the waiting area appearing tired and teary eyed. While escorting her into your office, you ask her how she is doing because she looks very sad. Christine begins to cry. Between her sobs, she shares with you that she didn't sleep much last night because her parents were fighting. "They're always fighting. They hate each other. I hate them. I wish they would stop," she volunteers. "They're always so self-absorbed and never listen to anything I have to say. It's as if I don't count at all. Every time I tell my mother how bad I'm feeling, she tells me to 'get over it' because there are lots of other people worse off than me. And my father, well, he doesn't even know I exist." As you continue to listen, she adds, "I can't take this anymore. I don't know what to do. I feel like I'm losing it. I've been doing some stupid things, and I don't want to do them anymore but don't know what else to do." She then rolls up her sleeves to reveal four parallel vertical scratches starting at her wrists and moving up her arm. The scratches are superficial, but of greater concern are the other scars you notice on her arm. As Christine continues to cry, she tells you that she has been cutting for 2 years and that she does it because she feels better afterwards. She has reached the point now where she cuts twice a week, feels like her friends have abandoned her because she has become "too needy," and feels even more lonely and helpless. With tears running down her cheeks, she whispers, "I don't know what else to do. I hate my life!"

These three scenarios are only a few examples of what is becoming a commonplace reality in the daily work of many counselors and health care professionals in schools and on college campuses. While the act of cutting, mutilating, or otherwise injuring oneself has occurred throughout human history (Favazza, 1996), there has been a seeming explosion in both the occurrence and the public awareness of self-injurious behavior over the past decade (Nock & Prinstein, 2005). Acts that are direct forms of harm perpetrated on the body, such as intentional and "delicate" cutting of the skin, have emerged as yet another common form of self-destructive adolescent behavior. The occurrence of these self-injurious acts is growing at a rate that has given mental health professionals pause. Self-injuring adolescents and young adults are beginning to compete for the clinical attention historically paid to those engaging in the better established, or more traditional, self-destructive activities of the adolescent years, such as substance abuse, eating disorders, or the myriad other high-risk, impulsive acts characteristic of this age group. Intentional self-injury is rapidly becoming the new adolescent pathology of the times and, as such, is still poorly understood.

SELF-INJURY: A NEW SYMPTOM FOR OUR TIME

Every age gives birth to new ways in which human beings give voice to their suffering, and our present age is no exception. Human beings have struggled throughout history to understand their own being-in-the-world and to make sense of the reality of suffering that being human sometimes brings. As our understanding of medicine, psychology, and the complexity of the human organism has become more sophisticated, we have moved from the more mythopoeic and, perhaps, simplistic explanations of difficult-to-understand psychological phenomena to ones that are more multifaceted and less dogmatic. For example, we no longer view those who experience hallucinations as "possessed" by demons or as inherently morally deviant. Rather, we are able to offer more informed explanations that speak to their symptoms as being a consequence of their genetic predisposition, neurochemistry, or developmental history, some combination of which may have contributed to their particular mode of psychological suffering.

Our understanding of psychological symptoms and the way we articulate that understanding are always culturally and historically situated (Berger & Luckman, 1967; Cushman, 1990). Our existence in a particular time and place unavoidably mediates what kinds of symptoms emerge from our suffering as well as how they manifest themselves in people's lives. How we are situated in a particular place and time also contextualizes how we construct meaning around those behaviors and symptoms so that we can more accurately categorize them into new and more refined syndromes or disorders. This evolution in understanding is clearly evidenced in the psychiatric community's ongoing revisions of *The Diagnostic and Statistical Manual of Mental Disorders (DSM)*, which will soon be published in its fifth iteration. We have seen this process play out throughout the brief history of the formal disciplines of psychiatry and psychology. For example, in Freud's Victorian Age, "hysterical neurosis"—the conversion of psychological distress into symptoms of physical paralysis—emerged as the new pathology of that time. In fact, the attempts at treatment of the new disorder gave rise to the development of psychoanalysis. More recently, the 1970s inaugurated eating disorders as the new, emerging "it" pathology—the new modality by which some young women manifested and lived out their particular form of psychic distress. And it appears that in our current time and place, self-injury is quickly emerging as the "psychopathology of choice" in many young people.

As a relatively new behavioral manifestation of psychological distress, the phenomenon of self-injury constitutes an extension of the continuum of self-harm that ranges from the more hidden forms of harm (e.g., overwork, poor eating habits, smoking) to the more active and dramatic forms of destructiveness (e.g., substance abuse, sexual risk taking, eating disorders, suicidality, and, now, self-injury) (see Turp, 2003). Although all forms of self-harm are ways of living out and communicating one's ambivalence, pain, and self-destructiveness, self-injury is an especially difficult and disturbing behavior because it perpetrates violence on the body (and onto the self) in direct, dramatic, and strident ways. It makes a powerful statement about the psychological distress of an individual and the distorted and harmful attempts made by that individual to manage and soothe her pain. It points to a sense of powerlessness experienced by the person and is often suggestive of a subtle and deeply buried trauma of psychological neglect, invalidation, and emotional abandonment suffered at the hands of a parent, a family, and, perhaps, even a culture. Self-injury, then, is a complex phenomenon that speaks loudly about an individual's emotional pain and about her attempt to assuage it.

Clinicians and mental health researchers are finding that self-injury is closely aligned and highly correlated, in both form and substance, to eating disorders, and they suggest that these are clinically interconnected syndromes (Farber, 2000; Levitt, Sansone, & Cohn, 2004). In fact, Conterio and Lader (1998) have dubbed self-injury the "new anorexia" of our time. They explain that self-injury and eating disorders denote similar psychological dynamics. Cutting, like depriving oneself of food, represents a powerful form of communication. The behavior is a plea to have one's voice heard, an attempt to break the silence that has been imposed by, in many cases, the very people who are most supposed to care and to listen. Cutting is a specific language of pain that communicates the suffering of past and current trauma, which is spoken loudly by the self-inflicted repetition of that trauma upon one's own body (Conterio & Lader, 1998; Farber, 2000; Nasser, 2004; Strong, 1998).

Self-injury is the "new anorexia" also in the sense of its sudden emergence and swift proliferation in our society (Conterio & Lader, 1998; Farber 2000).

It appears to be closely paralleling the evolutionary footsteps of its eating disorders counterparts. In the 1970s, anorexia nervosa was just beginning to be recognized as a growing problem among young women. By the 1980s, however, it had reached full status as the most highly publicized disorder of the day, and clinicians were seeing young women with eating problems in high schools and on college campuses in increasing numbers. These young women acted out their psychological pain on their bodies through a deprivation of nourishment that poignantly mirrored the emotional deprivation they otherwise experienced in their lives (Hund & Espelage, 2005; Piran & Cormier, 2005). When the phenomenon of anorexia entered public discourse, in the 1970s, it was seen as a mysterious and incomprehensible illness that was thought to be intractable. The very thought of starving oneself seemed bizarre and frightening, both to the general public, which heard anecdotal descriptions of the deviant eating behaviors, and to the health care professionals who had to treat these individuals. As attention and research increased, however, a clearer understanding of the phenomenon filtered through to the public via the mass media. As a result, anorexia became less of a taboo subject and therefore, eventually, less stigmatizing for its sufferers. Likewise, as clinicians developed greater understanding of the illness, they also developed greater sensitivity to the dynamics and pain behind the disorder. They were better able to look for the human being behind the behaviors and no longer be diverted by the disturbing nature of how these individuals acted out against themselves. As clinicians were able to put a human face on the illness, working with these individuals became a less frightening and burdensome task. This shift in attitude contributed significantly to the creation of greater tolerance for the morbid and disturbing nature of the disorder, which, in turn, allowed clinicians to become more open to increasing their understanding and competence in treating these patients.

The emergence and proliferation of and the response to adolescent self-injury are following a pattern similar to the one that occurred with eating disorders 30 years ago. While self-injury is not a new psychiatric phenomenon, it has only recently become the focus of significant clinical scrutiny. Traditionally, it had been trivialized, misidentified, or considered solely as a symptom of some other syndrome. We are now finding that self-injury has "come of age" as its own discrete expression of profound psychological pain (Favazza, 1996, 1998) and is fast becoming the new mode by which many young women (and some young men) are now learning to give voice to their suffering.

As eating disorders challenged the conceptual understanding and practical experience of health care professionals 30 years ago, the advent of self-injury as the latest adolescent mental health malady of the new century offers similar challenges. We are at the infancy of our understanding of this phenomenon.

In fact, it is so novel as a syndrome that it has yet to be considered a discrete disorder in and of itself by the American Psychiatric Association (2000) but appears only in the DSM-IV-TR as a partial criterion for the diagnosis of Borderline Personality Disorder. Because we still know relatively little about the phenomenon, the rate and intensity with which mental health professionals encounter these self-destructive behaviors in adolescents far exceeds their understanding and expertise.

SELF-INJURY IN THE PUBLIC EYE

Public awareness of self-injury has been raised in recent years through extensive media coverage. Television dramas, entertainment news programs, feature films, and the print media have all contributed to heightening consciousness about the growing incidence of self-injury. In particular, the widespread coverage of celebrities and other high-profile individuals who have publicly acknowledged that they have cut or otherwise injured themselves has had a profound impact on the public's willingness to begin to destigmatize the behavior and has opened the floodgates, as it were, for others to disclose their own behavior and seek treatment. Celebrities such as Princes Diana, Angelina Jolie, Johnny Depp, Drew Barrymore, Marilyn Manson, and Courtney Love have all publicly disclosed that they once inflicted on their bodies some form of direct and intentional injury. The phenomenon has also appeared in the plotlines of a number of popular television programs such as *Beverly Hills 90210* and *Seventh Heaven* and in feature films like *Girl, Interrupted* and *Thirteen* (Adler & Adler, 2005). The effects of its presence in the entertainment media have, in a sense, legitimated self-injury as a real phenomenon that warrants attention, and disclosure of self-injury by celebrities may have helped create an atmosphere that has given other injurers the courage to come forward and seek help.

The national print media have also made contributions to this discussion with feature articles that have raised the public's awareness even further about the growing "epidemic" (Nevious, 2005, April 19). The *New York Times*, the *Boston Globe*, the *Chicago Tribune*, *Time*, and *Newsweek* have all shed more light on the problem and have exposed some of the larger, more complicated issues related to the treatment and recovery from the self-damaging behaviors. The titles of some of these articles alone (e.g., "An Arm Full of Agony" [Kalb & Springen, 1998, November 9], "An Epidemic That Cuts to the Bone" [Nevius, 2005, April 19]), speak poignantly to a subtext of pain that has continued to capture the public's attention. And, as an unintentional consequence, the broad and sometimes graphic coverage has helped mobilize professionals to become better informed about the phenomenon and to learn more about assessing and treating adolescents who express this very powerful message of pain.

Self-Injury on the Internet

The other simultaneous development that has increased awareness and stimulated public discourse about self-injury has been the emergence of new Internet sites and chatrooms on the subject. Since the year 2000, the Internet has erupted with sites about and for people who self-injure. While not all sites are positive and pro-recovery, many are, in fact, devoted to helping self-injuring individuals better understand their behavior and offer support and resources to help in the recovery process. (A listing of a few of these sites is provided in Appendix III.) A number of the sites also provide discussion forums where injurers are able to anonymously and safely write about their struggles. Participants often share their stories, which resound with the pain of abuse and neglect and which speak deeply to their ingrained feelings of disconnection and invalidation. These sites provide a community of "understanding" that creates a safe space for participants to find greater courage to honestly share their experience and, as a result of doing so, to perhaps begin the process of unbinding themselves from their shame. Many of these sites offer opportunities to interact with others with similar experiences who, while not ready to relinquish their self-injury, may find comfort and develop hope through the anonymous, yet meaningful relationships they develop online.

What is clear is that the power of the anonymity of the Internet may make it easier for individuals to openly tell their stories. It affords participants the possibility of expressing those parts of their lives that may normally be inhibited in polite social conversation and to present more of their authentic selves (Adler & Adler, 2005). This authentic self-presentation and the experience of having that personal presentation accepted and supported can become a powerful foundation for the beginning of recovery. This supportive context can, in turn, then become the fertile ground to offer self-injurers hope to seek out assistance in more formal ways and begin the process of recovery in earnest. At the same time, the anonymity of the Internet can also create conditions under which individuals seeking connection and support can be influenced in negative ways by the relationships they develop online. Vulnerable individuals can be swayed by more forceful peers on the other end of the e-mail or the instant message. The danger is that self-injurers can become better at self-injury by learning from others they meet online (Whitlock, Powers, & Eckenrode, 2006).

Overall, though, the increased public awareness of adolescent self-injury resulting from greater media and Internet exposure has unmistakably generated a proportional increase in the identification and reporting of the behaviors constituent of self-injury. As a result of these shifts in public consciousness, counselors, nurses, coaches, administrators, student life personnel, pediatricians, and youth ministers—all those professionals who work closely with adolescents—are now finding themselves the first adults to learn about a particular adolescent's self-injuring behavior and, therefore, the first compelled to intervene and provide assistance. These are the people who have become our frontline responders to adolescents who, because of their pain, have paradoxically turned against themselves by "cutting away" at their own bodies as a way to ease and extinguish their distress and suffering.

THE PROBLEM FOR FRONTLINE PROFESSIONALS

To be sure, the Internet and the media's coverage of self-injury have significantly raised the level of awareness about the phenomenon among the general public, health care professionals, and self-injurers themselves. This increased consciousness has decreased the stigmatization that self-injurers have historically experienced and has allowed many to feel safer in disclosing their behavior to others, thereby taking the first step in seeking assistance. Counselors and other frontline health care professionals, however, have been caught off guard by this newly emerging mental health problem and by its attendant "epidemic of disclosure" of recent years (Levenkron in Edwards, 1998, November 9). Consequently, helpers on the frontlines—in schools, doctors' offices and emergency rooms, and on college campuses—have reported feeling inadequately trained and ill prepared to understand and work effectively with individuals who self-injure (McAllister, 2003; Rayner, et al., 2005; Roberts-Dobie, 2005).

Self-Injury and the School Counselor

The school setting has become one of the primary venues where adolescent mental health issues are first identified and where referral for treatment is often initiated (Dollarhide & Saginak, 2003). School counselors are, more often than not, the first mental health professionals that students encounter. In fact, school counselors may often be the first person to whom students would consider disclosing their personal problems, given the access and personal relationship they may have with them (Froeschle & Moyer, 2004). These professionals very often deal with the mainstream mental health concerns students bring to their attention—divorce, sexual abuse, substance abuse, dating violence, bullying, sexual identity exploration, and so on. Unfortunately, self-injury is rapidly becoming one of those problematic behaviors that compete for professional attention in schools. A recent survey (Roberts-Dobie, 2005) of randomly selected members of the American School Counselor Association (ASCA), the largest school counselor organization in the United States, found that most respondents (81%) reported having worked with a student who self-injured. However, unlike their experience working with more common mental health issues, where counselors generally feel a sense of competence and expertise, only 6% of the respondents reported feeling highly knowledgeable about actually working with the self-injuring student. Overall, they rated themselves highest on knowledge of symptoms of self-injury, followed by knowledge of the root causes of self-injury, but lowest on knowledge of intervention strategies and treatment.

The high school years bracket the age range when self-injurious behaviors typically begin (Conterio & Lader, 1998), and, therefore, school counselors are in a uniquely powerful position to intervene in the lives of these individuals (Roberts-Dobie, 2005). The problem that arises, however, is that if counselors do not feel competent and confident, as the survey suggests, their effectiveness in appropriately intervening will necessarily be compromised. In order to identify self-injuring behaviors and take appropriate action, school counselors not only must understand the dynamics of self-injury itself but, more important, must possess, at the very least, a rudimentary knowledge of the necessary steps to take when confronted with a self-injuring student. Roberts-Dobie (2005) notes that while there is much extant literature describing school counselors' work with other mental health issues such as suicidality and eating disorders, very little guiding literature exists regarding work with the self-injuring population in the school setting.

Self-Injury and Student Services Professionals on the College Campus

A recent study (Whitlock, Eckenrode, & Silverman, 2006) utilizing the largest sample to date of U.S. college students (ages 18–24) clearly suggests that self-injury is a serious problem on the college campus, as well. Seventeen percent (N = 490 of 2,875) of the respondents reported that they had practiced self-injury at some point in their lives, 7.3% within the last year. Twenty-one percent of all those who had self-injured had injured themselves more seriously than expected, but only 6.5% of all self-injurers ever sought medical attention for their injuries. Nearly 40% of all the respondents also reported that no one was aware of their self-injurious behavior.

If these data can be assumed to reflect trends across college campuses, then mental health and student life professionals in these settings find themselves facing a new student problem that must be addressed. The college or university setting, however, has its own unique problems for responders. First, most students in college are no longer minors and live independently. They are *not* a "captive audience" in the same way high school students may be. As a result, there are fewer opportunities for responders to be made aware of their self-injury unless the individual herself or people close to her reveal the information. Second, as the study confirms, self-injuring individuals on college campuses tend to avoid seeking professional help and, therefore, are less accessible and amenable to care. The implication of this, of course, is that college mental health and student life staffs must become increasingly sensitized to the presence of this new mode of self-destructive behavior in order to better identify and respond to individuals who may require help.

Self-Injury and Health Care Professionals

Self-injuring adolescents may also come to the attention of adults during a visit to the school nurse or at a routine visit to their pediatrician's office. In more serious cases, they may be brought to hospital emergency rooms to have their injuries treated. Unfortunately, as Conterio and Lader (1998) observe, "many medical professionals are just as uninformed as lay people about self-injury and how to treat it" (p. 27). They are inadequately trained to treat the *individual* who presents with the self-injury; therefore, they often simply attend to the physical wounds and neglect the person behind the injuries. In fact, their attitudes toward self-injurers have occasionally been observed to be hostile and unhelpful (McAllister, 2003; Rayner et al., 2005). Self-injurious behaviors are commonly interpreted as "manipulative" or "attention seeking," and the patients manifesting these behaviors are considered to be recalcitrant and unmanageable (Rayner & Warner, 2003). Medical professionals frequently report finding it difficult to connect to these patients on a human level. They, instead, divert their focus to patching up the wounds and sending the individual home. They report feeling helpless, ambivalent, and frustrated in dealing with these difficult-to-understand individuals (McAllister, Creedy, Moyle, & Ferrugia, 2002) and often become resentful at feeling "emotionally blackmailed" by them (Conterio & Lader, 1998). As a result of these attitudes, many of those who require medical attention because of their injuries have learned to present themselves to medical professionals as suicidal rather than as "pure" self-injurers, as the former approach is more likely to elicit compassion than the latter, which often evokes anger (Clarke & Whittaker, 1998; McAllister et al., 2002).

Frontline Responders, Countertransference, and the Crisis of Confidence

Do my scars embarrass you so much?
You make me feel like you do not want me near you.
The look on your face, your posture, the movement of your body, speak only
    of disgust.
I feel so alienated from you.
Like I was so alienated from my family,
particularly my mother.
She never heard my fear, my pain, my shame,
but was disgusted by me too.
I learnt to stay silent, and now
it is so much easier to let blood flow than words.

Tyler (in Smith et al., 1999, p. 130)

Self-injury is a complex and multidimensional phenomenon, and self-injuring adolescents are very difficult to treat. The difficulty in engaging these individuals in treatment resides not only in the resistant, almost addictive quality (Turner, 2002) of the behaviors themselves but also in the fiercely distancing emotions they elicit in others. Self-injurers inevitably evoke compelling countertransferential feelings in the helper. The potent yet primitive statement that self-injury makes to others is one of profound pain and rage that is unsettling and often overwhelming for those who try to help—even for the most seasoned clinician.

In a recent conversation, a colleague who has worked in the field as a school counselor for close to 20 years spoke precisely to the kinds of mixed feelings counselors can have in dealing with self-injuring adolescents. He noted:

> When a student walks into my office and begins to talk about one of her friends who is a "cutter," I immediately start feeling anxious and go into crisis mode. I think to myself: Is she suicidal? Is this a cry for attention? Is she being manipulative? Should I call her into my office immediately? Should I check in with her parents? Should I let the administrators know? I've felt confused about how to handle these situations. I often feel incompetent in knowing what the right thing to do is. And that pisses me off. I think what gets in the way for me sometimes is that, frankly, I'm a little freaked out by someone cutting themselves on purpose. And, I know I'm not supposed to feel scared, right? I'm the student's counselor. But I do, and it makes me want to avoid the situation altogether.

This reaction is typical of counselors and other health care professionals on the frontlines. The powerful feelings induced by self-injury destabilize clinicians' sense of competence and confidence, and these individuals often experience overwhelming feelings of helplessness (Connors, 2000). When feeling off-balance in this way, clinicians can also have extreme reactions to compensate for their feelings of impotence. On the one hand, for example, they might respond to the extreme pull of the self-injurer to be relieved of her pain. As a result, clinicians can be drawn into the client's dynamics and may develop such compassion and a "need" to be helpful that they become overinvolved and lose their sense of professional boundaries. Soon enough, though, they may discover that what they offer is not enough or is blatantly rejected and sabotaged. The clinician's stance can then easily shift from being overinvolved and supportive to being angry and rejecting of the client. This shift, in essence, plays out very dramatically the self-fulfilling prophecy for the self-injurer. It reinforces for her the belief that people are disgusted by her and her behavior and that no one truly cares or can help (Conterio & Lader, 1998).

The clinician's professional equilibrium is additionally challenged by the struggle to determine whether this self-destructive behavior is necessarily suicidal. The cuts may be superficial, but the blood that flows is certainly real. What happens if the client cuts herself too deeply and does serious harm? Should she then be responded to as if she were suicidal, although she clearly denies it? This confusion is further intensified by the visceral reaction that one can have at hearing how the self-injury is caused or by actually seeing the client's wounds and scars. The mere sight of blood can make some people nauseous, and seeing the wounds can produce deep feelings of disgust (Alderman, 1997); for one who is not prepared for the crudeness of the display, seeing someone's open wounds or healing scars can be quite alarming and even traumatizing (Connors, 2000).

These factors eventually contribute to many clinicians' developing negative attitudes toward self-injurers, and these attitudes in turn produce emotions in clinicians that are difficult to manage (Rayner et al., 2005). In a culture that openly values health and attention to self-care, intentional and repeated attempts at the wounding of one's own body become incomprehensible. Particularly for health care providers whose very professional identity and self-worth are predicated on their desire and perceived ability to actually be helpful to others, the seeming senselessness of self-injurers' actions can be devastating to the clinicians' own sense of competence. Helpers want to help, and being able to help is based on one's belief that he or she can actually be helpful to others and that his or her help will be accepted. The primitiveness and destructiveness of self-injury however, creates a scenario for helpers that flies in the face of their very self-identity and confidence in being helpers. As a result, they may become angry at and resentful toward their client, feelings that eventually may turn into guilt because of the common belief that "good clinicians aren't supposed to experience negative emotions about their clients." These destabilizing feelings are then often conflated by the clinician into feelings of being deskilled and incompetent, which strike directly at the heart of their professional confidence and their actual ability to provide good care to their clients (McAllister, 2003; Rayner et al., 2005).

This loss of confidence is ultimately responsible for what Connors (2000) refers to as *compassion fatigue*. Compassion fatigue occurs when clinicians come to feel so overwhelmed and helpless because of the pain and trauma of their clients that they have difficulty sustaining the capacity to respond usefully to those individuals. In these cases, it is easier to see self-injuring clients as uncooperative, self-sabotaging, and treatment resistant than to contain and be present to their powerfully primitive projections and behaviors.

The unfortunate outcome of this dynamic is that it leads the helper to therapeutically disengage from the self-injurer. When this occurs, counselors and other responders may ignore or be outright unwelcoming to students who self-injure (Austin & Kortum, 2004). They may make pejorative judgments about the character of the adolescent, and they may fail to follow through with a thorough assessment (McAllister et al., 2002). These defensive maneuvers on the part of helpers serve to restore in themselves a sense of equilibrium and allow them to protect themselves from their perception of having failed to be helpful. In the end, it is easier to locate the source of the difficulty in the client rather to look at one's own incomplete knowledge or unhelpful attitudes and beliefs (Rayner et al., 2005).

The problem is that as professional helpers disengage from their clients, they obviate those conditions so necessary to conduct appropriate assessments and to facilitate care—they do not empathically communicate acceptance and thus fail to build trust. As a result, clients may not return for follow-up care, and the opportunity for further intervention is lost. Inadequate assessments of self-injurers can be catastrophic, as it can increase the risk of repetition of the behaviors, and with the increase of repeated self-injury comes a significant greater risk (as much as an 18-fold increased risk) that the individual will eventually become suicidal (McAllister et al., 2002).

School and college counselors are usually in the best position to become involved in the lives of adolescent self-injurers. As such, they hold a great responsibility in making a positive first contact, as the nature and tone of that first contact is crucial to setting the stage for future treatment (McAllister et al., 2002). These professionals, in their ability to intervene early and well, serve as a bridge to more intensive and specialized later treatment (Roberts-Dobie, 2005). Therefore, their ability to be empathic, to engage, and to not be incapacitated by the behaviors are paramount in beginning to establish the trust so necessary for the adolescent to remain connected and receive help. In fact, when clinicians feel helpless in working with traumatized clients, they actually have a higher likelihood of feeling traumatized themselves. Through their feelings of helplessness, their sense of competence is directly challenged, and, with that challenge, their confidence as caregivers plummets, as well. If they perceive themselves as having the skills to address the needs of self-injurers, however, "they are more likely to feel worthwhile working with such clients and less likely to demonstrate negative attitudes" (McAllister et al., 2002, p. 583).

The chapters that follow are written with the intent to increase awareness for frontline responders about what self-injury is—its nature, dynamics, and manifestations—and to increase their ability to respond effectively by providing practical guidelines for engagement, assessment, and intervention. With an increased understanding of self-injury and the development of the appropriate response and practice skills, frontline responders can come to see more clearly the person behind the behavior and thereby increase the likelihood of remaining therapeutically engaged with the suffering individual.

SUMMARY AND CONCLUSION

When human beings harm themselves intentionally, it is a sign that something has gone dreadfully wrong (Farber, 2000). We have seen, in recent years, that the incidence of self-injury is on the rise and that adolescent self-injurers are coming to the attention of frontline health care professionals as never before. At the same time, these professionals—counselors, nurses, social workers, and others—are finding that working with self-injurers, even at the initial stages of engagement and assessment, is extraordinarily demanding. The work with this population tests one's professional know-how; it challenges one's ability to be empathic and compassionate; and it can turn a normally patient and persistent helper into one who withdraws and disconnects. The drama of self-injury and its complicated processes immobilize highly skilled and competent clinicians and usurp their confidence in their ability to provide appropriate clinical care to their clients.

The awareness of this dynamic is the starting point in developing the knowledge base and skills necessary to tackle this client population. Understanding that one's negative reaction to a self-injurer may be more typical than not may actually liberate us to more honestly assess our own skills and to work toward developing greater competence. The purpose of this first chapter has been to present self-injury as a rapidly growing symptom of adolescent distress, to highlight the likely role of counselors and other health care providers as frontline responders, and to paint a realistic picture of some of the personal challenges that may make it difficult for some to work with self-injuring adolescents. Nevertheless, the reality is that on the frontlines, we have no choice—self-injurers *will* be brought to our attention and *will* need our care.

To this point, Farber (2000) captures very poignantly the challenge of the work that lies before us:

> It is very difficult to treat patients who court death. It is a challenge to connect empathically with them, so we tend to resist the complex attachments that must develop if we are to treat these patients. It is much easier to see them simply as the sum of their symptoms, and to collude unconsciously with them in maintaining their symptoms and their sense of identity that is bound up in them. Understanding the mystery of self-harm ... means getting in touch with the darkest, most violent, and primitive aspects of ourselves, a venture into unknown territory that evokes fear. It means bending toward the patient's unconscious to face the monsters and demons in them and in ourselves. It means facing truths about ourselves, our families, and our society that we do not want to face. Trying to understand self-harm means entering into our patients' darkest states of being, to tolerate dwelling there for a time, confident in one's ability to emerge from it. (pp. 6–7)

In the next chapter we will turn our attention to defining self-injury, delineating its forms and manifestations, and to exploring the sociocultural factors that contribute to its growing proliferation.

CHAPTER 2

The Context and Features
of Adolescent Self-Injury

When I discovered the razor blade, cutting, if you'll believe me, was my gesture of hope. That first time, when I was twelve, was like some kind of miracle, a revelation.... All chaos, the sound and fury, the uncertainty and confusion and despair—all of it evaporated in an instant, and I was for that moment grounded, coherent, whole.

Caroline Kettlewell (1999, p. 57)

Adolescent self-injury is a complex and multidetermined phenomenon that is manifested in multiple and diverse ways (Farber, 2000). It defies any simple, surface logic and challenges our most basic human sensibilities as to what might drive its self-destructive nature. Self-injury appears to be paradoxical and contradictory. It is a calculated violent act upon one's body that is often intended to ward off unpleasant feelings and to, ironically, make oneself feel more "normal." As such, it makes a powerful statement about the individual's extreme distress and about her distorted, but temporarily effective, attempts to create a sense of order out of emotional chaos. The scars left by the act of self-injury are a visual manifestation of an individual's unspoken pain that not only is indicative of a problem for the individual sufferer but that, as we shall see, reflects a broader social and cultural context out of which the behavior emerges, takes root, and is ultimately fueled.

A WORKING DEFINITION

My body looks how I feel.

A Self-Injurer (in Rayner & Warner, 2003, p. 308)

A variety of terms have been used to label the cluster of behaviors that reflect an intentional but nonsuicidal aggression against oneself that causes damage to bodily tissue. Some of the more common terms include "para-suicide," "wrist-cutting syndrome," "deliberate self-harm," "delicate self-cutting," "self-inflicted violence," "self-abuse," "self-mutilation," and "self-injury" (Connors, 2000; Simeon & Favazza, 2001). The multiplicity of these labels can further complicate understanding, as some are suggestive of motive behind the behavior, whereas others are more sensationalistic, and some are even moralistic or pejorative in tone. For the purposes of this book, I have adopted "self-injury" as the primary descriptor for this cluster of behaviors that intentionally bring about bodily harm. To this end, I will use Walsh's (2006) formal definition of self-injury that is parsimonious yet highly descriptive. He writes that:

> *Self-Injury* is intentional, self-effected, low-lethality bodily harm of a socially unacceptable nature, performed to reduce psychological distress. (p. 4)

As Walsh (2006) explains, this definition is descriptive and nonexaggerative. It maintains that self-injury is intentional in that it is a willful act and *not* the result of accidental or an ambiguous act that may be unconsciously driven. It is a deliberately chosen act used by the self-injurer, often in a repetitive way. The behavior is self-effected in that it can be enacted individually or with the help of others. In some cases, particularly among adolescents, self-injurers may take turns at hurting each other—for example, slaps across the face or punches to the head. Therefore, while not directly causing their own injuries, the participants have deliberately engaged in a reciprocal exchange of hurting another and, in turn, allowing themselves to be hurt in kind.

The other important distinction to be made about self-injury is that the conscious intent of the act is *not* to commit suicide. Walsh (2006) uses the phrase "low lethality" to indicate that self-injury "involves those forms of self-harm that do modest physical damage to the body and pose little, or no, risk to life" (p. 4). This, of course, does not mean to imply that individuals cannot die from self-injury. In some circumstances, an injurer might accidentally cut too deeply; in addition, when she is under the influence of substances, a self-injurer might find that her judgment is significantly impaired, leading to a substantial increase in the level of lethality; if the injurer cuts on the neck or other high-risk body areas, the level of lethality can also increase. In the main, however, self-injurers do not articulate a desire to die through their self-injurious enactments. Rather, they speak of a desire to feel more alive through the act and to escape from the feeling of "inner deadness." A more thorough discussion of the differences and motivations between self-injury and suicidal intent is presented in Chapter 7.

The next component of Walsh's definition refers to the social unaccept-ability of the act of self-injury. Self-injury has existed throughout human his-tory, and, in some cultures, self-injury, scarification, and other forms of body modifications have been integral parts of those cultures' meaningful religious symbol systems or played other social organizing function (e.g., rites of pas-sage or signification of social status) (Favazza, 1996, 1998). Self-injury as understood in our contemporary cultural context has no legitimized social function, nor is it a sanctioned social ritual that bears particular meaningful-ness to the members of our society (Walsh, 2006). Therefore, to the extent that it resides outside legitimate social and religious functions, self-injury is considered to be aberrant and destructive.

Finally, Walsh (2006) observes that, while self-injury is not suicidal, it is clearly psychologically motivated. The individual engages in repeated self-injurious behaviors for the very practical purpose of reducing her psychological distress. The behavior comes to serve the primary function of regulating one's internal tension and affective states. It is a method of self-regulation that restores affective equilibrium in an individual who otherwise feels overwhelmed by her fears, vulnerabilities, or interpersonal disconnection. Self-injury has a very practical purpose—to restore emo-tional homeostasis—and for that purpose, it works—albeit only for the moment. When deprived of this outlet, the self-injurer is often likely to become increasingly panicked, disorganized, and even further distressed (Conterio & Lader, 1998).

WHAT CONSTITUTES SELF-INJURY?

A number of different models have been proposed that situate self-injury on a broad continuum of behaviors that range from simple bodily self-alteration (e.g., tattooing and body piercing) to hidden or passive forms of neglecting self-care (e.g., failure to eat healthy or failure to attend to medical needs) to deliberate self-harm (e.g., wrist and body cutting or self-inflicted cigarette burns) (Connors, 2000; Turp, 2003; Walsh & Rosen, 1988). It is important to distinguish these various behaviors in terms of the direct or indirect harm they cause as well as in terms of whether the individual's behavior is intended to be harmful or is primarily a reflection of the cultural phenomenon of self-expression through body art and piercings (Walsh, 2006).

Connors (2000, pp. 12–13) describes four general categories along this continuum of harm:

1. *Body alterations:* direct, self-chosen changes to the body, often to conform to cultural or group norms. Body alterations may or may not involve pain, and sometimes entail the use of anesthesia. The intent behind these common, socially sanctioned (at least by the subgroup, if not the dominant culture) actions is generally beautification or symbolic marking to indicate belonging. Examples are cosmetic surgery, tattoos, ear/body piercing, eyebrow plucking, and ceremonial or initiation scarring or marking.
2. *Indirect self-harm:* behaviors that can directly cause harm to the person's body and psychological wellbeing even though the apparent or conscious intent is not to harm the self. Examples are substance abuse, overeating, dieting, purging, smoking, staying in a damaging relationship, unnecessary surgery, and excessive exercise.
3. *Failure to care for self:* an inadequate ability to provide self-care or protect self. Significant mental health problems, inadequate economic resources, and lack of information may contribute to or exaggerate these forms of self-harm. Examples include excessive risk-taking, accident proneness, not getting necessary medical care, poor nutrition.
4. *Self-injury:* direct actions that injure the body that do not appear to fit the category of body alterations noted above. A few examples are cutting, burning, and head-banging.

The second and third categories (indirect self-harm and failure of self-care) are both indirect, or more passive, enactments of harm upon the self. They are, therefore, more obviously distinguishable from the more direct forms of self-harm suggested in the fourth category (self-injury). There is some debate, however, over whether different types of body modification (category 1) are actually more benign forms of self-injury. Since the late 1980s, body art through tattooing and body piercing has become much more common, and the nontraditional piercing of body parts other than earlobes has become increasingly more accepted (Koening & Carnes, 1999). While body piercing, tattooing, and other forms of body modification have been linked to adolescent self-esteem deficits, depression, anger, and aggressive impulses (Carroll & Anderson, 2003; Clay, Hagglund, Kashani, & Frank, 1996; Lehnert, Overholser, & Spirito, 1994), there are no clear data at this time to suggest that body modification is a form of self-injury or that self-injury is simply an intensification of the dynamics at play in using the body as a canvas for art. Others (Claes, Vandereycken, & Vertommen, 2005), while studying self-injury patterns in female eating-disordered patients, have found negative correlations between piercing and tattooing and self-injury. In fact, the strongest negative correlation was found between piercing and cutting.

Walsh (2006) acknowledges the difficulty in distinguishing when body art crosses the line into the territory of self-injury. With the permeation of body modification in its many varieties throughout contemporary culture, it would be inappropriate to designate all forms of body modification as self-injury. First, body modification (e.g., tattooing, piercing) is a socially endorsed activity, and, second, few who acquire tattoos or piercings would say they do so to relieve psychological distress (Walsh, 2006). Moreover, those who self-injure certainly do not consider their behaviors as having aesthetic merit. In fact, self-injurers often feel a sense of shame and disgust at the scars left behind by their injuries (Farber, 2000). Walsh (2006) provides a rule of thumb in distinguishing whether body modifications actually constitute self-injury. He notes that "If the individual presents with multiple forms of direct and indirect self-harm, then the clinician should be alert for self-destructive motivations associated with body modification. Otherwise, the client may just be part of the cultural phenomenon of body art and enjoy it as a form of self-expression. In the latter instance, it would be a mistake to pathologize the behavior" (p. 52).

The Forms and Manifestations of Self-Injury

Most individuals who self-injure learn to use a variety of instruments and methods to cause their injuries (Alderman, 1997; Clarke & Whittaker, 1998; Connors, 2000; Conterio & Lader, 1998; Farber, 2000; van der Kolk, Perry, & Herman, 1991; Walsh, 2006). Table 2.1 provides a nonexhaustive listing of methods of self-injury found across populations.

TABLE 2.1   Common Forms of Self-Injury

Cutting the skin
Body carving
Head banging
Burning the skin
Self-hitting
Interfering with wound healing/picking at scabs
Scratching skin to the point of soreness or bleeding
Hair pulling
Self-biting (especially inside the mouth)
Self-inflicted tattoos
Sticking oneself with needles or pins
Peeling layers of skin
Ingesting sharp or toxic objects to cause discomfort

Compiled from Conterio and Lader (1998); Farber (2000); Smith et al. (1999); Walsh (2006).

A number of separate studies provide a sense of the popularity of the various self-injury methods. In a mail-in survey of 250 self-injurers, 96% of whom were female, Favazza and Conterio (1988) found that the most common methods were cutting (72%), burning (35%), self-hitting (30%), interference with wound healing (22%), hair pulling (10%), and bone breaking (8%). Likewise, an unpublished study by Walsh and Frost (reported in Walsh, 2006) presents similar data. In their smaller sample (34) of adolescents, 23 of whom were female and 11 male, the researchers found that the more common forms of self-injury reported were cutting (82.4%), body carving (64.7%), head banging (64.7%), picking at scabs (61.8%), burning (58.8%), self-hitting (58.8%), self-piercing (52.9), and scratching (50%). In a more recent study of 101 female eating-disordered patients, 64.9% engaged in one or more types of self-injurious behavior. Forty-four percent engaged in cutting, followed by scratching (38.1%), bruising (26%), biting (19.8%), and burning (11.5%) (Claes et al., 2005). Finally, in a study of 440 adolescents in a community sample, cutting (41%), self-hitting (32.8%), and punching or hitting a wall (18%) were the most frequently reported methods.

These studies and the extant clinical evidence suggest that cutting is the most often used method of self-injury. Pao (1969) introduced the term "delicate self-cutting" to signify the controlled, superficial cutting performed by self-injurers that usually requires little, if any medical attention. Individuals who cut report that once they have learned to cut themselves, either they experience little or no pain or the pain they do feel is localized and much more tolerable than their diffuse emotional suffering (Farber, 2000). While wrists and arms are the most common areas of the body that are cut, some injurers expand their activities to other body areas, as well. A study of 240 self-injurers (Favazza & Conterio, 1989) indicated that they cut certain areas of their bodies more than others: wrists and arms (74%), legs (44%), abdomens (25%), heads (23%), chests (18%), and genitals (8%). The cuts may be simple lines or a word or symbol engraved in the skin, and the location of the cuts can often point to some hidden or veiled meaning for the injurer. Those who engage in the cutting of their genitals may cut their breasts or even their vaginal canals. Cutting one's breasts and genitalia is a self-injury that is profoundly more secretive and ultimately significantly more shame inducing than other kinds of self-cutting (McAllister, 2003). The risk of serious injury or even death increases when cuts move away from superficial ones on the arms and legs and move toward the face, neck, and genitals. Of grave concern, recently, is the practice among groups of adolescents of sharing cutting instruments and possibly exposing themselves to a host of infectious diseases, including HIV and hepatitis (Farber, 2000). The instruments used for cutting are also varied. Self-injurers use razor blades, scalpels, knives, scissors, shards of glass, pieces of metal, or other household items that will serve the purpose. They develop complex rituals around their self-injury and often develop very creative ways to inflict harm upon their bodies. Christine (in Smith et al., 1999, p. 11) illustrates her singularity of purpose and multimethod approach quite bluntly:

> I've tried most sorts of self-harm the most frequent being cutting or stabbing.... I smash bottles and on one occasion smashed a glass panel, but normally I use a scalpel or razor blades (all numbered and used in sequence until they are blunt).... I also burn myself ... with an iron or with boiling water or with cotton wool soaked in chemicals strapped to my hands. Blisters are pulled off and scabs are cut open.... I also bruise myself, hitting myself with anything that is available.

Diagnostic Classification

Until recently, self-injury has not been considered a clinical phenomenon in and of itself. In the past, it has either been identified as a failed suicide attempt or considered simply as a symptom of some other psychiatric condition, usually Borderline Personality Disorder (BPD) (Favazza, 1996; Muehlenkamp, 2005; Walsh & Rosen, 1988). Alternatively, others who self-injure have been given diagnoses such as Post-Traumatic Stress Disorder (PTSD), Dissociative Identity Disorder (DID), Bipolar Disorder, or one of a host of other diagnostic labels, ranging from Adjustment Disorder and substance abuse to psychosis and brain dysfunction (McAllister, 2003). These diagnostic labels often fail to capture the essence of the individuals' psychological dynamics and can be very misleading. For example, individuals suffering from eating disorders have a high rate of self-injury (Muehlenkamp, 2005; Sansone & Levitt, 2004), yet individuals suffering from eating disorders do not also necessarily suffer from BPD. While BPD is the often-preferred diagnostic label, and self-injurers do exhibit borderline features, it falls short of capturing the heuristic essence and clinical presentation of all self-injuring individuals.

Though a number of formal classification systems for self-injury have been proposed over the past 70 years, beginning with the work of Karl Menninger (1938) and continuing with the model offered by Pattison and Kahan (1983), no single paradigm has been widely adopted to date. More recently, the work of Favazza (1996, 1998) and colleagues (Simeon & Favazza, 2001) has made a significant contribution in clarifying these classification issues. Specifically, Simeon and Favazza (2001) propose a classification scheme composed of four categories. The first category, *Stereotypic Self-Injurious Behaviors*, "refers to highly repetitive, monotonous, fixed, often rhythmic, seemingly highly driven, and usually contentless (i.e., devoid of thought, affect, and meaning) acts, which can widely range in self-inflicted tissue injury from mild to severe or even life-threatening at times. They are … commonly but not necessarily associated with some degree of mental retardation, and appear more strongly driven by biology than other types of SIB" (pp. 6–7). The second category, *Major Self-Injurious Behaviors*, refers to the most dramatic kind of self-injury (i.e., castration, amputation, or eye enucleation) typically enacted by individuals suffering from severe psychotic pathology, although it has also been associated with intoxication, encephalitis, severe character disorder, and depression or mania. *Compulsive Self-Injurious Behaviors*, the third category in Simeon and Favazza's model, include behaviors that are repetitive and ritualistic and that typically occur multiple times per day, such as hair pulling (trichotillomania), nail biting (onycophagia), and skin picking or scratching (neurotic excoriations). Only trichotillomania is classified in DSM-IV-TR as a discrete disorder under the rubric of impulse control disorders.

The final category, and the one most relevant to the concerns of this book, is *Impulsive Self-Injurious Behaviors.* This type of self-injury is characterized by a preoccupation with harming oneself physically, a failure to resist the impulse to self-injure, the experiencing of a sense of tension prior to the act and a feeling of relief after the execution of the act, *and* the lack of conscious suicidal intent (see Table 2.2). Simeon and Favazza (2001) suggest that there are two subcategories of impulsive self-injurers, those who engage in the behaviors only a limited number of times in their lifetimes (episodic type) and those who do so frequently and habitually (repetitive type). They note:

> In the repetitive type, self-injury may become an organizing and predominant preoccupation, with a seemingly addictive quality, that is incorporated into the individual's sense of identity. The self-injury may become almost an automatic response to various disturbing internal and external stimuli, typically beginning in adolescence and persisting for decades…. It can be generally said that these behaviors frequently permit those who engage in them to obtain rapid but short-lived relief from various intolerable states. In this sense, they serve a morbid and pathologic but life-sustaining function. (p. 15)

Given the current classification system of DSM-IV-TR, Simeon and Favazza (2001) have proposed that repetitive self-injury be classified under "impulse control disorders not otherwise specified." They advise, however, that the distinction between compulsive and impulsive repetitive self-injury may sometimes be blurred. Likewise, Walsh (2006) notes that some self-injurers present with "*both* compulsive and impulsive self-injurious behaviors *at the same time*" (p. 19) and cautions against too hastily diagnostically dichotomizing these types of self-injurious patterns.

TABLE 2.2   Summary Description of Impulsive Self-Injurious Behaviors

1. Preoccupation with harming oneself physically
2. Recurrent failure to resist impulses to harm oneself physically, resulting in the destruction or alteration of body tissue
3. Increasing sense of tension immediately prior to the act of self-injury
4. Gratification or sense of relief when committing the act of self-injury
5. Lack of conscious suicidal intent associated with the act, which is not in response to psychosis, transexualism, mental retardation, or developmental disorder

Adapted from Simeon and Favazza (2001).

Despite the development of a number of classification systems like the one discussed, self-injury definitional problems persist. Some (Muehlenkamp, 2005) argue that self-injury is a unique clinical syndrome because it is common to both the clinical and the nonclinical population and because its features are distinct from those of suicidal behavior as well as from other established mental disorders. Consequently, the adoption of a new classification of self-injury syndrome would offer definitional clarity that would benefit both researchers and clinicians in their work with self-injuring individuals.

Prevalence

Notwithstanding the "epidemic of disclosure" of self-injury alluded to in Chapter 1, the increased public attention to self-injury, and the proliferation of research on the subject, the rates of adolescent self-injury are most likely underreported. There is still a paucity of epidemiological data on adolescent self-injury that can provide a clear picture of the rate of occurrence (Muehlenkamp, 2005). Much of the extant data to date are unreliable in framing the epidemiological evidence for a number of reasons. First, the lack of an agreed-upon operational definition for the phenomenon (i.e., the interchangeable use of terms like "self-injury," "self-mutilation," and "self-harm") makes it difficult to gather accurate data. For example, the use of some of these labels (e.g., "deliberate self-harm") may not distinguish between "self-injury" (as defined earlier) and suicide-related behaviors. In our current discussion, and as is examined in greater detail in Chapter 7, self-injury is actually understood to be seen as antithetical to suicide (Gratz, 2001). In a substantial segment of the literature about self-harm, this distinction is lost.

Second, while self-injury has become less stigmatized in recent years, it still remains a social taboo in many sectors of our society. We come to know the incidence of the behaviors only for those individuals who come to the clinical attention of health care professionals. Individuals who have self-injured in the past may not bring it up unless directly asked, and many clinicians still do not ask about self-injury in their initial assessments. Many self-injurers suffer in silence and deal with the behaviors privately and, therefore, remain under the epidemiological radar. In other cases, health care professionals may not label self-injury as such in order to protect the individual from the potential stigma of the behavior (McAllister, 2003).

Furthermore, much of the current research has been conducted with the clinical population. There are few extant studies that examine the rates of self-injury in the college-age population and even fewer that investigate self-injury in the secondary school setting. What is clear is that the rates are on the rise, not only in the United States but also around the world, according to the World Health Organization (Skegg, 2005).

Self-injurious behaviors typically begin at puberty and can continue for the next 10 to 15 years or even longer (Conterio & Lader, 1998; Favazza, 1998; Paivio & McCulloch, 2004; van der Kolk et al., 1991). Pattison and Kahan (1983) estimated that the prevalence rates of self-injury in the early 1980s was approximately 400 in 100,000 people. Conterio and Lader (1998) revised that estimate to 1,400 per 100,000 in the late 1990s. Assuming that these estimates are reliable, the numbers suggest that there has been a 250% increase in a 20-year period. Other reviews report prevalence rates of 14% among high school students (Yates, 2004) and 12% to 17% in the college-age sample (Whitlock, Eckenrode, et al., 2006; Yates, 2004). In their review of the literature, Nock and Prinstein (2005) note that self-injury is occurring at a rate of 4% in the general adult population and 21% in the adult clinical populations. The rates appear to be appreciably higher, however, in the adolescent population. They estimate rates ranging from 14% to 39% in adolescent community samples and 40% to 61% in adolescent psychiatric inpatient samples. Between 5% and 9% of adolescents from Australia, the United States, and England reported having self-harmed in the past year, with few episodes seeming to be true suicide attempts (Skegg, 2005). A study of 150 college students found that 35% of the sample reported a history of self-injury, and 15% reported a history of more than 10 incidences of the self-injurious behaviors (Gratz, 2006).

Results from a more recent study of college students with a much larger sample size (N = 2,875) indicated that 17% or 490 participants had practiced self-injury at some point in their lives, and 7.3% had practiced it in the past year. The respondents also indicated the age of onset of the behavior as follows: 5% reported that the behavior began prior to the age of 10, 24.9% between the ages of 10 and 14, 27% between the ages of 15 and 16, 34% between the ages of 17 and 20, 4.6% between the ages of 21 and 24, and 4.4% past the age of 24.

Ross and Heath (2002) have conducted the most direct investigation of self-injury in a community sample of adolescents to date. They surveyed 440 students in two schools, one in an urban and the other in a suburban setting. Students were administered an initial screening questionnaire, and, if they endorsed an item suggesting that they had ever hurt themselves on purpose, they were then selected to participate in a semistructured interview that served to clarify how the student should be classified. The participants were also administered the Beck Depression Inventory and the Beck Anxiety Inventory to assess the social-affective dimensions of self-injury.

The results indicated that, although the two schools differed in terms of ethnicity and socioeconomic status, the rates of self-injury did not. Using the initial screening questionnaire alone, 21.2% of students in the urban school reported having self-injured, while 19.6% of suburban students reported the same. After clarifying their responses through the interview, the researchers classified an average of 13.9% of participants as self-injurers. Fifty-nine percent of the sample reported that they began to self-injure in grades 7 or 8, 24.6% by grade 6 or earlier, and 11.5% during grade 9. The study also indicated that there was significant variation in frequency of behavior, that cutting was the most common method, and that adolescents who self-injured had higher rates of depressive and anxious symptomatology, suggesting greater socioemotional struggles in these individuals. Finally, 64% of self-injuring students used words such as "lonely," "sad," and "alone" to describe their affective state prior to their injuring themselves. Other data of note include that 77% of the self-injurers were White, 59% came from homes where parents were married, and 36% came from homes in which the parents were divorced or separated.

Gender Differences

Prevalence rates also differ significantly along the variable of gender. Whereas being male is a notable risk factor for suicide, self-injury is significantly more prevalent in females (Conterio & Lader, 1998). Globally, deliberate self-harm (which includes suicide attempts) is the primary reason for female medical admission for hospital care (McAndrews & Warne, 2005). Some reviews suggest that the prevalence of self-injury is three to four times higher in females than in males (Clarke & Whittaker, 1998) and that up to 90% of those who present for treatment are female (Conterio & Lader, 1998). What may account for this discrepancy? At a very basic level, much of the extant data are taken from clinical populations in which women are overrepresented (Yates, 2004). Additional explanations for this difference can be attributed to patterns of socialization. The gender-role socialization of females may make it more likely that anger will be turned inward, toward the self, rather than outward, as aggression against others. Conversely, males may be socialized to discharge their negative emotions against others, lowering their rates of self-injury (Clarke & Whittaker, 1998; McAllister, 2003). McAllister (2003) further posits that this difference in prevalence may also reflect the fact that women may experience more abuse as children than men; since childhood abuse is an important predictor of self-injury in later life, women may be at higher risk.

In recent years, however, the incidence of self-injury in the male adolescent population appears to be on the rise (McAllister, 2003; Walsh, 2006; Whitlock, Eckenrode, et al., 2006). In their community adolescent sample, Ross and Heath (2002) found that 64% of the self-injurers were female, while 36% were male. McAllister (2003) suggests that self-injury is "becoming more common in males perhaps because more males are identifying as surviving childhood abuse; males are becoming socialized to be emotionally literate; and society is becoming less tolerant of acting out behaviors such as verbal and physical abuse" (p. 181). There is some evidence, although generally mixed, that individuals who are gay, lesbian, or bisexual may be more likely to self-injury than heterosexual individuals (Whitlock, Eckenrode, et al., 2006). The risk for homosexual men may be higher than that for lesbian and bisexual women, but more data are needed to be able to make a more conclusive distinction in terms of self-injury and sexual orientation.

SOCIOCULTURAL CONTRIBUTING FACTORS

What, then, might account for such a dramatic increase in adolescent self-injury over the past 20 years? Certainly, the increased prevalence in self-injury has not occurred in a vacuum. The categories we use to understand our reality, even the pathological forms our behaviors may take, are always socially and culturally constructed (Berger & Luckman, 1967; Kuhn, 1970). Like other disorders that have emerged out of a particular time and place, reflecting the cultural condition of that time (see Cushman, 1990), self-injury has materialized as a new pathology of this particular time, specifically reflecting the cultural situation in which we currently find ourselves. Some would argue that self-injury is a behavioral subtext of a larger social disorder that is characterized by increased alienation and disfranchisement (Conterio & Lader, 1998; Walsh, 2006)—specifically, that within the deep structure of self-injurious behaviors lie issues relating to power imbalances, group marginalization, and social injustice (McAllister, 2003). From this perspective, the skin is seen as the literal and metaphorical border between one's inner world and the outer environment with which one has no choice but to have contact. And, if one experiences disenfranchisement from this outer social reality and feels diminished because her voice goes unheard, her skin actually becomes the canvas, or message board, through which her inner utterings are expressed (Clarke & Whittaker, 1998). By marking or damaging one's skin, the individual communicates in a visual language what might otherwise be difficult to articulate.

The skin also communicates one's sense of identity and how one views one's place in the various social circles of one's life. It can speak to how one feels about one's place in normative culture. It can suggest one's stance toward one's parents and authority. It can communicate the choice the individual has made about her membership in a particular subculture, and can therefore communicate her feelings about her place in the larger, mainstream cultural framework. To some extent, tattoos, piercings, and brandings all serve this function and have come to be seen as largely normative by the adolescent peer group. As such, adolescents have become desensitized to self-injury, viewing it as simply an extension of these popular forms of body alteration (Walsh, 2006). What self-injury does, in essence, is "up the ante" with attempts to communicate, in vociferous, visual, and self-destructive ways, to those who may not hear the self-injurer (i.e., parents, other family members, doctors, society) their tumultuous emotional states and the internal pain they carry with them.

There have also been significant shifts over the past 30 years in society's conception of what constitutes "normal" family structures and how children are reared. With the economic necessity requiring that both parents work and the high-stress lives many people live, less and less time is devoted to being present and to caring for children in important ways. Many parents are pulled in different directions and may find it difficult to be present to their children as they would like to be. On one hand, a child may feel neglected because of the parent's inconsistent psychological presence; on the other hand, she may feel psychologically intruded upon by the parent's compensatory and inconsistent attempts to be involved in and, perhaps, have control over the child's life. Ultimately, the inconsistency of parental psychological presence makes it difficult for the child to have its early basic relational needs met. That is, when there is parental absence, it is hard for the child to have and internalize the experience of being psychologically held, comforted, soothed, and emotionally contained. We know that early secure attachment in infancy can inoculate children from later difficulties in adult relationships and even against various forms of psychopathology (Schore, 1994). Without the experience of this "holding environment," the infant has difficulty developing a secure attachment to her primary caregiver. A secure attachment is emblematic of an internalized confidence that the world is a safe place, because, in being loved and taken care of, the child learns that she can tolerate the vicissitudes of life and not fall apart. She knows at an existential level that she can manage herself in relation to the world and that she can thrive within that world.

Further contributing to this sense of lack of secure belonging in the world is the high divorce rate, which has led to the progressive dissolution of nuclear and extended family units. Consequently, children have had increasingly fewer important adults in their lives who can help parent and care for them. They have come to be increasingly isolated from adults who can be of support to them and help them cope with both the normal developmental struggles of life and the more dramatic or traumatic events that children sometimes experience. Even for the more intact families, many parents work outside the home, and, therefore, latchkey children and those raised by relative strangers in day care have become more the norm than children who have a parent at home. The inconsistency resulting from these varying rearing arrangements often makes it difficult for the child to know how and where to discharge her feelings and to seek guidance in dealing with day-to-day decisions (Conterio & Lader, 1998). To this point, Farber (2000) comments that American culture's "thrust toward promoting self-sufficiency and independence, may well thwart the strong and intimate attachments that children need. . . . Preadolescents and adolescents more often than not come home from school to empty houses at a phase of their development when their need for parental attention and supervision is greater than most parents realize. Even with the best intentions, we may be producing and raising generations of touch-deprived and security-deprived children who are more vulnerable to abuse by others" (p. 188). As parental structure has decreased and as the number of structured rites of passage has dwindled, some adolescents are filling this void with self-injury (Conterio & Lader, 1998).

This dynamic is further complicated by the cultural ethos that has developed over the past 30 years and that is propagated by the popular media through music videos and song lyrics, television shows, and movies: the "feel good," "quick fix" mentality. The point of view propagated by this attitude is that we ought to feel good all the time and that if we don't, then there is something wrong with us. We seem to be continuously hungry for greater intensity in our experiences, more and different forms of stimulation, and higher highs, culminating in the inability to tolerate any emotional discomfort or pain. We have developed little tolerance for the difficulties of everyday life that are part and parcel of being human. Any degree of anxiety, sadness, or guilt is not to be tolerated and ought to be immediately alleviated (Farber, 2000). The philosophy is that "if it doesn't feel good, don't do it, and if it feels good, then you have to go for it." Our "quick fix" society says that one can and should remove any negative feelings as expediently as possible—pop a pill, take a drink, or eat that bag of chips—so that we can "feel" better (Conterio & Lader, 1998). What is lost in this mind-set, however, is that "feeling" better is not the same thing as "being" better. The emphasis on the "feeling in the moment" way of thinking negates the multidimensional reality of living, which includes the not-so-pleasant moments and affects that help us to understand who we are and how we might negotiate the ups and downs of living. This philosophy of life is undoubtedly transmitted to our children in both overt and very subtle ways, and, ultimately, it does not serve them well. In this way, the overinvolved and enmeshed parent unwittingly communicates that any delay of gratification is undesirable and should not be endured. Children do not learn how to work at or work through issues and situations in their lives. Therefore, in their rush to immediately "feel better," some adolescents have not learned the mechanisms through which they can appropriately and effectively self-soothe in times of distress.

Moreover, adolescents are subject to the daily pressures of life, which are difficult to escape. Competition in schools, multitasking and overextended lifestyles, and the emphasis on the accumulation of material goods are all cultural pressures that contribute to persistent low-level stress and anxiety in many young people (Walsh, 2006). This already-present low-level stress is then compounded by the other pervasive cultural forces that strike so powerfully at the self-esteem of young women, namely the overemphasis on physical appearance, with its accompanying unrealistic standards of beauty. Our body-focused culture helps us keep our gaze on the surface level of things and suggests that if we are pretty enough, thin enough, and sexy enough, then all is right with the world. This persistent and debilitating gender bias against women helps to create an atmosphere in which girls and young women are made vulnerable for objectification and for increased abuse and harm of many kinds (Conterio & Lader, 1998). The most tragic part is that many girls and young women buy into the cultural message that beauty is the only commodity worth pursuing in order to feel good about oneself and in order to be truly loved. When girls then fail to meet these unrealistic and impossible-to-achieve cultural standards, some turn to abusing or otherwise actively causing harm to themselves (Conterio & Lader, 1998).

Some young women have rebelled in very dramatic ways against this beauty- and body-focused pressure. Conterio and Lader (1998) have coined the phrase "the culture of ugly" to describe this rebellion against the beauty and sexual expectations placed on young women by our culture. They explain that

> people in their late teens and early twenties deliberately festoon themselves in ways that not only repel their seniors but also many contemporaries.... The droopy clothes mask their figures and sexuality; the makeup and accessories are meant to shock, to repulse. We see this "uglification" trend as part of the large-scale anxiety and backlash against sexual pressures placed

on our youth.... Uglification, in our view, is an unconscious effort by young people to protect themselves against premature sexuality. Self-injury is a pathological extreme form of this. (p. 7)

From a feminist perspective, self-injury can be seen as a direct response to the exploitative cultural standards of beauty and sexuality imposed on women. Self-injury is an attempt at reclaiming control over one's body and over one's identity in the face of the oppressive and disempowering cultural sexual ethos. Shaw (in Walsh, 2006, pp. 44–45) writes:

> Self-injury is uniquely distressing because it reflects back to the culture what has been done to girls and women. Whether or not it is a conscious process, by refusing to remain silent, by literally carving, cutting, and burning their experiences of violation and silencing in their arms and legs, girls and women claim ownership of their bodies and their subjectivity. They refuse to relinquish what they experience as true. This is a radical and threatening act because part of what holds patriarchy in place is girls' and women's silence.

THE VOICE OF PAIN

I had no voice, so I created my own. I danced on the edge of a blade and played with fire.

A Self-Injurer (in Austin & Kortum, 2004, p. 621)

Pain speaks of our bodily existence when spoken language cannot. Pain speaks and writes on and through the body, signifying what words cannot say. If the language of pain fails to communicate, if it cannot be heard or read by another, it becomes woven into the fabric of the "speaker's" existence.

Sharon Farber (2000, pp. 16–17)

The danger in our work as mental health professionals on the sometimes very harried and chaotic frontlines is that we react only to the immediate behavior that comes to our attention. We see the behavior as the problem, and we sometimes define the suffering individual by the behavior: "he's a druggie" or "she's a cutter." And, behind the shorthand descriptors used to depict our students or clients, we lose sight of the person and the pain behind the label. We can easily lose sight of the young girl who may have been sexually abused by an uncle or incested by a sibling, the young boy who may have been severely beaten by his alcoholic father; we lose sight of those, who for no fault of their own, were not held, hugged, made to feel worthwhile and alive by those who were in a position most able to do so. When these children, these victims of care offered without tenderness, find themselves in terrifying and traumatizing homes, they are powerless and trapped. They cannot overpower their abusive father when no other adult steps in to help. They cannot penetrate the walls around a neglectful mother who will not allow the child to express a need or a want. All they can do is withdraw into themselves, seek ways to avoid the madness, and hide in silence.

Silence is a prevailing theme in childhood abuse. Those who are repeated victims of childhood abuse are frequently warned to be silent. If they speak, they may experience further abuse or may not be believed at all. As a result, they are damned if they do and damned if they don't. Unfortunately, in most cases, the only available support may be from the people in the child's home, the family, which may be where the abuse has taken place in the first place. The child is then caught in a cycle of re-abuse but is unable to leave because, as conditional as her care may be, it may, in fact, be the only taste of care the child has ever had (McAllister, 2003). These children's experience of trying to communicate to others but finding that no one hears their voices only condemns them to further vulnerability and extinguishes any hopes they may have to be heard. Accordingly, they learn to live in silence, because what is communicated to them most intensely is that they have no right to speak and that their cries and pleas will not be heard. In short, their inner lives are invalidated, and they are implicitly told *that they don't matter.* Their suffering is not heard by those who are supposed to care, they have little or no value to those who are supposed to protect them, and they are of no consequence to those whose hearing they so desperately want. They learn that their words can't bring them affection, that they don't have the power to move the other to embrace them, give them understanding, or soothe their pain. And so they learn how *not* to use words to speak of their pain (Farber, 2000).

McLane (in Farber, 2000) has noted that if "expressive acts of pain are hindered …—if the wounding is not communicated …—pain reiterates. It is not resolved, but becomes part of the lived structure of the human being suffering it" (p. 17). When unspoken, *pain reiterates* and is transmuted into different forms through the use of different idioms. The idiom of self-cut skin, then, is a language that articulates long-standing pain emerging from the collection of past trauma that has deeply wounded the self-injurer and silenced her voice (Levenkron, 1998). We shall see in greater detail in the next chapter the role that trauma plays in the lives of self-injurers; and we shall also see the many ways trauma is experienced by self-injurers in both its simple and acute form—sexual or physical abuse—or in its more subtle and complex forms of neglect, emotional abandonment, and invalidation.

We shall see that self-injury is a way that earlier trauma is repeated, symbolized, and communicated to others. Those who suffered trauma at the hands of others are sometimes obliged to remember it by acting it out. It is a way of "telling without telling" the story of the original abuse (McAllister, 2003). Strong (1998) refers to self-injury as the "bright red scream," as the blood that flows from cutting one's flesh is symbolic of the tears that do not, or perhaps cannot, flow. The pain may be too great, or it may even have been forgotten. Amid the numbness, the injurer may have little or no understating of the nature of that pain. It often remains inchoate and, while experienced, is not framed in either thought or words. The flowing blood of self-injury, the "bright red scream," shouts what cannot be shouted. It points to pain that is deep, raw, and compelling, yet, at the same time, the violent act against the self comforts, soothes, and provides a "wounding embrace.... [It] takes the place of a hug, a compliment, a mother's kiss" (Conterio & Lader, 1998, p. x). It provides the injurer with a sense of being alive in an otherwise deadened existence. The pain of self-injury is about the attempt to feel, the effort to speak, and the hope for connection. It is the attempt, fueled by emotional deprivation, to make sense of an inconceivable personal history and to find oneself again. Merleau-Ponty (in Farber, 2000) captures this sentiment poignantly and expresses the hope for wholeness found in the darkness of the pain behind the acts of violence self-injurers perpetrate on their bodies. He writes: "Pain *refers* to the disintegration of the wounded person and to her need for reintegration, and *expresses the value* of the persons harmed, her wholeness, and her wished-for unwounded connection to the world" (p. 17). It is through their self-inflicted injuries that these individuals speak both the pain of their lives and their simultaneous hope for belonging and healing.

SUMMARY AND CONCLUSION

This chapter provided a formal working definition of self-injury, discussed its placement on the broader continuum of self-harm, and explored the powerful sociocultural factors associated with the behaviors in question. The prevalence of self-injury in the adolescent population has increased appreciably over the past 20 years, and, while historically self-injury has been a behavior seen mostly in females, recent surveys suggest remarkable increases in the rate among the male population, as well. Self-injury has become more prevalent in our society, in part, as a response to the changing cultural dynamics around child care and family structures, as well as to society's focus on physical beauty, its persistent message of instant gratification, and the "quick fix" approach to life's problems.

As a result of these overpowering forces, some children have great difficulty experiencing a sense of security and belonging in their lives and the belief that they will be loved simply for who they are. Some fail to learn how to make sense of this experience and have come to be deprived of the words to describe and release the pain they feel. Instead, some learn, in very effective ways, how to communicate their unexpressed and inexpressible distress through their destructive actions turned upon themselves. For self-injurers, those actions entail perpetrating violence against their own bodies that, in the end, serves to speak volumes about the profundity of their suffering and the disconnection from others that they feel.

In the next chapter, we explore the experience of trauma as the foundation for self-injury. We also broaden our definition of trauma to include forms that are more complex, hidden, and insidious, particularly within the context of faulty attachments with significant caregivers and the invalidating environments created through psychological and emotional neglect.

CHAPTER 3

The Experience of Trauma
and the Foundations for Self-Injury

Neurosis is always, initially, a legitimate act of protest.

Walter Davis (1989, p. 246)

*Often we choose pathology over the unknown. Pathological predictability is
safer than being present to what is.*

Richard Hycner (1991, p. 141)

Constructing a profile of a typical self-injuring adolescent is a complex task.
The development of self-injurious behavior involves many factors, and given
our present understanding of the phenomenon, it is not easily explained or
accounted for by any single determinant. The various characteristics of an
individual's genetic vulnerabilities, childhood environment, caregiving relationships, and traumatic experiences all differentially contribute to creating
the conditions that may compel an individual to enact violence on his or her
body. Similar life histories do not necessarily create individuals who respond
to the stress and the conflict of life in similar ways. For example, a life experience that may lead one person to withdraw, to isolate from others, and to
become dysphoric may be the impetus for another to develop a style of living
that engages more intensely with others and may actually immunize that individual from the onset of that dysphoria.

To date, much of the extant literature on self-injuring individuals has been
descriptive in nature. A preponderance of this research has been conducted on
the inpatient adolescent population or on those self-injurers identified as such
through their presentation for treatment. The resulting data and conclusions

drawn from this research must, therefore, be considered with caution, as they may not be consistently representative of nonclinical self-injuring adolescents (Yates, 2004). The symptomatology of the clinical sample may be significantly more severe than that for a nonclinical sample and may, in fact, indicate a potentiated effect created by the interaction of a host of comorbid clinical conditions (e.g., eating disorder, depression, anxiety, pathological personality features) from which the individual also suffers. The fact that many of the samples used in current research have been taken from clinical populations also points to the implied resources and access to services these individuals may have. Much of the literature identifies self-injurers as middle- and upper-class White females. Again, caution must be taken in interpreting these conclusions, as those from a lower socioeconomic class may not necessarily possess the same resources or access to appropriate pathways to treatment available to those with greater financial means or other cultural or socioeconomic privileges.

Keeping these sampling biases in mind, we find that the general profile of adolescent self-injurers that emerges in the literature is quite consistent. Self-injurers are usually female, in their 20s and 30s. They began to self-injure in their early teens, are middle and upper class, are intelligent and well educated, and are emotionally inarticulate—that is, they lack a language to express their inner life, have difficulty forming intimate relationships, have a high likelihood of also suffering from mood swings, depression, anxiety, eating disorders, poor impulse control, low self-esteem, anger, and irritability, and feel profoundly disappointed in themselves; in most cases, they report having experienced some form of childhood maltreatment, neglect, or trauma (Conterio & Lader, 1998; Farber, 2000; Hodgson, 2004; Nock & Prinstein, 2005; Stone & Sias, 2003; Walsh & Rosen, 1988). Recently, there has been a growing number of qualitative studies that have recruited participants from nonclinical settings such as Internet chatrooms and college campuses (e.g., Adams, Rodham, & Gavin, 2005; Conte, 2004; Hodgeson, 2004). These studies (although, in most cases, participants were self-selected) provide both corroborating evidence for and greater clarity on some of the developmental and experiential characteristics that begin to round out the tentative sketch we have of adolescent injurers. Even with this additional information, however, a single profile of a "typical" adolescent self-injurer has yet to be conclusively identified.

While descriptive information about self-injurers is abundant in the literature, the connections and interrelatedness among the identified characteristics as well as an analysis of the pathways that lead to self-injury have, to date, been poorly articulated. We know what many of the individual characteristics of self-injurers are, but we know little about how they may interact and build upon each other to potentiate a self-destructive act of violence upon one's own body. How do the feelings of helplessness, worthlessness, and voicelessness that seem to underpin the dynamics of self-injury actually develop? What are those core environmental and psychological conditions that put that particular developmental process in motion? How do we begin to both link and unravel the many factors that place a young person at risk for self-injury? Yates (2004) notes that self-injury research lacks a unifying theoretical framework that does precisely this—organize its many descriptors into a causal or developmental conceptual model. He proposes that a developmental psychopathology understanding of self-injury can provide the much-needed rubric for organizing the extant data in order to begin to identify and to articulate developmental pathways that may contribute to the emergence of self-injurious behaviors. To this end, informed by recent work in the study of trauma from a developmental psychopathology perspective (Cook et al., 2005; Cicchetti & Toth, 2005; Ford, 2005; Kinniburgh, Blaustein, Spinazzola, & van der Kolk, 2005; Straker, Watson, & Robinson, 2002; van der Kolk, 2005; van der Kolk et al., 1991; van der Kolk, Hostetler, Herron, & Fisler, 1994; Yates, 2004), this chapter explores the central developmental processes that may lead to self-injury, organized around the most widely observed characteristic of self-injuring individuals, the experience of childhood trauma. It examines the role of trauma—both simple and complex—in the derailment of the normative developmental patterns in children. The notion of *complex trauma* is distinguished from the more simple acute kinds of trauma, and the hidden forms of trauma found in the earliest attachment relationships are also discussed. The chapter concludes by exploring the link between the experience of maltreatment and invalidation and the adolescent's turn to the body in violence. The specific biological, psychological, social, and behavioral developmental effects of the exposure to trauma are then reviewed in Chapter 4.

TRAUMA AS THE DEVELOPMENTAL CORNERSTONE FOR SELF-INJURY

The exposure to trauma, particularly in childhood, has a powerful and pervasive effect on the biological, psychological, and social adaptive functioning of the individual (see, for example, Briere & Spinazzola, 2005; Cicchetti & Toth, 2005; Conterio & Lader, 1998; Cook et al., 2005; Farber, 2000; Fonagy, Gergely, Jurist, & Target, 2002; Paivio & McCulloch, 2004; Simeon & Favazza, 2001; Suyemoto, 1998; van der Kolk, 2005; van der Kolk et al., 1991; Walsh, 2006; Walsh & Rosen, 1988; Yates, 2004). It can shape the individual's sense of self, her dexterity in managing her internal life, and how she adapts and functions, given the challenges of the external world.

It impacts the development of what Bowlby (1969) referred to as "internal working models" that provide psychological and behavioral templates that dictate both one's stance toward the world and how one will navigate its stressors and travails. The experience of trauma can be foundational to development. It can significantly impede the evolution of those fundamental capacities for self-regulation and interpersonal relatedness. As such, exposure to trauma sets the groundwork for the emergence of those conditions that can give rise to dysfunctional personality features, incapacitating clinical conditions, and a range of self-destructive behaviors that includes self-injury.

The research literature has identified a number of salient characteristics of self-injurers. For purposes of clarity and organization, the prominent experiential, personality, and clinical constructs that have been shown to correlate highly with self-injurious behavior have been grouped into three broad categories: Trauma Exposure, Personality Characteristics, and Comorbid Clinical Features (see Figure 3.1). Each of these categories, in turn, contains specific characteristics that have been identified in self-injurers. The position posited here maintains that the exposure to trauma functions as the developmental cornerstone of the emergence of self-injurious behavior. Trauma, in its many iterations, often gives rise to a chain of events that can establish pervasive pathological trends for the individual. For example, one's pathogenic experiential history may provoke undue anxiety in the individual that makes psychological demands that are beyond her developed capacities. As a result, the individual's sense of security and comfort are undermined, and the reduction of the overwhelming anxiety becomes the focal point around which the individual's psychological and emotional energies are mobilized. The persistence of this dynamic usually leads to the learning of generalized defensive strategies that, while effective for the short term in reducing discomfort, ultimately prove ineffective as a global coping mechanism. The pathogenic experiential history of these individuals deprives them of the requisite experiences for the learning of adaptive behavior and healthy self-regulatory functioning (Millon, 1996).

The exposure to trauma—both simple and complex—is associated with the development of maladaptive personality features (Axis II diagnostic conditions), as well as the more discrete clinical syndromes we descriptively identify through Axis I categories, such as Major Depressive Disorder, Generalized Anxiety Disorder, Posttraumatic Stress Disorder, and Dissociative Identity Disorder. As Figure 3.1 illustrates, it is hypothesized that the maladaptive personality features and the clinical syndromes emerge from and may be exacerbated by the experience of trauma and, at the same time, interact with each other to influence their mutual development. The longer-term effect of this interactive

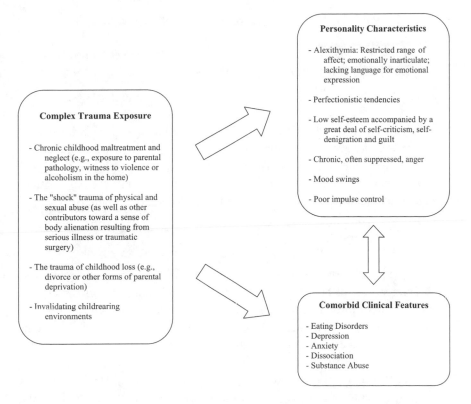

Personality Characteristics

- Alexithymia: Restricted range of affect; emotionally inarticulate; lacking language for emotional expression

- Perfectionistic tendencies

- Low self-esteem accompanied by a great deal of self-criticism, self-denigration and guilt

- Chronic, often suppressed, anger

- Mood swings

- Poor impulse control

Complex Trauma Exposure

- Chronic childhood maltreatment and neglect (e.g., exposure to parental pathology, witness to violence or alcoholism in the home)

- The "shock" trauma of physical and sexual abuse (as well as other contributors toward a sense of body alienation resulting from serious illness or traumatic surgery)

- The trauma of childhood loss (e.g., divorce or other forms of parental deprivation)

- Invalidating childrearing environments

Comorbid Clinical Features

- Eating Disorders
- Depression
- Anxiety
- Dissociation
- Substance Abuse

FIGURE 3.1. Experiential, personality, and clinical features associated with individuals who engage in self-injury.

relationship is that the individual becomes increasingly predisposed to the experience of additional trauma in the future.

While there is significant overlap and interaction among the characteristics that may coexist in the profile of a self-injurer, no specific feature in and of itself is either necessary or sufficient to explain the cause of self-injury. That is, no single traumatic event or experience, personality characteristic, or co-morbid clinical condition can exclusively predict self-injury. Some survivors of extreme trauma never engage in self-injurious behaviors. Likewise, not all individuals diagnosed with Borderline Personality Disorder take a razor to their skin. Thus, self-injury is multidetermined. The precise conditions and factors, as well as the combinations and directional sequencing of those factors that may give rise to self-injury, are still unclear and warrant further investigation. The extant preliminary evidence, however, does indicate that the experience of trauma is a central factor in the lives of most self-injurers (Connors, 2000; Farber, 2000; Walsh, 2006; Walsh & Rosen, 1988).

RETHINKING THE NOTION OF TRAUMA

I hurt my skin where it could not be seen and felt as though I'd beaten the abusers by destroying my body before they could.

Dee (in Smith et al., 1999, p. 9)

Every life and every childhood is filled with frustrations; we cannot imagine it otherwise, for even the best mother cannot satisfy all her child's wishes and needs. It is not the suffering caused by frustration, however, that leads to emotional illness but rather the fact that the child is forbidden by the parents to experience and articulate his suffering, the pain felt at being wounded.

Alice Miller (1980, p. 254)

Farber (2000) observes that self-harm, in its various forms, communicates something powerful about personal trauma. While there is no direct, unequivocal cause-and-effect relationship between trauma and self-injury (i.e., not all victims of trauma engage in self-injurious behavior), much of the current research does establish a compelling connection between the experience of trauma and the reenactment of that trauma upon the self in various forms, including through self-injury (e.g., Briere & Spinazzola, 2005; Cicchetti & Toth, 2005; Conterio & Lader, 1998; Cook et al., 2005; Fonagy et al., 2002; Paivio & McCulloch, 2004; Suyemoto, 1998; van der Kolk, 2005; van der Kolk et al., 1991; Walsh, 2006; Walsh & Rosen, 1988; Yates, 2004). The experience of trauma may, in fact, be *the* core condition that sets the stage for the development of self-injurious behaviors. Yates (2004) proposes a *traumagenic* hypothesis that addresses precisely this link by pointing to the negative impact of trauma on levels of competence that typify normative development. He sees the emergence of self-injury as a compensatory strategy for relational and regulatory adaptation, resulting from trauma-induced deficits in adaptive functioning. Childhood trauma, in general, and child maltreatment in particular, serve to undermine the normative developmental processes regarding the emerging sense of self, the ability to regulate affect and control impulsivity, and the ability to establish appropriate relational patterns that are requisite for healthy engagement with others. Yates (2004) observes:

> A developmental psychopathology model of [self-injury] suggests that, as in typical development, individuals who self-injure strive to achieve a bounded sense of self with a coherent personal narrative. However, in the context of traumatizing childhood experiences, particularly maltreatment, these individuals may not develop adaptive self and other expectations,

effective tools for the perception, interpretation, and integration of experience, competent arousal modulation strategies, and/or the capacity to engage in fulfilling and meaningful relationships with social partners. This model posits that [self-injury] is a compensatory regulatory and relational strategy that aims to achieve connectedness, self-preservation, symbolization, affect regulation, and/or self-other boundary differentiation despite vulnerabilities at the motivational, attitudinal, instrumental, emotional, and/or relational levels of competence. (p. 58)

The experience of trauma sets in motion a chain of reactions that propels the individual to establish self-protective strategies and coping mechanisms that, while serving adaptational purposes, ultimately thwart normal developmental processes. Accordingly, we must consider how the experience of maltreatment and relational trauma in childhood actually create the conditions whereby that trauma is repeated upon one's own body through self-injury. How does early and repeated trauma thwart the development of internal regulatory mechanisms that allow the child to negotiate the external world and tolerate frustration in an adaptive way? What are the pervasive developmental effects of this trauma on the child's emerging sense of self and on her ability to form healthy attachments to others? In order to fully address these questions, we will explore in greater detail the notion of childhood trauma and review recent developments in the traumatic stress field on the nature of complex trauma and child maltreatment and its impact on normative development.

Complex Trauma Defined

Trauma is most typically understood through the diagnostic criteria for Post-Traumatic Stress Disorder (PTSD) set forth in DSM-IV-TR. According to this perspective, trauma is said to develop as a result of exposure to events that involve actual or threatened death or serious injury or a threat to one's physical integrity; the individual's response to these events involves fear, helplessness or horror (American Psychiatric Association, 2000). However, this diagnosis fails to adequately capture the multiplicity of traumatic exposures that individuals may suffer throughout critical developmental periods that do not constitute the out-of-the-ordinary, extreme stressors that are acute, shocking, and imminently life threatening (e.g., violent personal assault, severe automobile accident, torture, exposure to a life-threatening illness). While the PTSD diagnosis articulates some of the psychological sequelae of the trauma (e.g., persistently reexperiencing the traumatic event through intrusive recollections, dreams, or physiological reactivity), it fails to capture the pervasive developmental effects of the trauma of childhood that may be of a less dramatic or "shocking" nature but that may, in fact, be persistent and chronic (van der Kolk, 2005). Not all traumatized children are necessarily exposed to acute events or experiences that rise to the level of rape, physical attack, or a life-threatening accident. They may, however, have the chronic experience of being raised in an alcoholic household, suffer through the mental illness of a parent, or experience ongoing psychological or emotional abuse and neglect at home, or a combination of these. These are all examples of potentially traumatizing environments that pose significant developmental challenges for children.

The term "complex trauma" has emerged in the traumatic stress field to broaden the understanding of the idea of the one-time event of simple, acute trauma that represents the conventional understanding of the phenomenon, as delineated by the PTSD diagnosis. Van der Kolk (2005) notes that the term "complex trauma" describes

> the experience of multiple, chronic and prolonged developmentally adverse traumatic events, most often of an interpersonal nature (eg, sexual or physical abuse, war, community violence) and early-life onset. These exposures often occur within *the child's caregiving system* and include physical, emotional and educational neglect and child maltreatment in early childhood. (p. 402, emphasis added)

The traumas children sometimes experience may include abuse or neglect, traumatic medical or surgical procedures, or being the victim of an accident or a witness to community violence. These forms of trauma represent those that are more commonly understood to be consistent with the diagnostic criteria of PTSD. The notion of "complex trauma," on the other hand, broadens the criteria for what can constitute a traumatic experience. It includes wider experiences of *maltreatment* that denote the contextual structure of the child's aberrant caregiving experiences. Cicchetti and Toth (2005) posit that, at the most basic level, child maltreatment is the experience of "a toxic relational environment that poses considerable risk for maladaptation across diverse biological and psychological domains of development" (p. 410). It represents a profound failure of the family environment to provide opportunities to the child that foster normative developmental processes. Instead, maltreating families create a pathogenic relational milieu that undermines development and poses substantial risk across a broad spectrum of functional domains. These theorists have delineated four categories of child maltreatment: (a) physical abuse; (b) sexual abuse (i.e., sexual contact or attempted contact with caregiver or other adult); (c) neglect (both the failure to provide minimum care and the lack of supervision); and (d) emotional maltreatment, which involves persistent and extreme thwarting of the child's basic psychological and emotional needs (Cicchetti & Toth, 2005).

The pathogenic relational environments created in maltreating families traumatize children through the very nature of the relationships fostered in the family, thus making the trauma interpersonal. Consequently, trauma need not result from the experience of an acutely shocking event like incest but may result from the more subtle and insidious nature of the destructive relationships created by the caregivers, for example, through active verbal abuse, on one hand, or emotional disengagement, on the other. The implicit message communicated in the interactions that occur in maltreating environments is that the child lacks inherent worth and is not deserving of the parent's time, attention, kindness, or love. The real self of the child is, essentially, disconfirmed. To this point, van der Kolk (2005) observes that "most trauma begins at home; the vast majority of people (about 80%) responsible for child maltreatment are the children's own parents" (p. 402).

Children growing up in maltreating family environments suffer profoundly. Their developing capacities to function well in different areas of their lives are frustrated. They rarely have secure childhoods, and their resulting symptomatology tends to be pervasive and multifaceted. They are likely to become depressed, as well as to be vulnerable to various medical illnesses, and they frequently exhibit a variety of impulsive and self-destructive behaviors (van der Kolk, 2005). The repeated developmental disruptions these children are subjected to from their invalidating parents increases the probability of maladaptation and psychopathology that, in turn, have serious implications for the child's ability to develop and maintain a stable sense of self and to develop secure attachments in later life (Cicchetti & Toth, 2005). Even at the earliest stages of life, maltreating families create hidden traumas that can become foundational for the invalidation of a child's hopes for legitimacy, acceptance, and worth that self-injuring adolescents so often crave.

The Hidden Trauma of Faulty Attachment Relationships

Love and violence, properly speaking, are polar opposites. Love lets the other be, but with affection and concern. Violence attempts to constrain the other's freedom, to force him to act in the way we desire, but with ultimate lack of concern, with indifference to the other's own existence or destiny.... [Here,] violence masquerade[s] as love.

R. D. Laing (1967, p. 36)

Whatever the baby's genetic endowment, the mother's ability or failure to "re-late" is the sine qua non *of psychic health for the infant. To find a good parent at the start is the basis of psychic health.*

Harry Guntrip (1986, p. 467)

The centrality of the experience of a secure and facilitative rearing environment in early life cannot be underestimated. Beginning with the most basic interactions an infant has with its primary caregiver and continuing to the nurturance and support given in later childhood, these early social transactions—especially with the mother during infancy—become indelibly imprinted onto the inner life of the developing child. These early relationships become templates that sculpt the child's capacity to enter into all later emotional relationships. Schore (1994) observes, "These early experiences shape the development of a unique personality, its adaptive capacities as well as its vulnerabilities to and resistances against particular forms of pathologies. Indeed, they profoundly influence the emergent organization of an integrated system that is both stable and adaptable, and thereby the formation of the self" (p. 3).

These early attachment relationships are formative because they facilitate the structural development of the brain (Fonagy et al., 2002; Schore, 1994, 2003a, 2003b). Positive emotional experiences (e.g., formation of secure attachment with the primary caregiver) or negative ones (e.g., separation or loss of caregiver or other trauma) may create a permanent fissure in the still-developing immature brain structures that can limit the functional capacities of the individual in later life. Secure and facilitative environments protect the child from becoming overwhelmed by the external world and allow the child to internalize a sense of stability and safety that fortifies her developing sense of self and inoculates her from the fear of psychological fragmentation. Through secure attachment relationships and validating childhood environments, the individual comes to develop the critical capacity to create and maintain an internal sense of emotional security that is buttressed with the fundamental knowledge (conscious and unconscious), that one is loved and that during times of stress, one can cope—both by regulating one's own emotions and by going to others for interactive soothing (Fonagy et al., 2002; Schore, 1994, 2003a, 2003b).

Secure Attachment

The universal human need for the development of close affectional bonds with a primary caregiver is a precondition for setting in motion the normal development of human beings (Fonagy et al., 2002; Schore, 1994). The primary goal of this attachment system is to provide the infant with the experience of security through the caregiver's function as the primary regulator of the infant's emotional experience. As the caregiver becomes attuned to the fluctuations of the infant's moment-by-moment needs and responds effectively to those needs, the caregiver has, in effect, provided the mechanisms for the regulation of the infant's internal emotional states. Through this process

> The infant learns that arousal in the presence of the caregiver will not lead to disorganization beyond his coping capabilities. The caregiver will be there to reestablish equilibrium. In states of uncontrollable arousal, the infant will come to seek physical proximity to the caregiver in the hope of soothing and the recovery of homeostasis.... Secure infants' behavior is based on the experience of well coordinated, sensitive interactions where the caregiver is rarely overarousing and is able to restabilize the child's disorganizing emotional responses. Therefore, they remain relatively organized in stressful situations. Negative emotions feel less threatening and can be experienced as meaningful and communicative. (Fonagy et al., 2002, p. 37–38)

Van der Kolk (2005) observes that securely attached children learn to regulate their affect and behavior by anticipating the caregiver's response to their needs, which, on the whole, have been experienced in the past as consistent and beneficial. They learn to trust how they feel and how they understand the world and, thus, develop confidence in their ability to react to whatever the world may present. The experience of being understood by their caregiver instills in them the sense that they "can make good things happen," and, if they may be at a loss in a particular situation, they possess the internal resources not to be overwhelmed and can freely seek assistance from others. Parents of secure children are themselves secure (Fonagy et al., 2002) and are able to remain calm in assisting their distressed children to restore a sense of safety and equilibrium. What the child internalizes through the experience of secure attachment—being well cared for by an attuned parent—is the sense that she deserves to be protected and well cared for, and, thus, she develops the desire and the competence to follow suit and take good care of herself. Farber (2000) has suggested that "If the attachment figure remains available and responsive, providing protection, help, and comfort when needed, the child then can develop the psychological, emotional, and cognitive skills necessary for mastery and a firm sense of security in the world" (p. 74).

Insecure Attachment

Attachment systems occasionally go awry, however (Farber, 2000). Caregivers, who themselves may have been insecurely attached in childhood, fail to create the conditions that allow the infant the opportunities to thrive in safety.

When basic attunement to the infant's needs and appropriate responses to those needs are *not* offered by the caregiver, the infant is inadequately protected from her own anxiety and fears, as well as from the real dangers of being in the world (e.g., going hungry). Some insecurely attached infants, those designated as *anxious/avoidant*, have typically had experiences in which their emotional arousal was either not restabilized by their caregiver or was actually overstimulated and aroused by intrusive parenting. The *anxious/resistant* infant, on the other hand, as a result of the unresponsiveness or underresponsiveness of the parent, has developed a low threshold for threat and becomes preoccupied with having contact with the caregiver in order to elicit a nurturing response but is ultimately frustrated when that care does not materialize in the expected or hoped-for manner. The most insecurely attached children, those designated as *disorganized/disoriented*, experience the caregiver as the source of both fear and reassurance. The radically mixed experiences they have of their caregivers significantly impede any development of internal coherence (Fonagy et al., 2002). The internal confusion generated by such inconsistent parenting creates an environment of fear and bewilderment that mobilizes the child's resources away from the activities of safe and carefree play and toward finding psychological safety and security, as these are not experienced in the person and presence of the caregiver. Fonagy and colleagues (2002) explain that

> caregivers of disorganized infants frequently respond to the infant's distress by hostile-helpless ... dissociated or disorganized, frightened or frightening ... behavior. It is as if the infant's emotional expression triggers a temporary failure on the part of the caretaker to perceive the child as an intentional person, and she responds with massive withdrawal, communication errors, role confusion, or negative-intrusive frightening behavior. Consequently, these children come to experience their own arousal as a danger signal for abandonment. . . . [It] brings forth an image of the parent who withdraws from the child in a state of anxiety or rage, to which the child reacts with a complementary dissociative response. . . . When confronted with a frightened or frightening caregiver, the infant takes in as part of himself the mother's feeling of rage, hatred, or fear and her image of him as frightening and unmanageable. (pp. 356–357)

Van der Kolk (2005) adds that when

> caregivers are emotionally absent, inconsistent, frustrating, violent, intrusive, or neglectful children are likely to become intolerably distressed and unlikely to develop a sense that the external environment is able to provide relief. Thus, children with insecure attachment patterns have trouble relying on others to help them and are unable to regulate their emotional states by themselves. As a result, they experience excessive anxiety, anger, and

longings to be taken care of. These feelings may become so extreme as to precipitate dissociative states or self-defeating aggression. (p. 403)

The experience of being chronically overstimulated or intruded upon by one's caregiver taxes the child's resources by keeping her focus constantly directed toward the external world. The child who is overstimulated, intruded upon, or neglected is essentially forced to become hypervigilant toward the caregiver. The child remains in a predominant reactive mode: Will my parent yell at me? Do I need to protect myself now? I'm hungry. Will I be fed? Will my parent become upset by what I'm feeling now or by what I want? The need for this vigilance precludes the child's turning inward to the life of fantasy and the activity of play that is so crucial for normative development. It diverts the child's attention from her internal states—what she feels and thinks—such that she begins to disconnect what is experienced internally from the reality of the outer world. The child's beliefs, distorted as they may be, about the nature of his or her experience, in essence, become reality. The caregiver's lack of attuned presence and responsiveness fail to contain the child's inner turmoil and anxiety and place the child in the position of having to manage her own overpowering affective states. Rather than feeling "emotionally held" and "psychologically contained," the child feels impinged upon. The child's psychological boundaries are violated. In these instances of poor caregiving, the child is traumatized not by, for example, the acute trauma of physical or sexual abuse but rather by the long-standing effects of the quality and nature of the caregiver-child relationship itself. Every negative interaction between the parent and the child impinges on the normative developmental processes of the child, and the cumulative effect is the subtle and often hidden, yet pervasive, experience of psychic trauma (Farber, 2000).

Maltreatment and the Invalidation of the Self

The cause of trouble is that parents somehow fail to get it across to the child that he is loved for his own sake, as a person in his own right.

W. R. D. Fairbairn (in Guntrip, 1986, p. 449)

Caregivers of insecurely attached infants were often insecurely attached children themselves (Fonagy et al., 2002). They simply become caught up in the perpetual intergenerational cycle of repeating the trauma perpetrated against them. Their own inability to be present, attentive, and attuned speaks to their own emotional deprivation and suffering, which prevents them from being able to love their children well. Those who have suffered trauma and humiliation at the hands of their own parents learn to dehumanize themselves and others, and they exact a kind of morbid revenge by becoming destructive to their own children (a process that is rarely a conscious one). In effect, they behave in a way as to implicitly abdicate their parental role. Rather than providing security and comfort, they create a sense of profound instability in the child's center of safety by engaging in what in their minds are seemingly innocuous acts or harmless comments. Letting the infant wait for prolonged periods of time to be fed or to have its diaper changed; not holding the child close so that her skin touches that of its caregiver's and so that she can hear the caregiver's beating heart and feel the undulating movements of her chest as she breathes; laughing when the child is in pain; or not allowing the child to express anger and frustration are all examples of ways of parental relating that force the child to turn inward to make sense of the intense and confusing emotions she may feel. These are modes of caregiving that, in the end, are subtle but profound injuries to the child's spirit and emerging sense of self.

Linehan (1993a) sees these "invalidating" moments as fundamentally communicating to the child that, in essence, her inner life and private experiences are unacceptable. The child's expression of inner thoughts is often met with erratic, inappropriate, or extreme responses that serve to dismiss or trivialize her experiences. The child's encounters with painful or overwhelming emotions are disregarded, and the intents and motivations behind the child's behavior are summarily negated. This profound experience of invalidation tells the child that her understanding of her own experiences is wrong and not to be trusted and that the "wrongness" of her experiences is a direct result of her own character and personality defects. The subtext of the communication is not so much that the child has *done* something wrong but that the child *is* something wrong, and when this is communicated, the child experiences a profound felt sense of emotional and psychological abandonment by the parent. Sarah (in Smith et al., 1999) comments precisely on this sort of experience:

> My mother never seemed to like me. Nothing I did seemed to please her. She never cared what happened to me. I'm sure she knew he was raping me but she did nothing. I must have done something to cause such hatred. It must have been my fault just as it is my fault that all my relationships fail, why I'm alone. Now she's dead and I can never make the relationship between us right. I'm so angry at myself. Why didn't I sort it out before she died? (p. 39)

The consequences of this kind of experience are profound. Van der Kolk (2005) notes that, as a result of maltreatment and the accompanying implicit invalidation, the child comes to believe that the many negative attributions that emanate from the caregiver and are directed toward her are indeed true.

She internalizes the caregiver's injunctions and comes to believe that the caregiver is correct, that she, the child, *is* the source of the problems—she *is* the one who is defective. The caregiver is spared in this transaction. It is safer for the child to take on the responsibility for her "badness" (as must clearly be the case, given the treatment received from the one who is supposed to care for and protect her), rather than risk losing the parent's love. The negative voice of the parent—her mood swings and inconsistency, her shame and guilt, her own hostile projections—reflected in the dyadic relationship becomes internalized by the child and functions as the internal compass that guides her self-definition and accompanying behaviors, both in the present and in later life. The child has no choice but to internalize the punitive experience and make it her own—it is a matter of her own survival. By internalizing the negative voice (and, ultimately, the person whose voice it is), the child is acting in the belief that doing so will protect her from the possibility of future harm. The act of internalization serves to shield the child from the overwhelming emotions she feels; it helps to preserve some semblance of a relationship with her parent and, ultimately, functions to give her some illusion of control over her otherwise unmanageable experience (van der Kolk, 2005).

Van der Kolk (2005) further points out that the child depends on her caregiver for her very survival. Therefore, when she is ensnared in a toxic and maltreating relationship with an abusive or neglectful parent, the child is literally trapped. She is not able to end the relationship or to protect herself by other means, as an adult in a similar situation can. When faced with a traumatizing family, the child experiences a crisis of loyalty and organizes her behavior in ways that allow her to survive within the family. The child learns to keep the secret of her abuse, and she learns to acclimate to her situation through helpless compliance or through any other way she has learned that ensures her survival (van der Kolk, 2005).

The Turn to the Body

I stand in awe of my body, this matter to which I am bound has become so strange to me.

Henry David Thoreau (1906, p. 78)

There is only one antidote for mental suffering, and that is physical pain.

Karl Marx (in Berlin, 1939/1981, p. 133)

The end result of exposure to complex trauma is the invalidation of the child's sense of self (Fonagy et al., 2002). The trauma of the boundary violations that occur as a result of traumatic attachment systems or maltreatment in the family or the acute trauma of abuse attacks the foundation of the child's bounded identity and emerging self. She experiences the devastating feeling of being unwanted when the caregiver fails to respond to her attempts to elicit care. Her voice is essentially *silenced*, and the development of her inner life—her ability to think and feel and equate those activities to the reality of her experience—is severely stunted. The child is not given the freedom to explore her world in safety and to think about and feel what she experiences. Her safety from future harm depends upon her ability to replicate her caregiver's thoughts and feelings and to anticipate her caregiver's desires and moods. This dynamic is clearly fostered by the caregiver's own stance toward the child. For example, mothers of disorganized children often experience themselves as merging with their child and understand their child to be merely an extension and replica of themselves (Fonagy et al., 2002). In these cases, the child is forced to exert energy in protecting herself in order to avoid being subsumed or annihilated by the caregiver's need for merger, rather than being free to focus on those activities of fantasy and play that facilitate her developing sense of self. Because the child's overwhelming feelings have not been sufficiently contained and regulated by an attuned caregiver, the child has failed to develop the ability to reenact for herself the soothing usually experienced by "mothering" received early in one's life. She has failed to internalize those mechanisms, mediated through the experience of care, that allow her to feel worthwhile and valued, as well as to remain whole in the face of challenges from the external world. She needs the other for her self-definition. She needs to incorporate the caregiver, who may in fact be the abuser, into herself in order to help provide any semblance of self-coherence. Resisting the possibility of psychological abandonment effectively means internalizing the intolerable, hostile "alien" other who dismisses, invalidates, and abuses (Fonagy et al., 2002).

When the emotional and psychological core of one's identity is invalidated, the individual has no recourse but to turn to the body for solace. When the child's emotional world has been constricted by a punitive or neglectful family environment and her attachments have been insecurely formed, her ability to develop the use of fantasy and imagination to help her contain and express her experience becomes stifled. And when this happens "there is nothing left to do but call upon one's own body" (Farber, 2000, p. 160).

Fonagy and colleagues (2002) understand the body to be a channel for managing unprocessed mental states. When psychic reality is poorly integrated, the body becomes the bridge for the continuity of the sense of self. This shift is particularly critical during adolescence, when changes in the body have greater implications for identity than during other times of life. Unprocessed emotions and mental states come to be represented in and through the body. Physical attributes such as appearance and weight come to represent the individual's internal states—one's sense of well-being, control, and self-worth. How one feels is equated with how one looks. In eating disorders, for example, the person's distorted perception of seeming fat is not a result of her looking fat but a result of the "things" perceived to be inside her that she can manipulate, control, or get rid of. When the abusive or neglectful caregiver is internalized, the individual has internalized the hostile or alien other and has transformed it into themselves, or, more accurately, their "bad" self. An attack on the body, as in self-injury, is an attack on this alien other, experienced as in one's own body. The attack is both an attempt to be rid of that internalized alien other and a way for the individual to experience a greater sense of integrity of self. As Fonagy and colleagues (2002) explain, by sacrificing the body, the self-injurer can, paradoxically, preserve the self.

Farber (2000) observes that when "the world is too much to bear, when there is not that feeling of containment derived from oceanic experiences with the mother, the child may find self-injury to be a way of separating from her, cutting or scratching herself away from her mother.... The physical pain she inflict[s] upon herself can be understood as the wish to destroy the maternal object that she has unconsciously introjected" (p. 163). Claire (in Smith et al., 1999) speaks to this process quite explicitly:

> I hate her so much, my whole body sometimes feels explosive when I think of her or even if someone mentions the word mother. I can't get her away from me, she is with me day and night. She lives and breathes me. I feel her inside and out. When I inhale I feel she fills even more of me. When I exhale, I feel that the breath I breath is infected by her, so I try not to breathe on anyone in case they are made bad by her breath. There is no way away from her, she is with me day and night. The torment is killing me. I sometimes think people can see my mother inside me. I feel covered and smothered by her. I want to hurt her, kill her. I cut her flesh away from mine. It is the only way that I will be free of her. (p. 41)

Lucy (in Smith et al., 1999) cut away at her body so that she could cut away at the object of her sexual abuser's lust. She explains:

> He used to say how lovely my breasts were. Pert he called them. Said they were like pure marble. He said my nipples would stand out showing how much I wanted him, but I didn't, I never did. Well they are not lovely now. My breasts are a mass of scars ... sometimes I cut inside my vagina too. That's how he made me feel, as if I was being cut apart inside. (p. 10)

In the final analysis, self-injury becomes an attempt to blot out and forget the unthinkable experience of abuse, neglect, or lack of care. It is an effort not to feel what cannot be tolerated. It is an attempt to eclipse the psychic pain experienced from parents who might be enmeshed, overinvolved, rigid, controlling, or dominating and who have decimated the self-injurer's spirit. By attacking the body, the self-injurer finds a new voice to utter her protest, to make meaning of the pain, and to assuage the horror of the trauma by enacting it repeatedly upon herself (Farber, 2000).

SUMMARY AND CONCLUSION

One of the most common characteristics in the profile of self-injurers is the experience of trauma. That trauma may have been of the simple, acute nature, in which the individual was exposed to the immediate fear of the possibility of dying, was the victim of a violent act, had a serious medical condition or multiple surgeries, or was sexually assaulted. On the other hand, the individual may have been exposed to a more complex, yet subtler and hidden form of trauma. In the latter case, what traumatizes is not the acuity of the experiences as much as their chronicity. The exposure to complex or hidden childhood trauma suggests that a child has experienced, or is currently experiencing an environment that may be physically or emotionally neglectful or one in which she is criticized or otherwise maltreated by parents or other caregivers. It suggests that chronic exposure to the possibility of harm, continual rejection, or both creates insecurity and fear. These environments are traumatic because the important attachment relationships within them are themselves traumatizing. The child's inner world fails to be acknowledged, and her emotional and psychological needs fail to be attended to appropriately. In some cases, the resulting developmental dynamics compel these individuals to learn to make sense of their experience, to cope with their pain and fears, and to manage their life in ways that become self-destructive and retraumatizing. Some of these individuals become attached to the experience of trauma and recreate that trauma by turning to the body and enacting violence against themselves through self-injurious means.

In the chapter that follows, we turn to a review of the principle effects of the exposure to trauma across developmental domains and begin to explore how the stage may be set for a person to turn to self-injury in response to his or her traumatic attachments and experiences.

CHAPTER 4

The Developmental Effects of Complex Trauma

Pain—psychological pain, surely, but perhaps even physical pain as well—is about the resistance to the motion of life. Our attempt to deny what has happened and is happening causes us pain.

Robert Kegan (1982, p. 265)

The developmental impact of childhood trauma is substantial. Exposure to complex trauma results in the faulty development of the core capacities for self-regulation and interpersonal relatedness (van der Kolk, 2005). Children exposed to complex trauma are at risk for additional trauma exposure in adolescence and adulthood and, because of the cumulative effects of chronic exposure, develop a host of psychiatric and addictive disorders and chronic medical problems, as well as impairment in vocational and interpersonal functioning (Cook et al., 2005). Survivors of chronic trauma often also develop particularly enduring attachments to trauma and to the experience of suffering (Farber, 2000). The attachment to the suffering of the original trauma may become imprinted in the child's regulatory process and actually serves as a source of comfort. A common example is the abused child who develops a greater attachment to the abusive parent than to the other. The abusive parent is *not* always abusive; he may, at times, demonstrate moments of considerable tenderness and care. Farber (2000) suggests that in essence, "'a warm enemy is better than a cold friend'—Mixing the bonds of love with the bonds of violence can produce a strong but confusing attachment" (p. 229).

The developmental effects of childhood trauma exposure range from the complex disruption of affect regulation and disturbed attachment patterns to rapid shifts in emotional states and bodily dysregulation, to self-destructive behaviors and feelings of ineffectiveness and self-hatred (van der Kolk, 2005). In their comprehensive review of the complex trauma literature, Cook and colleagues (2005) identify seven primary domains of impairment in children exposed to trauma—Attachment, Biology, Affect Regulation, Dissociation, Behavioral Control, Cognition, and Self-Concept. Table 4.1 lists each of the seven domains and provides specific examples of the behaviors and symptoms associated with each. While the scope of this book does not permit a comprehensive discussion of the domains of impairment resulting from childhood trauma, the model articulated by Cook and her colleagues (2005) can serve as an organizing template for the existing research on self-injurers. As we shall see, research that attempts to profile self-injurers has essentially identified many of the common childhood experiences, personality characteristics, and comorbid conditions present in survivors of childhood trauma as presented in Table 4.1. Again, while no direct causal link has been established between the experience of complex trauma and self-injury, some type of trauma—either simple or complex—may be a necessary but not sufficient condition for the development of *impulsive self-injury*. The following sections of this chapter present brief reviews of current research arranged according to the identified domains of impairment of children exposed to complex trauma.

TRAUMA AND SELF-INJURY

To date, the exposure to trauma is the most highly correlated factor with self-injury (Connors, 2000; Conterio & Lader, 1998; Farber, 2000; Favazza, 1996; Suyemoto, 1998; van der Kolk et al., 1991; Walsh, 2006; Walsh & Rosen, 1988; Yates, 2004). In reviewing the childhood experiences of self-injurers, a number of traumatic events emerge as significant. These traumatic incidents occurring prior to the onset of puberty include parental loss or deprivation, chronic illness or major surgery, sexual or physical abuse, and emotional neglect. In fact, up to 79% of clinical and community samples of self-injurers have reported a history of child abuse or neglect (Yates, 2004). Some examples include the work of van der Kolk, Perry, and Herman (1991), who reported finding that childhood physical and sexual abuse as well as parental neglect and separations are highly correlated with self-injury. Of the 28 subjects in their study who reported self-injurious behavior, 22 (79%) provided histories of significant childhood trauma, and 25 (89%) reported serious disruptions in parental care. They point out, however, that while "childhood trauma contributes heavily to the initiation of self-destructive behavior, lack of secure attachments maintains it. The subjects who had experienced prolonged separations

TABLE 4.1   Domains of Impairment in Children Exposed to Complex Trauma

I. Attachment	IV. Dissociation	VI. Cognition
Problems with boundaries	Distinct alterations in states of consciousness	Difficulties in attention regulation and executive functioning
Distrust and suspiciousness		
Social isolation	Amnesia	
Interpersonal difficulties	Depersonalization and derealization	Lack of sustained curiosity
Difficulty attuning to other people's emotional states		Problems with processing novel information
	Two or more distinct states of consciousness	Problems focusing on and completing tasks
Difficulty with perspective taking	Impaired memory for state-based events	Problems with object constancy
II. Biology	**V. Behavioral control**	Difficulty planning and anticipating
Sensorimotor developmental problems	Poor modulation of impulses	Problems understanding responsibility
Analgesia	Self-destructive behavior	
Problems with coordination, balance, body tone	Aggression toward others	Learning difficulties
	Pathological self-soothing behaviors	Problems with language development
Somatization	Sleep disturbances	Problems with orientation in time and space
Increased medical problems across a wide span (eg, pelvic pain, asthma, skin problems, autoimmune disorders, pseudoseizures)	Eating disorders	
	Substance abuse	
	Excessive compliance	**VII. Self-concept**
	Oppositional behavior	Lack of a continuous, predictable sense of self
III. Affect regulation	Difficulty understanding and complying with rules	Poor sense of separateness
Difficulty with emotional self-regulation	Reenactment of trauma in behavior or play (eg, sexual, aggressive)	Disturbances of body image
Difficulty labeling and expressing feelings		Low self-esteem
Problems knowing and describing internal states		Shame and guilt
Difficulty communicating wishes and needs		

Cook et al. (2005). Complex trauma in children and adolescents. *Psychiatric Annals, 35,* 390–398. © SLACK Incorporated. Reprinted with permission.

from their primary caregivers, and those who could not remember feeling special or loved by anyone as children, were least able to utilize interpersonal resources during the course of the study to control their self-destructive behavior" (p. 1669). Favazza (1996) reported similar findings in that a history of childhood abuse was present in 62% of his sample, with 29% reporting both sexual and physical abuse, 17% reporting only sexual abuse, and 16% reporting only physical abuse. Yates (2004) concluded from his review of the literature that the strongest associations tend to be between self-injury and sexual abuse, particularly the intrafamilial abuse of parent-child incest. The percentage of survivors of incest who engage in self-injury has been shown to range from 17% to 58% in various samples. The association between self-injury and abuse is strongest when the abuse is chronic over a long period of time and when it is perpetrated by an individual known to the victim, such as a family member.

Walsh and Rosen (1988) provide still further evidence regarding the relationship of childhood trauma, other negative childhood and adolescent experiences, and self-injury. The childhood profile of self-injurers that emerged from their study indicated a history that included significant family losses via divorce or placement outside the home (e.g., foster care); chronic illness, major surgery, or both; victimization through physical or sexual abuse; and exposure to violence, impulsivity, and alcohol abuse in the home. They also identified four adolescent conditions—recent loss, body alienation, peer conflict, and substance abuse—that also correlated highly with self-injury. In fact, the authors found that the coupling of these characteristics with the identified childhood conditions listed earlier accounted for 67% of the variance in a stepwise-regression analysis of predictors of self-injury. Body alienation—the adolescent's stance of disrespect, discomfort, and debasement of her physical self—emerged as the single most predictive variable of self-injury, followed by childhood loss and childhood abuse. What is particularly noteworthy, however, is that body alienation was the only factor associated with each of the four childhood conditions (childhood loss, physical or sexual abuse, illness or surgery, and family violence or alcohol abuse). The implications of this finding suggest that childhood trauma in its various iterations (whether it be trauma to the body via major surgery or sexual abuse or loss) all intensify the adolescent's disconnection from her body, which may lead to her experiencing the body as separate from the self; it may then function as the reservoir of psychological pain that results from the individual's shame and guilt.

A more recent study (Gratz, 2006) of female college students lends further support to the connection between the exposure to complex trauma (in this instance, childhood maltreatment) and self-injury. In a sample of 249 female college students, the experience of childhood maltreatment was the variable that was most highly correlated with the occurrence of self-injury ($r = .37$, $p < .01$).

Also significantly correlated were the experience of emotional neglect (r = .27, p < .01), physical abuse (r = .26, p < .01), overprotection (r = .22, p < .01), and sexual abuse (r = .19, p < .01). The results showed that the experience of childhood maltreatment reliably distinguished women who self-injured from those with no history of such behavior. These findings are consistent with current theoretical and research literature on the connection between the experience of trauma and self-injury.

ATTACHMENT

Children exposed to the complex trauma of maltreatment or disorganized attachment systems in early life suffer attachment difficulties in adolescence and adulthood (Cook et al., 2005). When the child-caregiver relationship is the source of the trauma—when the parent is too distant, unpredictable, punitive, or distressed—children do not learn to join others in collaborative problem solving when their own internal resources are overwhelmed. In adolescence and adulthood, their attachment styles reflect survival-based patterns that are disorganized and rigid and that mobilize around themes of the avoidance of abandonment, failure and betrayal, or the coercive control of others to mitigate the possibility of blame, intrusiveness, and hostility (Cook et al., 2005). Historically, clinicians have had a tendency to ascribe self-injurers the diagnosis of Borderline Personality Disorder (BPD), in which the nature of attachment in relationships is a primary criterion. While the diagnosis of BPD may be overutilized, the features related to the intensity and instability of relationships are exhibited by many self-injurers. They have difficulties trusting that others will be loyal and that they will care for them. They have difficulties with maintaining interpersonal boundaries, and their relationships tend to be erratic and emotionally volatile. Many, because of their attachment to trauma, are drawn to relationships that recapitulate attachment patterns of the past that were abusive and traumatic. Their inability to see others as potential allies who can help them negotiate life when their own resources may be inadequate creates a cyclical approach-avoidance pattern in their relationships that inhibits any semblance of secure attachment and, in effect, functions to isolate them further interpersonally (Adler & Adler, 2005; Conterio & Lader, 1998; Farber, 2000; Fonagy et al., 2002; Hawton et al., 2003; Levenkron, 1998).

BIOLOGY

While there is a paucity of neurobiologic research related to self-injury, there is some preliminary evidence that lower levels of the neurotransmitter serotonin are associated with self-injurious behaviors (Favazza, 1996; Grossman & Siever, 2001; van der Kolk et al., 1991; Yates, 2004). Serotonin is a presynaptic neurotransmitter that facilitates the conduction of impulses between neurons in the brain. A reduction in serotonin is associated with an increased risk of impulsivity and aggression toward self and others. Studies show that self-injuring individuals tend to have lower levels of serotonin than noninjuring individuals. The fact that some medications (e.g., SSRIs) that increase serotonin production in the brain tend to be efficacious in reducing the incidence of self-injury provides tentative indirect support for the serotonin hypothesis (Favazza, 1996; Grossman & Siever, 2001).

Another biological system that may be involved in the etiology and maintenance of self-injury is the Endogenous Opioid System (EOS) (Favazza, 1996; Grossman & Siever, 2001; Yates, 2004). Some self-injurers claim marked anesthesia during the act of the self-injury, and it is postulated by some that enhanced brain opioid activity may underlie the behavior. The *addiction hypothesis* related to opioid production suggests that the EOS has been so overstimulated by repeated acts of self-injury for the purpose of relieving dysphoria that the individual develops a tolerance for endogenous opioids and experiences withdrawal symptoms and so must reactivate the system to be anesthetized again (Grossman & Siever, 2001). The *pain hypothesis*, on the other hand, posits that individuals who self-injure have a constitutionally lower sensitivity to pain than noninjuring individuals. It is hypothesized that there may be an overproduction of endogenous opioids in these individuals or that they may possess neuroanatomical flaws that actually distort their perception of pain (Grossman & Siever, 2001; Yates, 2004). While a number of biological characteristics of self-injurers have been tentatively identified and appear to be similar to the characteristics of other victims of maltreatment and trauma (Cicchetti & Toth, 2005; van der Kolk, 2003), our understanding of the neurobiological aspects of the phenomenon is still far from complete.

AFFECT REGULATION

While our current understanding of the biology of self-injury is incomplete, the research literature is replete with data illustrating that self-injuring individuals have significant problems with affect regulation (e.g., Conterio & Lader, 1998; Farber, 2000; Favazza, 1996, 1998; Fonagy et al., 2002; Paivio & McCulloch, 2004; Simeon & Favazza, 2001; van der Kolk et al., 1991; Walsh, 2006; Walsh & Rosen, 1988; Yates, 2004). In fact, one of the functions of self-injury (which is discussed in further detail in Chapter 5) is that it, in essence, serves as an affect-regulatory mechanism for the individual who has difficulty naming, understanding, and managing emotions. Because self-injurers (and other survivors of trauma) have difficulty labeling and understanding their internal states and putting words to what they feel, they shift their complex psychological problems to the level of the body. These deficits have been equated with the construct of *alexithymia*—literally, "having no words for feelings"—which has been characterized as a deficiency in emotional intelligence (Paivio & McCulloch, 2004). When feelings become overwhelming and psychological tension increases to intolerable levels, self-injurious behavior functions as a means to ventilate that tension and bring the individual back to a state of affective equilibrium.

For self-injurers, words, as avenues to deal with emotions, are ineffective. To speak about what one feels for the purpose of relief does not work. Rather, relief is experienced only *after* the cutting or the burning or whatever other form of self-injury is used. Difficulties in affect regulation—not having fluency with emotional awareness and language (alexithymia)—appears to function as an important transmission mechanism between the experiences of childhood maltreatment and its reenactment through self-injury. Individuals who have difficulties regulating how they may feel at a particular moment by using their internal, self-soothing mechanisms turn to self-injury as a means to reestablish emotional equilibrium (Paivio & McCulloch, 2004).

Gratz's (2006) recent study, discussed earlier, also supports precisely this conclusion. While childhood maltreatment was the highest correlate to self-injury in her study, *emotional inexpressivity* was the most highly correlated variable with the maintenance of self-injury over time ($r = .32$, $p < .01$). These findings are consistent with others in the literature (e.g., Paivio & McCulloch, 2004) that have suggested that the inability or unwillingness to express thoughts, feelings, and other internal experiences through words is a central feature of self-injurers. These findings also support the notion of the nonverbal expressive role self-injury can play in the lives of self-injuring individuals.

DISSOCIATION

Typical of many survivors of trauma is the experience of alterations in states of consciousness, such as dissociation (Cicchetti & Toth, 2005; Cook et al., 2005; Kihlstrom, 2005; van der Kolk, 2005; van der Kolk et al., 1991; van der Kolk et al., 1994; van der Kolk, Roth, Pelcovitz, Sunday, & Spinazzola, 2005). When trauma overwhelms the psyche and the individual's ability to process and integrate her experience is taxed, she may emotionally and psychologically disconnect from the experience (and, in essence, forget the trauma) so that she may protect herself from its unbearable psychological pain. This "going numb" or "cutting oneself off" from those feelings is not a conscious act but is an automatic response to the actual trauma or some recollection or reenactment of the trauma (van der Kolk et al., 1994). Examples of dissociative responses include depersonalization, derealization, fugue states, and dissociative identity disorder (American Psychiatric Association, 2000).

The behavioral consequence of dissociation is a zombie-like state of automatization. One's conduct or actions become automatic, reactive, and avolitional. There is little conscious choice, careful planning, or even awareness of the motivations underlying one's behavior. The individual remains disconnected from her inner world, and her internal motivations lie outside her realm of awareness (Cook et al., 2005). By dissociating, the individual compartmentalizes painful feelings related to past traumatic experiences, which helps her disengage from her inner world—from the awareness of her painful memories, overwhelming thoughts, and insufferable feelings.

The relationship between self-injury and dissociative disorders is well established (e.g., Connors, 2000; Conterio & Lader, 1998; Farber, 2000; Favazza, 1996; Saxe, Chawla, & van der Kolk, 2002; van der Kolk et al., 1991; Walsh, 2006; Walsh & Rosen, 1988; Yates, 2004). Many injurers report feeling numb, disconnected, or blank prior to the self-injurious behaviors. In their disconnected, altered states of consciousness, they experience both psychic numbing and physical analgesia (Saxe et al., 2002). They often report that they feel little to no pain during the act itself. They explain that the injury itself is a way to "jolt" them back from that disengaged, altered state. It makes them feel alive and reconnected to themselves. For these individuals, self-injury may actually serve as a mode of regulating their dissociative states—from feeling numb, cutoff, and unreal to feeling embodied and alive again. The problem, however, is that, while dissociation provides protection from intolerable and unmanageable affects, it does so at a high price. Dissociation is ultimately very inefficient as a coping mechanism. While it may protect from overwhelming affects, "it also results in a subjective sense of deadness, of disconnection from others, and of internal disintegration" (van der Kolk et al., 1991, p. 1669).

BEHAVIORAL CONTROL

Self-injuring individuals often demonstrate patterns of behavior that operate at the extremes. They typically manifest behavior that is either overcontrolled or undercontrolled in a number of ways. They develop rigid behavioral patterns and inflexible character structures that serve to retain a sense of mastery and control over their world and relationships in the face of the overwhelming experience of childhood trauma. They frequently develop behavioral regulatory difficulties in areas of functioning commonly experienced by survivors of complex trauma (Cook et al., 2005). For example, they may exhibit poor modulation of impulses, aggression toward self and others, perfectionism, pathological self-soothing behaviors, eating disorders, substance abuse, oppositional behavior, and other features or behaviors that may be associated with comorbid clinical conditions and personality pathology. Co-existing with self-injury are typically a number of other important clinical features or discrete psychiatric disorders that merit some attention on their own.

Personality Disorders

Historically, self-injury has most often been associated with Borderline Personality Disorder (BPD) (Alderman, 1997; Andover, Pepper, Ryabchenko, Orrico, & Gibb, 2005; Conterio & Lader, 1998; Favazza, 1998; Muehlenkamp, 2005; Suyemoto, 1998; Walsh & Rosen, 1988). In fact, as mentioned earlier, self-injury is one of the formal criteria for the diagnosis for BPD in DSM-IV-TR. While not all self-injurers fit the BPD diagnosis, some of those who meet the full criteria do engage in self-destructive behaviors that include self-injury. The controversy surrounding BPD and self-injury stems from our inadequate diagnostic understanding of self-injury; it has, according to some, been too hastily equated with the borderline diagnosis, and the relationship may be "exaggerated" (Yates, 2004). Some point out that a borderline personality is simply a post-traumatic outcome (Connors, 2000) and that the label merely describes the characterological organization resulting from the sequelae of traumatic experience. That is, many individuals who have been severely traumatized (particularly within their own families) develop personality features consistent with the BPD diagnostic criteria. What is clear, however, is that, descriptively, many of the features of self-injurers and those of individuals diagnosed with borderline personality disorder *do* overlap. While the diagnosis of BPD has acquired a pejorative connotation implying that the BPD patient will be intractable and difficult to treat, the diagnostic conceptualization is highly descriptive and often exceedingly representative of features presented by self-injurers. Like those diagnosed with BPD, self-injurers do have difficulties with regulating their impulses and modulating anger; they do have unstable relationships and operate within them to avoid real or imagined abandonment; they do experience mood swings and chronic feelings of emptiness and often demonstrate severe dissociative symptoms. While the case may be that the full criteria for BPD may not be met, self-injurers often do exhibit significant borderline personality features (Farber, 2000; Fonagy et al., 2002). To this point, Conterio and Lader (1998) note, "Perhaps more than any other description, the borderline diagnosis captures the quality and tenor of some self-injurers' relationships: they are full of mistrust, fear, vulnerability and unpredictability. Rather than implying a pejorative view of the person, we think the borderline diagnosis highlights the suffering of the individual and the obstacles that impede her from forging safe and trusting bonds with people" (p. 178).

Eating Disorders

The co-occurrence of eating disorders and self-injury is exceedingly high (Conterio & Lader, 1998; Favaro, Ferrara, & Santonastoso, 2004; Favazza, 1998; Sansone & Levitt, 2002, 2004; Walsh & Rosen, 1988), and their dynamics along the self-harm continuum are extraordinarily similar and may actually be a function of the same psychological processes (Conterio & Lader, 1998; Farber, 2000). The implication here is that the relationship between self-injury and eating disorders goes beyond statistical association. Both sets of behaviors are typical of females with onset during adolescence; both are linked to the felt sense of body dissatisfaction and need for self-punishment; both serve similar psychological functions in terms of regulating affect and experiencing emotional relief; and both function as maneuvers to reclaim control over one's life by taking possession and controlling one's own body (Favaro et al., 2004). Comorbidity rates between self-injury and eating disorders have been shown to range from 25% in some studies (Sansone & Levitt, 2004; Favaro et al., 2004) to 75% in other clinical samples (Favazza, 1998). Despite some variability in the epidemiological data, self-injury has been clearly shown to have specific links to eating disorders, and the prevalence of adolescents who engage in both kinds of activities who present for treatment is exceedingly high (Conterio & Lader, 1998).

Depression and Anxiety

Depressive symptomatology and anxiety are prominent sequelae of exposure to trauma and are conditions that are also highly associated with self-injury (Andover et al., 2005; Briere & Spinazzola, 2005; Nock & Prinstein, 2005; Suyemoto, 1998; van der Kolk, 2005; van der Kolk et al., 1994). While self-injurers may be diagnosed with a discrete mood disorder such as major depressive disorder or bipolar disorder or with an anxiety disorder such as PTSD, not all self-injurers meet full diagnostic criteria for mood or anxiety disorders. In most cases, however, depressive symptomatology and anxiety are prominent features of the self-injurer's clinical picture. These symptoms, while present, may actually be obscured by other common comorbid features such as impulsivity, affective lability, and the problematic behaviors that emerge as foreground issues, relegating the depression or anxiety to a background or secondary position. Self-injury may actually be a means to manage anxiety and depression. Therefore, the act of self-injury itself may modulate one's depressive or anxious states, making those symptoms less prominent in both the self-injurer's subjective distress and the assessing clinician's diagnostic formulations. The fact that self-injurers are not usually consciously suicidal or outwardly manifest suicidal behavior may further obfuscate the underlying mood issues that may warrant clinical attention.

Substance Use

The use and abuse of substances, like self-injury, are used for the regulation of mood. Whether we need a cup of coffee in the morning to provide us with a little jolt so that we can begin the day or a glass of Chianti in the evening to help us relax and unwind, we are regulating our mood with the assistance of substances. In more extreme cases, we may use illegal drugs to alter our mood in more rapid, significant, and intense ways (Alderman, 1997). Although some variability exists in how substances may be used by self-injurers, a link between the two has clearly been established in the literature (Claes et al., 2005; Yates, 2004). For example, in a sample of 34 poly-self-destructive adolescents, 77% reported sniffing glue, 53% reported the frequent use of alcohol, 85% reported the use of marijuana, 32% cocaine, and 42% LSD (Walsh, 2006). In another study, 56% of self-injurers acknowledged a problem with alcohol, and 30% reported having used illegal substances (Conterio & Lader, 1998).

Mood-altering substances are utilized in different ways by self-injurers and may pose differential risks depending on the nature and context of how they are used. In my own clinical observations, I have seen self-injurers who abstain completely from the use of substances. Some of these individuals also demonstrated issues around body image and food intake. For them, the use of substances implied a sort of contamination of their body, which they tried to prevent at all costs. Having their mood altered by substances would signify a loss of control over themselves and their bodies, which would be difficult, if not impossible, for them to tolerate. For these individuals, the use of substances was anathema. On the other hand, for other self-injurers, substance use is simply one step along the mood-alteration continuum. For some, substance use is the more frequent and preferred method for altering their mood and numbing themselves to unpleasant feelings. When the intensity of those feelings overwhelms them and the use of substances fails to modulate those emotional states sufficiently, these individuals may turn to self-injury as a more direct means of discharging their negative affects in the attempt to find psychological relief. Self-injury becomes the preferred method at the next level of intensity on the mood-altering hierarchy that these individuals use in order to manage their distress and feel better.

The risk of a lethal self-injury can also increase when substances are present. For example, a recent self-injury case at a local college that escalated to very high levels of lethality involved a 19-year-old self-injuring female freshman who had a history of alcohol abuse. Upon learning that her boyfriend of three months wanted to end their relationship, she embarked on a drinking binge. After she left the bar, she returned to her dorm room, found her cutting implements, and began to cut herself. Because of her level of intoxication, she cut herself deeper than she normally did. She left her dorm, wandered throughout campus bleeding, and, shortly thereafter, passed out on the grounds, where she was found by campus security and transported to the hospital. She reported to her therapist that her intent was not to commit suicide but to "try to stop feeling so bad" now that she had been left by her boyfriend. She explained that she had always cut while sober because she knew the alcohol "made things get out of hand." The use of substances, while not always a factor with self-injury, is often an associated factor and can raise the level of lethality of the injury when the appropriate conditions are aligned.

COGNITION

Prospective studies have shown that maltreated or neglected children demonstrate significant deficits in cognitive functioning that include impairments in abstract reasoning, attention, and executive functioning skills, as well as in overall I.Q. They show deficits in their ability to process novel information, to focus and to complete tasks, to plan and to anticipate, and have difficulties in understanding responsibility (Cook et al., 2005). Unlike outwardly suicidal individuals, whose cognition is severely constricted and whose cognitive possibilities are dichotomously organized (e.g., "If my boyfriend leaves me, I will kill myself"), self-injurers, more often than not, tend to be disorganized in their thinking. Rather than to think they have no choice in their actions, they believe they have some choice in how they respond to situations in their lives. Unfortunately, the array of options is also limited. They include in their arsenal of problem-solving alternatives self-harming choices like self-injury (Walsh, 2006).

Decisions to self-injure are fueled by the distorted thinking patterns that develop as a result of the exposure to complex trauma. Maltreated or neglected children come to organize their view of the world around their experience of having been victimized and rejected (Farber, 2000). The core beliefs of these children become appropriately distorted around self-blaming and self-defeating themes. After all, how could a child coming from an invalidating environment not feel somewhat responsible for her psychological abandonment by her caregivers: "It's my fault my mother doesn't love me." "There's something wrong with *me*. I don't deserve to be loved and cared for." "If only I were a better daughter, my father would not have abused me as he did." These core beliefs fuel the sequential cognitive distortions that eventually lead to the decision to act destructively and, for some, to act out this self-blame on one's body.

SELF-CONCEPT

The cognitive deficits and distortions discussed in the preceding section play a significant role in undermining the development of a stable and integrated sense of self of children exposed to trauma. These children struggle to define a knowable, continuous, and predictable identity. They often have difficulties with boundaries, suffer from low self-esteem, and are racked with shame and guilt. Cook and her collaborators (2005) explain that

> repetitive experiences of harm, rejection, or both by significant others, and the associated failure to develop age-appropriate competencies, are likely to lead to a sense of self as defective, helpless, deficient, and unlovable. Children who perceive themselves as powerless or incompetent and who expect others to reject and despise them are more likely to blame themselves for negative experiences and have problems eliciting and responding to social support. (p. 395)

Adams and colleagues' (2005) recent online qualitative study of self-injurers between the ages of 16 and 26 provides corroborating evidence for this sense of a disintegrated, unstable self-concept and low self-esteem. They found that the most prominent theme across self-injurers' accounts of the self was the notion of validation—the desire of self-injurers to "maintain a sense of self that is legitimate, defensible, and acceptable, both internally (to themselves) and externally (to others)" (p.1300). In explicating their internal conflict between the perceived valid and invalid self, participants had distinctly negative tones to their self-judgments:

> I don't like myself. Fat ugly and stupid.

> Well i hate myself, i hate who i am. i hate who i see when i look in the mirror … i'd change everything pretty much. And it would be great. (p. 1300)

They felt highly inadequate about themselves and felt that, because they were worthless, they deserved the pain and life they had:

> there's just too much about me that is wrong … too many things that need to be fixed but i can't fix them because they are just who i am as a person. i feel totally worthless and feel like there's no hope for me, that I don't deserve anything good, even stuff i already have/I deserve the pain and suffering … I deserve all misery that is given to me. (p. 1301)

Many expressed a dire need for others to acknowledge their value before they could accept it themselves and felt they needed to be excessively submissive to others so as to sustain their hopes that they would be validated and accepted by them. They expressed the conflict of wanting to be themselves but feeling that their "true" selves needed to remain hidden in order for them to be accepted by others:

> I also have this big thing where I need people to reaffirm how good or bad a person I am.

> I think that I feel okay about myself. Maybe that is because I have so many people helping me feel that way. Left alone to my own thoughts, they stray to the negative.

> I feel that i have to conform to others opinions of me, and act how i'm expected to act…. But i can't keep living up to their expectations because it is crushing the person i really am by pretending to be someone else. (p. 1304)

> I wish I could change to be the person people want me to be. Or just accept me as I am. (p. 1305)

The final theme that emerged from the study was the participants' hope, despite their self-injurious behaviors, to be seen as normal by others:

> I'm also more f****d up in the head than most people. Looking at my cuts this morning made me feel sick—it reminds me that I'm, screwed up, that my head doesn't work the same way as everyone else's.

> I really want most people to treat me completely like everyone else. I'm not a freakshow…. I am a totally normal person.

> i want people to treat me like i am human, because i am. i may cut myself, but I am still human, i still bleed like they do, cry like they do. i just want people to look at me like i'm human, not some insane psycho that harms herself.

> I want them to realize that there is more to me than just a girl who cuts herself. When people look at me, I want them to see more than just the scars. (p. 1305–1306)

The experience of invalidation through maltreatment and neglect invalidates the core self of the individual, leaving a ruptured, unstable, and fragmented center that the self-injurer strives to legitimize. For the self-injurer, the body becomes the battleground for this struggle. The experience of trauma may not be articulated through words, spoken even to oneself, but the body is both the canvas and the playing field where pain is communicated and attempts at self-healing are played out.

SUMMARY AND CONCLUSION

While a definite profile of a "typical" self-injurer is not easily captured, this chapter presented the major environmental and clinical features commonly associated with individuals who engage in self-injury. The notion of complex trauma was utilized as the primary organizing rubric to describe the foundational experiences of many children exposed to maltreatment and neglect, prominent in the profiles of self-injurers. Self-injury is multidetermined and results from the complex interplay of a number of biopsychosocial factors— issues ranging from one's biological vulnerabilities and predispositions to the quality of early attachment relationships to abuse experienced in the home to the quality of support systems the individual has at her disposal. For purposes of organization and clarity, the central features of individuals who self-injure have been presented as discrete characteristics within particular developmental domains (see Table 4.1). It is important to keep in mind, however, that there is significant overlap and interaction between the many features described. For example, depressive symptomatology, dissociative states, and borderline personality disorder were discussed as separate features of self-injurers. The reality, however, is that these characteristics, like many of the othesrs discussed, are very much interrelated and usually exist coextensively with one another. Particular personality features transact with Axis I clinical conditions to, at times, potentiate those conditions, or, at other times, serve as an impetus for action or change. It is therefore difficult to tease out the interactive effects of, for example, borderline personality features, affective and cognitive regulatory difficulties, and eating disorders, as they all independently and synergistically may coexist in the profile of self-injurers. Self-injury appears to develop out of a context of trauma-induced deficits that lead to the development of comorbid conditions that contribute to the poor adaptive functioning of the individual and to the emergence of the compensatory behaviors they use to manage their lives.

Having reviewed the primary environmental, relational, and developmental context that may set the stage for self-injury, we now turn to the exploration of the phenomenological meanings and subjective motivations that may lead individuals to engage in acts of direct harm against their bodies.

CHAPTER 5

The Phenomenology of Self-Injury: The Attempt to Turn Pain Into Self-Healing

The great art of life is sensation, to feel that we exist, even in pain.

Lord Byron (in Khulsa & Stauth, 1999, p. 45)

No cut on my body will ever embody what I feel inside, but it's a start.

Dana (in Adler & Adler, 2005, p. 354)

Self-injury, in all its forms, challenges the limits of conventional wisdom and rationality. Individuals who have clearly suffered—who carry the pain of loss, abuse, and neglect—willingly trade in their psychological anguish for the self-inflicted wounds on their bodies. The unendurable suffering they have experienced as a result of the trauma in their lives or of the nurturance vacuum (Levenkron, 1998) they have felt in their own families compels them to distance themselves from the reality of those experiences. They drive those memories out of consciousness and disable their ability to think and reflect on the horror of those experiences and are, therefore, unable to construct a meaningful narrative of their lives. How do children make sense of their parents' words and actions when the parents communicate rejection and invalidation: "Why does my mother criticize me all the time? Why does she never listen to me—what I might think or feel? Why does she not love me?" or "Why does my father drink so much? Why does he never speak to me when he's sober? Why does he make me so afraid of him? Doesn't he love me?" or "Why won't my mother believe me when I tell her that her brother is touching me in my private parts and makes me feel bad? Why does she still let him baby-sit me? Why won't she protect me? Doesn't she love me?" How does a child make sense of a parent's behavior that does not create safety or protect her from others who may harm her? How does a child comprehend her own feelings and hopes when her internal world is not listened to and honored by the people she looks to most for understanding and acceptance? How does she hold in her mind the terror that the people who are supposed to prize and love her are the very source of distancing and uncaring?

The experience of invalidation and of these unthought and unspoken, yet deeply felt, questions that arise in the child speak to a profound sense of discomfirmation of who the child is and what she can become. Even the slightest recognition from another confirms one's presence in the world. A responsive smile, a gentle touch, an expression of concern, an act of kindness all confirm the presence and relevance of the individual, and, when they are absent, the child is discomfirmed as a human being. Laing (1969) outlines precisely this process. He observes that there are families where there is little genuine confirmation of personhood by the parents between each other and toward their children. The interactions in these families are marked by "pseudo-confirmation"—"by acts that masquerade as confirming but are counterfeit" (p. 83). Here, the child is confirmed only to the extent that he embodies the parent's image of who he should be, but the reality of who he *is* and *wants to be* is never attended to. The child is confirmed only when he lives out the "fiction" he is taken to be without the actual person behind the fiction being known and validated. This is a child who does not seem to be (outwardly) abused or neglected, but it is the child who has been the victim of subtle and systematic discomfirmation—usually occurring without the awareness of the participants. The unfortunate result of this dynamic is that the child's false self is the part that is validated and, accordingly, emerges as the only self that is acknowledged and prized. This, however, leads only to the child's feeling guilt, shame, and anxiety because he is not really the "false self"—the person his parents take him to be. The tragedy in all this, according to Laing (1969), is this:

> Confirmation of a false self goes on without anyone in the family being aware that this is the state of affairs. The [pathogenic] potential of the situation seems to reside largely in the fact that it is not recognized by anyone; or if the mother or father or some other member or friend of the family is aware of this state of affairs, it is not brought into the open and no effort is made to intervene—if such intervention were only to state the truth of the matter. (p. 84)

When the truth of the child's reality is denied, the child must mobilize to contain and transform her overwhelming affects in order to preserve some semblance of psychological integrity and to avoid disintegration. And, when one's psychological reality is poorly integrated, the body takes on an "excessively central role for the continuity of a sense of self" (Fonagy et al., 2002, p. 405). By transferring one's hurt to the body, one can sacrifice the body for the sake of keeping the mind more coherent and whole; relegating one's pain to the body provides the mind, at least for the moment, with a calming sense of well-being. Self-injurers seek physical pain to, in effect, distract themselves from and bypass their emotional turmoil. They turn to the body to divert their attention from those psychic realities over which they have little or no control. They are able to alter their mood states by focusing on pain in a deliberate and controlled way, unlike the inchoate emotional ache they feel powerless to otherwise endure. Although highly counterintuitive, self-injury works. It soothes and temporarily relieves emotional suffering. Some have described it as a "wounding embrace" (Conterio & Lader, 1998) to illustrate its role as a replacement for the warmth and intimacy usually experienced in loving relationships. Self-injury reduces tension and restores a sense of psychological equilibrium; it provides one an otherwise unfelt sense of control over her life (Walsh, 2006). It is highly effective in addressing psychological pain and becomes, over time, a desperate yet comforting attempt at self-healing despite its morbid and unpleasant manifestations (Clarke & Whittaker, 1998; Favazza, 1996).

THE PSYCHOLOGICAL FUNCTIONS OF SELF-INJURY

Feeling unreal and distant disconnected with life,
I pick up razor blades,
Relieved at the sight of them I cry,
Not totally aware, I cut into my skin,
Jolted back into reality by the act,
Checking that I'm still alive that I'm still real,
For a short while I am in control, for a short while I am at peace.

(Gardner, 2001, p. 3)

In general, self-injury, whether done to control or to better adapt to one's psychological pain, suggests that wounds to the skin can serve contradictory functions—one causes oneself direct harm by drawing blood and mutilating bodily tissue even as, at the same time, one may hope to restore one's life and feel whole through these self-destructive acts. As Nasser (2004) points out, self-injurers do not pursue death; through attacking their bodies, they attempt to defy it. They attempt to alter the deadness they feel inside and hope to expand consciousness through their acts so as to free themselves from their voiceless, yet enveloping internal anguish. Adolescence is a critical developmental period in which individuals attempt to give voice to the powerful feelings they have felt but have heretofore not been able to express. The demands for separateness and individuality that emerge during this period of life set the stage for the overt manifestation of the signs and symptoms that reflect the individual's internal conflicts. Up to this point, the child has been able to distance herself from the power of her spirit-wounding experiences, but in adolescence, with the onset of major biological changes and their accompanying developmental tasks, feelings of rage, anger, rebelliousness, and falling in love all surface and overpower her psychic and emotional capacities (Miller, 1980). The intensity of an adolescent's true feelings about her parents and her traumatic experiences or the reality of having been psychologically invalidated can overwhelm her and cause her to seek an outlet for those feelings in extreme and sometimes destructive ways. For one who has felt invalidated and rejected, to separate oneself from the object of one's oppression means that, essentially, she must destroy that person. But since that person (and her abuse and invalidation) has been internalized, the adolescent's only tolerable recourse is to turn her aggression inward upon herself and her body (Fonagy et al., 2002).

Themes From Recent Empirical Research

Self-injury serves a number of psychological functions that often overlap and usually operate simultaneously (Suyemoto, 1998). Recent empirical investigations have identified various themes that speak to the function of self-injury, and a number of these themes are highly consistent across studies. For example, Osuch, Noll, and Putnam (1999) found six factors that accounted for 85% of the variance in their sample of 99 self-injuring inpatients. The identified factors consisted of (1) Affect Modulation, which includes general affects or the specific affect of fear, anger, shame, guilt, or suicidality; (2) Desolation, which is similar to the affective regulatory function of factor (1), but the specific affects that were modulated in this case are isolation and emptiness; (3) Punitive Duality, which involves both the theme of self-punishment and the conflict between one's internal and one's external locus of control; (4) Influencing Others, which refers to the attempt to influence others through self-injury; (5) Magical Control, which also refers to the attempt to control or influence others, but, in this case, to do so in a confused, complicated, or perplexing way (illustrated in respondents' simultaneously endorsing contradictory items such as "to 'protect' important people in my life" and "to hurt someone important in my life"); and (6) Self-Stimulation, which refers to the attempt both to release tension (as in a release "that feels like sexual release") and to stimulate oneself (in a manner reminiscent of a "high" experienced through drug use).

Brown, Comtois, and Linehan (2002) found similar trends in their sample of 75 self-injuring women. Ninety-six percent of their respondents endorsed at least one item from the *Emotional Relief* subscale that included statements such as "To stop bad feelings," "To relieve feelings of aloneness, emptiness and isolation," and "To obtain relief from a terrible state of mind." Sixty-one percent endorsed at least one item from the *Interpersonal Influence* subscale (e.g., "To shock or impress others," "To get back at or hurt someone," and "To communicate to or let others know how desperate you are"), and 54% endorsed at least one item on the *Feeling Generation* subscale (e.g., "To stop feeling numb or dead" and "To feel something, even if it was pain"). The most frequently endorsed items on the *Individual Reasons* subscale were self-punishment (63%) and anger expression (63%).

In their online study of reasons why people self-injury, Warm, Murray, and Fox (2003) found that 96.7% of the 243 respondents agreed with the notion that self-injury is a way of expressing emotional pain; 95.6% agreed that it was used as a coping strategy; 89.6% noted that it was a means to release anger; and, 87.6% saw it as a way of staying in control. The majority of the respondents in this study did not view their behaviors as attention seeking or as an attempt to manipulate others, contradicting views presented in other research. In terms of what the respondents thought self-injury was not, they endorsed items that reflected their belief that it was not merely a female problem, that it was not a failed suicide attempt, and that it was not a sign of madness.

Examining a functional model of adolescent self-injury consistent with leaning theory, Nock and Prinstein (2004, 2005) suggest that reasons related to automatic reinforcement (i.e., the regulation—both increase and decrease—of emotional or physiological experiences) were the items most frequently endorsed by inpatient adolescents. Respondents endorsed items that were both automatic-negatively reinforcing (e.g., "to stop bad feelings") and automatic-positively reinforcing (e.g., "to feel something, even if it was pain"). They also found that social reinforcement was a significant factor in influencing the occurrence of self-injury. Individuals endorsed items that reflected both social-negative reinforcement (i.e., the desire to escape interpersonal task demands), such as "to avoid punishment from others," and items that reflected social-positive reinforcement (that involved gaining attention or materials from others).

Broad Functions of Self-Injury

Suyemoto (1998) observes that a major difficulty in attempting to understand the intrapsychic and interpersonal functions of self-injury is the overdetermined complexity and contextual embeddedness of the behavior. Self-injurious be-haviors have multiple functions, and the same individual will engage in dif-ferent behaviors at different times to meet different psychological needs. Lucy (Smith et al., 1999) comments:

> Talking about it over and over in therapy, I realized that I do it in different ways at different times. When I'm filled with feelings connected to him, I tend to cut myself. When I am angry, really angry and frustrated I'm more likely to hit myself, bruise myself. When I feel cut off, blank, as if I'm both alive and dead at the same time, it's then that I tend to burn myself. It is as if I haven't the energy to hurt myself in a more active way. (p. 11)

As a result of the multiple psychological uses of self-injury, it is very dif-ficult to clearly distinguish and differentiate one subjective function from another. For purposes of organization and clarity, I group the multiple func-tions of the behavior that have been reported in the literature into four broad categories—(1) Regulating affect, soothing emotional wounds, and managing dissociation; (2) Seeking mastery over pain and past trauma; (3) Commu-nicating pain, controlling others, and seeking nurturance; and (4) Securing and authenticating a sense of self. Thematically similar functions reported in the literature are arranged and incorporated into one of the four organizing categories. Following Suyemoto's (1998) approach, the descriptions that fol-low are an attempt to both differentiate and integrate the various functions of self-injury while remaining cognizant of their interrelated and overlapping nature.

Regulating Affect, Soothing Emotional Wounds, and Managing Dissociation

> It's like a relief. I do it every couple of weeks just to get relief ... from pressure that builds up inside.... [I] just, just feel that there's a pressure building up inside of you that you have to do something about. That you feel like you're going to explode if you don't. And cutting is a way to release that.
>
> Himber (in Suyemoto, 1998, p. 543)
>
> [The] only way I could calm myself down was to cut myself.... And it worked!
>
> Kristy (in Conte, 2004, p. 175)

The most commonly articulated explanation for wounding the body offered by self-injurers is that it provides them with a sense of deep relief from the emotional turmoil they feel. Self-injury serves to express, externalize and manage intolerable and overwhelming feelings (Farber, 2000; Favazza, 1996; Suyemoto, 1998; van der Kolk et al., 1991). As we have seen in Chapters 3 and 4, individuals who self-injure have often been exposed to insecure early attachment relationships, abuse, neglect, and other forms of complex trauma that interfere with the development of the ability to make sense of and manage their emotions. In one's infancy and early childhood, one's primary caregiver functions as the external regulator of emotion, and, as she is able to contain the child's affect and hold it for the child so that the child is not overwhelmed by it, the child learns to internalize the caregiver's calm responses to stress, tension, and uncertainty. The experience of this external soothing when in distress helps the child feel a greater sense of security in the world—that her needs will be taken care of—and helps in the development of the child's ability to tolerate and effectively regulate its internal, emotional world in later life (Fonagy et al., 2002; Schore 1994, 2003a, 2003b).

The problem is that many self-injurers, for whatever reason, have not had those requisite rearing experiences that create the conditions for the optimal development of their internal self-regulatory mechanisms. Consequently, they are forced to turn to other methods of dealing with their overpowering emotions and soothe their distress. Farber (2000) observes that "The parent's inability to contain the child or think about the child's mental experience, and thus mirror it for him, may later, in adolescence, promote a desperate quest for alternative ways to containing psychological experience, which may involve various forms of destructive and physical expression toward the self" (p. 163).

It is often the case that, later in life, the unbearable levels of emotional pain from which the self-injurer seeks relief result directly from the individual's perception of the stability or instability of her current interpersonal relationships. The levels of distress usually arise in response to real or imagined losses in her important relationships, when she believes that the relationship will soon end or that she will be abandoned. The operative emotion may be anger at the other for leaving or at the self for having failed in the relationship, or it may simply reflect the pain of feeling rejected. The self-injurious behavior functions as an attempt to mediate the intensity of feelings (e.g., anger, anxiety, pain) that cannot be expressed verbally (Suyemoto, 1998).

While the nature and sequence of self-injurious events vary according to each individual's own psychological and behavioral idiosyncrasies, a number of stages have been identified that describe typical patterns reported by self-injurers. Simeon and Favazza (2001) summarize the sequence:

> First is the precipitating event, often involving real or perceived loss, rejection, or abandonment. The second stage is the escalation of the intolerable affect, whether dysphoric or numb. Attempts to forestall self-injury (the third

step) are followed by its execution (fourth), which is often accompanied by partial or total analgesia. The fifth and final stage is the aftermath, which commonly involves at least short-lived relief. (p. 17)

The act of cutting serves as a calming function in both expressing and relieving the anguish self-injurers experience. It externalizes their pain, it alters their physiological state by triggering their endogenous opioid release, and it allows them to transition from an intense and heightened condition of psychological arousal to one of greater tranquility. In fact, the very anticipation of the act of self-injury can begin the soothing process and deescalate the building inner tension that so desperately seeks release (Farber, 2000).

Sarah (in Smith et al., 1999) describes the process that leads to her sense of relief:

> Once I let myself decide to do it, the relief seems to begin. I sort of go into a bit of a haze, I do things sort of automatically. I go out to buy my blades, tissues, bandages and melanin strips. I've got hundreds of blades at home but I like to get new ones each time, it's part of it. I think about what I'm going to do, where, how I'm going to do it. It's all part of it. I then go to the bathroom, sit on the mat and take everything out of the wrappers and place them all around me in the same order. I break the razors and by then I already feel much better, much calmer. (p. 35)

In addition to regulating intense feelings and soothing emotional distress, self-injury functions to regulate one's reactions to dissociative states. As discussed in Chapter 4, one of the common sequelae of the exposure to trauma is a dissociative response by the victim. Individuals report feeling numb or disconnected from their feelings and experience a sense of depersonalization in which they feel like automatons living in a dreamlike state within their bodies. They feel detached and estranged from their selves, and they experience themselves standing on the outside looking in at the events of their lives; they feel disconnected even from their bodily sensations. While dissociation emerges out of self-protective necessity—it helps victims detach, distance themselves, and push out of consciousness the reality of their past abuse or trauma—it also deleteriously disconnects them from their inner lives.

For these individuals, self-injury can function as the light switch, as it were, to help them transition to and from their dissociative states. When they dissociate, they experience an anesthetized, deadened sense of self and often lack the certitude that they are actually alive. Self-injury functions to alleviate this dead state of consciousness. When experiencing emptiness, disconnection, deadness, and lack of feeling, they can be jolted back into reality by the act of self-injury; in essence, they once again begin to feel and believe that they actually are connected to their bodies and actually exist. As one self-injurer put it, "When I cut myself and see the blood, it's very reassuring, because I can see for myself that I'm still alive" (Walsh, 2006, p. 8). Stacey (in Conte, 2004) reflects further on how self-injury ends her dissociative states:

> My body's there, but my mind's not there. I'm thinking about something else. I'm off in "la-la land." My mind is just racing. I'm just gone. It's like I'm stoned. I look like I'm stoned. I'm in like ... more like ... an imaginary world? Like you're there but you're not there. Like [your] body's there but your head is somewhere else, your mind is someplace else. I was very foggy.... And the pain ... and the blood makes everything real. It does. (p. 172)

Seeking Mastery Over Pain and Past Trauma

> *[If] I was feeling horrible, and I took up this knife and this razor blade, it gave me the power that I was lacking. Like, if my mom was being a bitch that day or ... I felt someone had made fun of me.... Once you do that—even if it is to yourself—you're the one that's causing the pain.... [It] overrides the pain that you were feeling before and compensates for it. So, sort of like you're in charge of the pain.*

> Claudia (in Conte, 2004, p. 176)

Self-injurers often feel out of control in their lives. Because they have often felt that their inner worlds have gone unheard and uncared for, or because they have been victims of acute or complex trauma that left them feeling damaged and invalidated as human beings—perhaps believing that they don't count in the eyes of those who are supposed to love them most—they experience great powerlessness in their efforts to control others or even their own destinies. Self-injurers, like other self-destructive individuals, invert the experience of pleasure and pain. They reverse what is painful and experience it, on some distorted level, as pleasurable. They derive a sense of control over their situation by actively attacking their bodies rather than feel the powerlessness of being wounded by the pain inflicted on them by others. For them, it is better to create their own pain and control it than it is to be the victim of another kind of pain that they cannot control (Farber, 2000). As victims of abusive or invalidating parents, for example, they had little or no control over their worlds. They could not control whether their alcoholic father would come home drunk and physically beat them or want to have sex with his "little princess." They could not control whether their intrusive or psychologically devouring mother would invade their psychological boundaries and belittle, berate, and crush their young spirits. They could not protect themselves from the traumas to which they were subjected. Now, however, they are the ones in control of their pain. And, by externalizing their internal pain to their bodies and, in essence, reenacting their original traumas, they seek to master those unremembered feelings of being powerless and out of control in the face of their abusers and thereby keep under control both their felt sense of pain and their responses to it.

Self-injurers' own stories speak to their desire for control over their lives—to feel a sense of power, to master feelings of self-hatred, or to overcome the feeling of uselessness:

> [B]y doing it physically, it would make it seem more real and it would actually get rid of the emotional pain for awhile, because you are concentrating on the physical pain.... But emotional pain I see as something that's in you and you can't really see it, you just feel ... so that you're not able to really remedy it, in a sense. But, by cutting yourself, or burning yourself, or whatever people do, you see the reality of it so then it gives somewhat of a temporary cure ... for how you're feeling. (Amy in Conte, 2004, p. 175)

> Freshman year of college I cut my leg a couple of times, just because I was overcome by these feelings of self-hatred. And that, I really started to think, well, I can't control that, so I will control *this*. (Claudia in Conte, 2004, p. 176)

> I kind of hated everything at that point.... I felt useless.... Like, that's just how I felt about me, in respect to everything. Like, I couldn't get anything right, and like, it just got to a point where ... I wanted to be in control of ... something, really. And ... that ... that wound up being it. The self-injury. (Kristy in Conte, 2004, p. 176)

Walsh and Rosen (1988) suggest that individuals with particularly traumatic histories may choose self-injury as a way to relive, recapitulate, and reshape those traumatic histories. Within a single act, self-injury can express the collective impact of their childhood and adolescent experiences. They act out all of the familiar roles of their past: "the abandoned child, the physically damaged patient, the abused victim, the (dissociated) witness to violence and self-destructiveness, and finally, the aggressive attacker" (p. 75). What is carried with them is a profound self-hatred that becomes the internalized abuse of the abuser. When feeling distressed, they turn the aggression inward. As one self-injurer puts it: "I want to cut when I feel angry, lonely/alone, confused. I feel I have no right to my feelings. I feel disgusting and dirty. I don't know what else to do. I want to hurt. I deserve to hurt" (Smith et al., 1999, p. 93). Through their self-punishment, they take vengeance on themselves for their own failings and for the wrongs done to them by significant others in their lives (Conterio & Lader, 1998). In doing so, they divert the aggression from external others—for example, the abusive parent—onto themselves in an attempt to preserve any semblance of hope for reparation for that lost relationship and in an attempt to recuperate the love and validation that were lost.

This sense of mastery and control over their past traumas is actually a mechanism that provides a sense of hope in the face of their despair over their pain-filled lives. Walsh (2006) observes that "most self-injuring people find it reassuring that cutting, burning, or some other form of self-harm is available whenever they may need it to reduce distress. The control that self-injury offers is antithetical to hopelessness. The future is not one of endless inescapable pain because self-injury often works as a tension-reduction mechanism" (p. 14). In fact, as is discussed at greater length in Chapter 7, self-injury is often counterintentional to suicide. It can actually be a preventive measure against suicide in that it serves as a compromise between the life force and the death drives of the individual; it is not an attempt to escape unendurable pain but to control it and keep it manageable (Suyemoto, 1998).

Communicating Pain, Controlling Others, and Seeking Nurturance

Whilst I was rushing downwards, there appeared before my eyes one who seemed hoarse from long silence.

Dante Alighieri (1950, p. 12)

A recurrent theme in the lives of self-injurers is their inability to put into words the pain they have experienced in their lives. Their unuttered anguish is transferred to the visible signs on the body. The body comes to speak what they themselves are unable to articulate. Those who have no voice have usually had it taken away in some manner. For example, the individual who has suffered the invalidation of her inner core by a caregiver learns to retreat inward and de facto abdicates the right to have a voice and speak her needs, desires, and hopes. She is acted upon, as opposed to being reacted to by an attuned, respectful caregiver. And so, when pain is not heard, let alone allowed expression, it "becomes woven into the fabric of the 'speaker's' existence" (Farber, 2000, p. 17). Many self-injuring adolescents speak precisely to this point when they say that no matter what they have done or not done, they have failed to capture their parents' attention sufficiently for them to listen, be present to them, and respond to them. As a result, they turn to a more vociferous form of communication—that of blood, scars, and the physical wounding of the body.

For the individual who feels alone, isolated, and forgotten, where no clearing has been made where her inner self can emerge and be confirmed and validated, self-injury can serve as a highly socially reinforcing act (Suyemoto,

1998). Self-injury is learned through familial modeling of abuse, leading the individual to believe that self-injury is right and that, in some distorted way, pain is linked to caring. This is similar to the abused child's powerful attachment to the abusing parent; while the child may be seriously abused by that parent, she may also experience moments when the parent expresses regret for her abuse and even provides care, tenderness, and nurturance. A powerful, difficult-to-sever link is thus established between the abusive parent and the child. The occasional acts of kindness serve as the intermittent reinforcement and acceptance that the child so desperately hungers for. With regard to self-injury, while there is much secrecy and shame associated with self-injurious behavior (Adler & Adler, 2005; Conterio & Lader, 1998) and many injurers hide their activities for prolonged periods of time, the reaction of others upon discovering the wounds or scars can be reinforcing in a number of ways.

First, the shock and horror (not to mention the vicarious traumatization) that others may experience can give the injurer a sense of power and control that she has heretofore never felt. While her verbal expressions of rage or pain may have been dismissed in the past, the graphic cuts on her body may not be so easy to ignore or write off. For some, self-injury is a powerful form of communication because it creates a sense of shock in others, and the injurer may take a secret delight in provoking extreme reactions, including revulsion and disgust, in others. For some self-injurers, the injuries represent cries to people outside the family who are invited to take notice of the trauma being caused in the family and to intervene in some way. Erin speaks of wanting others to know about the abuse she suffered at the hands of her father:

> I was hurting and I wanted people to know.... And that obviously the eating disorder didn't send a big enough sign. So I felt like I needed to take it a step higher.... So, and I definitely would always cut myself or injure myself in places that usually people would notice. That if I cut myself on my wrist or my forearm I would almost make a point to wear a short-sleeved shirt. So that someone would ask me about it and I would have to create a story but I would want to make the story a little shady so people would press it more. (Conte, 2004, p. 179)

Others try to be seen and acknowledged by their parents, who remain otherwise oblivious and disconnected. Claudia notes:

> I left clues for my mom to find.... I left the razor blade out and she would just take it away, and never say anything. And I confronted her about it later and she said, of course, that she had no idea. My mom. Bad mom. (Conte, 2004, p. 180)

Self-injury can be a desperate attempt to make others notice that the injurer exists and is in pain and hungers for connection.

Self-injurious behaviors can also be reinforcing in that the individual may actually receive positive attention from others. Family, peers, and caregivers can all rally around the injurer and provide the much-desired nurturance that the individual has heretofore not received. They may find that caregivers want to help and understand, and therefore the behavior achieves the desired secondary effect of bringing others closer and placing the self-injurer at the center of attention. Here again, nurturance and care are linked with pain. Sue explains:

> Doing my diary made me realize that when I was lonely or wanted someone to comfort me or feel sorry for me I would hurt myself, usually on purpose but make it seem like an accident. I talked this through in the group and remembered when I was little I used to go to the school nurse with cuts and grazes and she would cuddle me and make me feel better. People always seem so much nicer to you if they think you've had an accident. (Smith et al., 1999, p. 99)

The positive reinforcement received through self-injury is no more compelling than that received through peer relationships. The modeling and reinforcement of self-injury are powerful contributors to the contagion effect (discussed in Chapter 9). Adolescents see that this injurious behavior may be rewarded with attention, status, or admiration and so learn to imitate the behavior in order to garner the same desired attention or support (Walsh & Rosen, 1988). Sometimes adolescents engage in self-injurious activities together, encourage each other, teach each other new methods, and even compete with each other for the most severe or the deepest cut or for the greatest number of injuries (Suyemoto, 1998). These individuals find connection around their injurious acts and fortify their relational bonds through support for the behaviors. A former patient of mine once reported making a pact with three other friends; they agreed that, while they all committed to trying to stop cutting, should one of them relapse, the other two would also cut in order to demonstrate solidarity with the one who was more vulnerable and was not able to live up to her commitment.

Securing and Authenticating a Sense of Self

> *Every pleasure or pain has a sort of rivet with which it fastens the soul to the body and pins it down and makes it corporeal, accepting as true whatever the body certifies.*

> Socrates (in Plato, *The Pheado,* 81)

As noted in Chapter 4, self-injurers often experience a diffuse sense of self and struggle with maintaining both psychological and interpersonal boundaries. Their exposure to early life environments, characterized by insecure attachment relationships, parental invalidation or abuse, or the witnessing of violence or other serious traumas to the self or the body, interfered with the normative developmental processes that lead to the emergence of a bounded and coherent sense of self. These individuals fail to develop what Schore (2003a) describes as "the critical capacity to create and maintain the internal sense of emotional security [that] comes from the inner (but not necessarily conscious) knowledge that during times of stress, one can cope. Coping can occur either by autoregulation or by means of going to others for interactive regulation" (p. xvii). The development of these self-regulatory functions, which typically results from the experience of attuned mirroring in infancy and the experience of nurturance, care, and validation throughout childhood and adolescence, facilitates the emergence of a circumscribed and bounded self that stands in contradistinction to the selves of others. During recurrent episodes of disengagement from caregivers who are abusive, distracted, or even dissociative as a result of their unresolved relationship with their own traumas, children experience periods of drastic loss in affective and communicative responses that undermine their sense that a self actually exists and that it possesses the power of agency in their life (Fonagy et al., 2002).

Suyemoto (1998) explains that when a self-injurer experiences a crisis of perceived abandonment, with its accompanying intense emotions that threaten to overwhelm the self, she comes to equate the loss of the other as the loss of the self, because her diffuse boundaries are inadequate to contain that difference. Self-injury, then, serves as a stopgap measure to avert a loss of self and to establish new boundaries around the self by piercing the skin—the most obvious border between self and other—with the blood and scars as visible indicators of one's existing self. With the emergent strivings for separation that surface during adolescence (not to mention the biological changes of puberty and the concomitant demands of sexual maturation), the individual battles to emerge from the enmeshment with the self of the parent—a self that has been internalized and appropriated as a core part of the adolescent's own constitutional self (Fonagy et al., 2002).

Self-injury functions to defend against these feelings of merger by allowing the injurer to experience her own agency and vitality through the physical sensation of the act and by the reality of the resulting blood and scars even as she attempts to destroy the internalized other that suffocates, oppresses, and punishes. Amanda (in Hodgson, 2004) comments pointedly about her desire to cut away at the bad within her:

Cutting, even at 11 is not REALLY such a foreign idea. We cut the brown part off our apple when we eat it, we cut the dead leaves off house plants, we cut the grass when it no longer looks neat and tidy, heck, we even cut out our body parts when they no longer work right. Even small children want you to cut the part they don't like off (like crust off bread). Everybody cuts the bad out. (p. 162)

For the self-injurer, the body (and the harm inflicted upon it) functions as a transitional object of sorts (Suyemoto, 1998). Together, the body and its wounding connect the individual's inner and outer worlds—link her fragmented inner parts to the whole of who she is, her real self to the internalized alien self, and her numb and morbid internal experience to her secret hopes for greater meaningful connections with others and an end to her pain.

SUMMARY AND CONCLUSION

Individuals engage in acts of self-injury for a number of reasons, the most obvious of which is that it works! It provides a subjective psychological experience that helps the injurer organize her internal world, manage her emotions, cope with and control her pain, communicate feelings to others, and help confirm for herself that she is indeed alive. Self-injury functions as an attempt to be alive and to connect to others despite feeling rejected and unworthy. It is the individual's attempt to make contact with her psychological pain by transferring it to the body so that she can control it, reshape it, and transform it into attempts at self-healing. Self-injury represents an effort to cure oneself of one's loneliness, disconnection, and self-hatred. Emotional pain is replaced with a pain of a different sort that functions to soothe, act as the "friend" who listens, provide a hug, and be an ever-present source of comfort. Self-injury, as destructive as it may be, is, in the end, an attempt to affirm the self, paradoxically, through visible attacks on the body. It is an articulation of the injurer's fundamental desire for legitimacy and validation; the adolescent, lacking a clear sense of self within, turns to attacking her body and using her physical being to give coherence and psychological meaning to her efforts at reconstructing her personal narrative.

The next section of the book shifts from examining the nature and functions of self-injury to the engagement, assessment, and treatment of self-injurers. Chapter 6 explores the challenges of engaging self-injurers and offers a conceptual framework for developing an effective therapeutic posture in engaging these individuals, who, because of the very nature of their problems, have difficulty connecting to others and allowing others to be positive influences in their lives.

PART II

Engagement, Assessment, and Treatment

What has been wounded in a relationship must be, after all, healed in a relationship.

A. G. Rogers (in Connors, 2000, p. 130)

What we do not need is an educator, someone who "has plans" for us, nor a psychoanalyst who has learned that in the face of childhood traumas the main thing is to remain neutral.... No, we need precisely the opposite: a partial companion, someone who can share with us the horror and indignation that is bound to rise when our emotions gradually reveal to her, and to us, how the little child suffered, what it went through all alone when body and soul were fighting for years on end to preserve a life threatened by constant danger. We need such a companion—what I have called an "enlightened witness"...

Alice Miller (2005, pp. 22–23)

CHAPTER 6

Engaging the Self-Injurer: Making Contact With the Person Behind the Behavior

The capacity to give one's attention to a sufferer is a very rare and difficult thing.

Simone Weil (2001, p. 64)

In my encounter with my patient I am continually engaged in committing and recommitting myself.... I am not committed to something or someone; rather, I commit myself in my engagement with my patient.

James Bugental (1987, p. 249)

Engaging individuals who deliberately injure their bodies is a very difficult undertaking. The sight of flowing blood or a seeming highway of scars on a girl or young woman's arms can challenge the understanding and expertise of the most seasoned counselor or health care professional. In fact, self-injury is such a complicated and disturbing phenomenon that licensed psychologists consistently rate it as the "most distressing and stressful client behavior ... [and the] most traumatizing to encounter professionally" (Deiter, Nicholls, & Pearlman, 2000, p. 1188). The behavior evokes such powerful reactions of fear, confusion, and anger in helpers that it understandably distracts and distances them from being present to the person in need. As discussed in Chapter 1, these intense countertransferential feelings often destabilize the helper's clinical sensibilities. They can cloud one's typically thoughtful and sound therapeutic judgment by creating a sense of urgency that obviates patient, empathic attempts at understanding and engagement (Connors, 2000).

The primitiveness and shock of self-injurious behavior makes so vociferous a statement that the behavior itself is acutely thrust into the foreground. The act of cutting or otherwise wounding the body so forcefully captures the attention of others that the *individual* behind the behavior is easily obscured. When the focus is placed on the gruesome reality of the act, we can forget that self-destructive behaviors are often *symptoms* that point to deeper and more compelling pain. We can easily overlook the suffering person who has been brought to the point of mutilating her body in order to make a statement about the anguish she experiences. As a result, the urgency felt by helpers in stopping the act often eclipses a more complete understanding of the purpose and meaning of the behavior in the person's life. In these intense encounters, we can forget that people usually are the way they are (and do what they do) for a reason and that the first step in helping any person in psychological pain is not to "fix" her or make her pain go away but simply to understand her. When people do not feel understood, they are less likely to trust and engage meaningfully with others. Therefore, by understanding that our clients resort to self-injury as a means of dealing with their difficult-, if not impossible-, to-articulate psychological pain, and by communicating this understanding to them, we can begin to set the initial conditions for engagement and for building the kind of relationship that can lead to real healing.

This chapter explores the processes and challenges of therapeutically engaging self-injurers on the frontlines. In doing so, it examines the scope and limitations of the work that can take place in schools or on the college campus, and it considers what may need to be addressed in more intensive, longer-term treatment that should take place elsewhere. An underlying assumption for the ensuing discussion is that self-injuring individuals are difficult to engage because, at the most basic level, they lack the adequate internal resources for healthy attachment, because of the relational traumas experienced in their developmental histories (see Chapters 3 & 4). Therefore, in order to address these inherent challenges, I present a broad conceptual framework for engaging these individuals. A fundamental premise underlying this framework is that an appropriate starting point for helpers is an appreciation of the wisdom behind the self-injurer's resistance to help—that there is meaningfulness to their resistance and that their behavior makes sense. The chapter then explores some of the common problems resulting from this resistance and the helper's reaction to it and highlights the importance of sensitively maintaining firm but flexible boundaries in working with this population. The chapter concludes with a discussion of the general attitude, posture, and qualities of the effective helper that will create the conditions in which the self-injurer's affect can be better contained, her value as a person in her own right can be affirmed, and a framework for safety can be created.

ROLES FOR THE FRONTLINE RESPONDER

It is surely a critical feature of what we have to offer the patient that our view of him and of what he says is larger than his own.

David Shapiro (1999, p. 76)

While there has been a significant increase in the number of self-injuring individuals coming to the attention of mental health professionals in schools and on college campuses, the actual frequency of adolescent self-injury is still poorly assessed and underidentified (Whitlock, Eckenrode, et al., 2006). Those professionals on the frontlines—school counselors, social workers, nurses, college counseling center personnel, residence hall directors, and others—often carry the burden of being the first person to identify a self-injuring student and, therefore, the first obliged to intervene. As the frontline contact for self-injurers, these professionals often play (perhaps unknowingly) a crucial role in the complicated pathway to treatment that is typical for these individuals. Their incomplete understanding of the phenomenon, however, coupled with its disturbing manifestation, frequently evokes in them extreme emotional reactions that interfere with their effectiveness as helpers. These reactions are often anchored at one end of the continuum by feelings of disgust and helplessness that keep them away from the injurer and, on the other end, by the kind of guilt that leads to a need to "do for" the injurer, which culminates in overpowering fantasies to rescue the individual (Rayner et al., 2005). Obviously, neither of these extreme reactions creates the conditions for effectively engaging the self-injurer, nor do they optimally work to facilitate appropriate care. In fact, when filtered through these powerful emotions, the helper's own expectations of her role in addressing a self-injurer may become distorted or wholly unrealistic. What, then, are the reasonable roles and practical goals for frontline professionals working with this population?

I will answer this question by first noting those roles that may be impractical and unrealistic. First, it is important to keep in mind that the etiology and nature of self-injury are complex and multidetermined and that its emergence and maintenance have been typically reinforced by biological, psychological, and social factors over the course of years (Connors, 2000; Farber, 2000; Favazza, 1996). To expect that self-injurious behaviors that are well entrenched in the behavioral repertoire of an individual will cease easily and quickly is a setup for serious disappointment. As such, the role of professionals on the front lines is not to "cure" the individual of self-injury. It is not to suddenly intervene in such a way that will induce the individual to stop injuring herself. Embarking on the path to achieve this immediate end is often futile. The fact is that self-injury is *not* the core problem of the individual, although it may appear to be so. Rather, it is a symptom and a symbol of deeper underlying suffering. To miss this point is to miss the individual behind the behavior and, conversely, to miss the opportunity to connect with the injurer through the experience of understanding his or her pain. Furthermore, as discussed in Chapter 5, self-injury is psychologically meaningful to individuals who engage in the behavior and serves very practical healing functions; it soothes and provides psychological relief in times of emotional distress. To attempt at a "quick fix" misses this point entirely.

A second role that may be inappropriate for the frontline responder (depending on one's setting, of course) is to take the individual on as an ongoing counseling or therapy client. We know that effective treatment of self-injury is a long-term process and is multidimensional (Bateman & Fonagy, 2004; Farber, 2000; Linehan, 1993a; Walsh, 2006). The behaviors themselves are not always necessarily the exclusive focus of treatment but are addressed in the context of the underlying relational trauma and its sequelae that operate to fuel and sustain them. The self-injurer must develop a clearer understanding of her past traumatic attachments and can begin to integrate that understanding (and the new coping skills she develops) in the context of an ongoing therapeutic relationship. Only then can the individual become freer to let go of those modes of coping and self-regulating that may have been self-destructive. This process necessitates a more intensive kind of psychotherapy, over longer periods of time, than is possible in settings like schools or college campuses.

For example, the availability, consistency, and intensity required for the psychotherapy suggested here is beyond the scope of what can generally be provided by a counselor or other mental health professional in a school setting. First, there is the issue of competence and expertise in dealing with these students in a more intensive therapeutic mode. While not always feeling qualified, some school counselors may nevertheless feel obliged to meet with the student regularly and to provide counseling aimed at altering the student's self-injurious behavior. Unfortunately, believing that one in the role of a school counselor can provide the long-term therapeutic presence needed in the treatment of a self-injurer, while being responsible for the hundreds of other students, is unrealistic. Further, the school calendar, with its many breaks, holidays, and summer vacations, makes it impractical to sustain the consistent working relationship needed with this population. Likewise, treatment becomes difficult on the college campus when session limits, which many college counseling centers now impose, preclude any opportunity for the therapeutic attachment requisite for substantive clinical work to occur. The issue of summer breaks and extended vacations is operative in this setting as well, and such breaks disrupt the flow of treatment.

Among the many roles that frontline mental health and health care professionals can play, there are three that are essential across settings with regard to the self-injuring population: (1) being an educator, (2) linking systems and coordinating care, and (3) serving as a conduit to treatment (Roberts-Dobie, 2005). The first and second roles are discussed in greater detail in Chapter 9; however, a brief description of these roles is also appropriate here. Frontline responders are typically the local experts in matters of health and self care. As such, they are in a unique position within their community to educate others—teachers, administrators, residence hall personnel, parents, and so on. They can educate the community about a host of practical issues, including the significance of the self-injurious behaviors and how to respond to self-injurers, and can explore possible strategies for facilitating referrals. In their capacity as educators, frontline professionals can play an important role in creating a knowledgeable community of care that is well informed and appropriately responsive to the needs of the individuals under their charge.

The second role, linking systems and coordinating care, is closely associated with the first. By educating others and being identified as the local expert about these kinds of mental health issues, one implicitly begins to create linkages within the community that may play a role in a particular self-injuring individual's "circle of care." For example, the school counselor can be the liaison among school administrators, teachers, parents, and treating clinicians around issues that impact the self-injurer while at school. Or, the college counseling center psychologist can work with the deans and residential life staff around the needs of a self-injurer who is returning to the residence hall after being released from emergency care. Building bridges between the various stakeholders in one's setting can serve the very valuable purpose of creating an environment that will be optimally therapeutic for the self-injurer.

However, the most important role that the frontline responder can have that directly impacts the life of a self-injurer is that of being a conduit to treatment. The school counselor or nurse, or the student life personnel on the college campus, can be in the best position to effect a referral for the self-injurer to someone who can begin to provide optimal therapeutic care. The goal of assisting an individual in finding someone to provide appropriate help may, in fact, be the most useful goal to be achieved on the front lines. But, despite the seeming simplicity of this goal, it may be difficult to achieve. Often, self-injurers come to the attention of frontline professionals indirectly—a coach refers a student to the counselor's or nurse's office in the school; an RA in the residence hall discovers that one of her residents self-injures and calls the counseling center for guidance; or friends of a self-injurer come to a professional as a trusted adult for assistance. In many cases, self-injurers are ashamed of their behaviors and do not *directly* seek help themselves (Conterio & Lader, 1998; Whitlock, Eckenrode, et al., 2006). In fact, initially, many may not even want to change their behavior, and, when this is the case, engaging them around their self-injurious acts and insisting on their need for treatment will be ineffective (Connors, 2000; Farber, 2000).

While connecting a self-injurer to treatment is a primary goal for front-line professionals, it is important to keep in mind that it cannot occur in a vacuum. That is, the goal of helping someone transition into treatment cannot supersede the goal of coming to *know* the self-injurer and *understanding* the goals *she* may have for herself. It is out of this context of understanding that action can eventually emerge. While helping a self-injurer willingly decide to enter therapy is a monumental first step in addressing her psychological pain and the resulting destructive behaviors, it cannot be overemphasized that achieving this goal is predicated on the nature, quality, and tone of the helper's interactions with the injurer. Self-injuring adolescents, or most adolescents, for that matter, respond positively to adults whom they trust and whom they believe truly have their best interests in mind. If one approaches them, therefore, in an authoritarian, punitive, or shaming way, or if one attempts to impose his agenda on the injurer or communicates that he knows what's best for her, then he decreases the possibility of developing an effective working alliance and reduces one's ability to be helpful.

As we shall see, the work of engagement begins with understanding the relational difficulties inherent in the lives of most self-injurers and by being cognizant of how those difficulties will almost certainly play out in interactions with any professional who attempts to intervene. Therefore, the relationship becomes the foreground for any attempt at help, and it is in this context that the injurer can best be engaged to pursue further treatment.

THE PRIMACY OF RELATIONSHIP

All real living is meeting.

Martin Buber (1958, p. 11)

Oh, the comfort, the inexpressible comfort of feeling safe with a person, having neither to weigh thoughts nor measure words, but pouring them all right out, just as they are, chaff and grain together; certain that a faithful hand will take

*and sift them, keep what is worth keeping, and then with the breath of kind-
ness blow the rest away.*

Dinah Maria Craik (in Gabbard & Lester, 1995, p. xi)

The quality of the helping relationship is fundamental to the possibility for
change in any human being. Most schools of psychotherapy posit that the
therapeutic relationship serves as a central component in the change process
(Corsini & Wedding, 2005; Frank & Frank, 1991), and reviews of psychotherapy
outcome research clearly support this assertion (Lambert & Ogles, 2004; Orlinsky, Ronnestad, & Willutzki, 2004). Moreover, recent neuropsychobiological
research provides preliminary evidence that the secure attachments created
in psychotherapy relationships facilitate the regulation of the patient's brain/
mind/body systems and that the brain's plasticity allows for integration of the
emotional learning that accompanies successful psychotherapeutic experiences
(Schore, 2003b). The power of a positive therapeutic relationship and a strong
connection with a therapist are especially vital in work with self-injuring individuals. In fact, some clinicians contend that the quality of the relationship is
perhaps *the* most important single component that allows for the engagement
of the self-injurer in the often difficult, long-term healing process (Bateman
& Fonagy, 2004; Connors, 2000; Farber, 2000; Ivanoff, Linehan, & Brown,
2001; Linehan, 1993a).

Therefore, frontline responders need to be particularly attentive to issues of
relationship in working with self-injuring adolescents. As discussed in Chapters 3 and 4, one of the core problems experienced by many individuals who
self-injure are difficulties in attachment and in developing stable relationships.
Frequently, instances of self-injury are triggered by relationship problems that
are viewed as precipitating real or imagined abandonment. The relational trauma often experienced by self-injurers taints the very notion of relationship,
and the postures these individuals adopt toward their relationships in general
are exceedingly precarious. When trusted individuals in one's life are the very
source of abuse, neglect, or invalidation, the individual's conflicted desire to
be in relationship is heightened. The inconsistency and unreliability of early
significant attachments become paradigmatic of future relationships and create
great ambivalence. On one hand, these individuals long to be connected with
others; on the other hand, because of disruption in their developing sense of
personal coherence caused by unstable past primary relationships, interpersonal closeness often evokes highly anxious and terrifying emotional states,
leading to behaviors that distance others. For these individuals, intimacy suggests both being engulfed and swallowed up so that their voices will again not
be heard and allowing another person yet again to subsume their inner selves.

These fears lead to lives characterized by chaotic, insecure, and volatile attach-ments, in which one's self-destructive behaviors are perpetrated in response to those unhealthy attachments. Farber (2000) notes that a central theme of many patients whose lives are organized around self-injury

> is that "there is no one there" for them, a theme that speaks of a lack of secure attachments; earlier in life there was no home emotionally in a consistent and reliable way. To have nobody (no body) makes one turn aggressively to one's own body in order to feel that there is somebody (some body) there. "I feel alone and I am afraid that no body is there anymore.... I cannot trust anyone and nobody puts his trust in me. Nobody, no body! I have only my own body ... " (p. 353)

For these individuals, struggling with relationships is more often the norm than not. Relational instability is a hallmark for many of these persons and undoubtedly emerges whenever others demonstrate genuine caring and attempts to be helpful. Consequently, there is little reason to believe that these dynamics will not play out with the counselor, nurse, or other frontline responder when she attempts to be helpful in intervening with the self-injuring adolescent.

The implications of self-injurers' dynamics, then, are significant for how any frontline responder needs to think about the process of engaging them. The foundational starting point for engagement is to keep clearly in the fore-ground the interpersonal life of the self-injurer and the necessity of working to establish a reasonable helping relationship with her before anything else can take place (Bateman & Fonagy, 2004). Again, this process begins not by "fixing" the individual or imposing one's own goals on her (perhaps to stop the self-injurious behaviors or to get her into therapy tomorrow) but by listening with the intention of understanding. Connors (2000) suggests that *presence* is at the heart of this process. She notes that most self-injurers may not have had "sustained experiences with a present and engaged other" (p. 135). The experience of having someone actually *be there*—willing to engage and be involved, willing to listen to her voice and her pain, and will-ing to take the risks in order to understand—is quite foreign to them. Because trusting others is difficult for these individuals, we should take care not to expect that they will trust those of us who attempt to be helpful despite our good intentions. However, in spite of the self-injurer's difficulties in trusting those who try to help, helpers should work to remain consistent, reliable, attentive, and nonjudgmental; that is, the helper should strive to remain trust-worthy in spite of not being trusted.

The quotation from Alice Miller that introduces Part II of this book sug-gests that survivors of childhood relational trauma are best helped by the kind of individual whom she describes as an "enlightened witness." Connors

(2000) refers to an "emotional witness" in a similar light, illustrating the quality inherent in one who can be present and engaged. This notion of *witness* is also implied by Farber (2000) when she notes that people decide to go into treatment because of the wish to end suffering and to be "known and remembered by another" (p. 363). To have another compassionately see one's life for what it actually is and to be with that person in spite of it communicates a powerful message to one who may believe that no one cares enough to be present. To witness is to be willing to listen to the person's perspective while refraining from imposing one's own views or abusing one's own power (Connors, 2000). A witness affirms another's truth that may heretofore not have been seen and acknowledged. It is in the seeing and the not shying away from what is seen—from this truth—that the witness confirms the life of the individual and lets her know, unambiguously, that she is not crazy and that she is not alone.

Truth is what ultimately heals us; to the extent that others have denied the truth of our experience, so do we become alienated from ourselves and from others in the world. To the extent that we can come to embrace our own truth—the truth that, perhaps, we were not loved well by a parent (someone who was supposed to have been "for us" rather than "against") and that, perhaps we came to believe the lie that we deserved the abuse or neglect we received—then we begin to reconnect ourselves to the reality of our experience and can begin in earnest the journey toward greater wholeness. Bateman and Fonagy (2004) assert that it is the "experience of being understood that generates the experience of security" and, I would add, provides the experience of validation—both of which are enormously vital to engaging and working with self-injuring adolescents. In the end, what is communicated to these individuals through these "holding" experiences is that they are accepted and valued in their own right regardless of what they've done, what they do, or what changes they will and will not make in their lives.

The problem is that, despite their training and experience, helpers sometimes lose faith in the fact that the relationship itself can *be* the primary medium for helping others heal. We helpers sometimes assume that we know better of clients' experience than they do, and we forget to ask *them* what may actually be helpful. For example, a study that compared the perceptions of self-injuring adult women with those of mental health professionals regarding which strategies were helpful to self-injurers in managing their behavior illustrates precisely this point (Huband & Tantum, 2004). Table 6.1 illustrates the rankings by both clinicians and self-injurers of 14 intervention strategies used to help patients manage their self-injurious behaviors. Although the sample for the study was small (N = 10 self-injurers) and consisted of adult women between the ages of 21 and 48, the results are nonetheless notewor-

TABLE 6.1 Self-Injurers' and Clinicians' Rankings of Strategies Helpful in Managing Self-Injury

Self-Injurers' Views	Strategy	Clinicians' Views
1	Having available a long-term relationship with one key worker	8
2	Being encouraged to talk about and express feelings from your past	2
3	Being given a 24-hour emergency contact telephone number	11
4	Getting counseling or psychotherapy	5
5	Taking prescribed medication	13
6	Having contact with staff who don't show a lot of emotion about self-injury	6
7	Being asked about any sexual problems in your past	7
8	Regular discussions taking place between all staff involved in your care	1
9	Being admitted to hospital	14
10	Having staff pay minimum attention to your wounds	9
11	Having others take charge of sharp objects	12
12	Being encouraged to care for your own wounds yourself	4
13	Being encouraged to have contact with only certain staff	10
14	Being taught relaxation techniques	3

Adapted from Huband and Tantum (2004) with permission. *Psychology and Psychotherapy: Theory, Research, and Practice.* © The British Psychological Society.

thy in their demonstration that clinicians and clients can hold very different views of what is helpful. Self-injurers rated "Having a long-term relationship with one key worker" and "Being encouraged to talk about and express feelings from your past" as most helpful in managing self-injury, while clinicians ranked these variables eighth and second, respectively. The preferred strategy for self-injurers was the development of a long-term relationship with a helper, again underscoring the centrality of relationship in the entire helping process.

Clinicians, on the other hand, ranked "Regular discussions taking place between all staff involved in your care" first and "Being taught relaxation techniques" third. Self-injurers ranked these same items eighth and fourteenth (last), respectively. The authors of the study conclude that "It can be argued that the nature of an intervention is less important than the way it is experienced ... we found that a strategy was more often recalled as helpful when implemented by staff recalled as being caring, promoting autonomy or acting competently. The same strategy was more often recalled as unhelpful when delivered by staff recalled as showing a lack of concern, overprotection or incompetence" (Huband & Tatum, 2004, pp. 423–424). The implication of this study is that the clinicians' sensitivity to engagement and relationship building potentiated the power of their interventions for their clients. Conversely, without positive relationships, potentially helpful interventions were diluted of their effectiveness.

APPRECIATING THE WISDOM OF RESISTANCE

Resistance is the residue of an attempted dialogue cut short in midsentence.

Richard Hycner (1991, p. 137)

There is room for the idea that significant relating and communicating is silent.

W. D. Winnicott (in Gabbard, 1996, p. 208)

People who engage in acts of self-injury have often been categorized in that class of clients who are difficult to engage and who are occasionally summarily labeled as "treatment resistant" (Connors, 2000; Farber, 2000; Linehan, 1993a). While the reality is that individuals who self-injure do pose a treatment challenge, the popular usage and a common misunderstanding of the concept of *resistance* greatly contribute to making this a self-fulfilling prophecy. As the first quotation suggests, resistance is about an interrupted dialogue, which by definition requires the participation of more than one person. Self-injurers resist connections with others and resist movement toward self-care because their past experience in dialogue—being heard and being allowed to speak—has been painfully distressing and profoundly wounding. When we, as helpers, see their resistance as only their lack of cooperation in getting better, we too become responsible for rupturing a dialogue with them and, in turn, contribute to fortifying their hardened stance. Before we turn to discussing the kinds of "resistances" that can be expected from self-injurers, let us briefly consider the general notion of resistance and explore its self-protective function and its inherent wisdom.

Hycner's (1991) insights on the nature of resistance can significantly inform our understanding of both our clients' *and* our own impediments that interfere with genuinely engaging others. He notes that, fundamentally, resistance is a form of self-protectiveness. It speaks to the vulnerability of the person who resists and points to the pain experienced in making contact with other human beings. From an outsider's perspective, the individual may seem walled off and unreachable, but, from the person's own subjective understanding, his resistance can be understood as the attempt to avoid psychological injury. It represents the individual's belief that he lacks the internal resources to adequately deal with these perceived external threats. The problem is that resistance is often anachronistic, that is, it is not a response to the current situation but is a remnant from old conflicts and hurts. Hycner (1991) writes:

> Resistance can be a *deep* expression of something this person *desperately* needs and it's the only way he knows how to take care of himself. Much like the child who at an early age learns to say no, that no becomes one of the first ways of discerning and asserting one's identity as distinct from that of one's parents. The resistance in a sense is an internalized, yet truncated, care-giver. It becomes a substitute for the parents who might have protected the child and set limits.
>
> Unfortunately, unlike a real care-giver, resistance is primarily defensive rather than nurturant. In fact, the paradox is that resistant behavior closes off the nurturance that could come from others. We are busy defending against real and imagined threats, and thus push away those who might best provide a nurturing and healing interaction. Resistance protects, yet concurrently keeps the person from growing: It cuts off a dialogue with the world. (pp. 139–140)

Essentially, resistance is a person's way of being-in-the-world. It is a means to finding security in unfriendly surroundings. It provides predictability and safety and is ultimately an integral part of who the person has become. Therefore, attempts to pound against the resistance in order to break it or eliminate it fail to truly enter the person's world and block the development of any real helping relationship (Hycner, 1991).

Appreciating that resistance has value and wisdom can allow for an altered stance of receptivity in the helper. The appreciation that people are the way they are—that they are resistant for a reason—can free the clinician to make contact with the person more fully and authentically. To attempt to impose a solution or a goal—*my* solution or goal—on the person will, paradoxically, only strengthen and fortify his resistance to change and to being different from who he is. It is helpful to keep in mind the clinical paradox that the more *I* want from my client—that is, the more I want him to get better, or to be a certain way, or to do certain things differently—the more I increase the resistance and the less therapeutic leverage I ultimately have with him (Searles, 1979). To this point, Hycner (1991) adds:

> Resistance is not to be castigated, but rather to be embraced. Resistance is not to be broken through, but rather to be incorporated. The only way to get to where you want to be is to accept where you are, even if where you are isn't where you want to be. What is required for growth is an integration of seemingly opposed polarities. It is the paradoxical valuing of all of one's self, including those parts perceived as undesirable, that begins the road to recovery. (p. 144)

The failure to appreciate this inherent paradox is the contribution to client resistance that we, as helpers, make. Linehan (1993a) incorporates these insights into several of the basic assumptions she proposes for conducting Dialectical Behavior Therapy (DBT) (a recommended treatment for self-injurers that is discussed further in Chapter 8). Three of the Linehan's assumptions, if embraced by helpers, would reduce their contribution to creating resistance to treatment. These assumptions are that (1) patients are doing the best they can, (2) patients want to improve, and (3) patients cannot fail in therapy. With regard to the first assumption, Linehan (1993a) asserts that because patients' behavior is "frequently exasperating, inexplicable, and unmanageable, it is tempting to decide that the patients are not trying.... The tendency of many therapists to tell these patients to try harder, or imply that they indeed are not trying hard enough, can be the one of the patient's most invalidating experience in psychotherapy" (p. 106). In short, rather than align with their patients' efforts and the resources they possess at the moment, the clinician devalues their struggle and, in turn, fuels the resistance.

The second assumption is closely associated with the first in that it speaks to the assumption by many clinicians that a patient's failure to improve sufficiently or quickly enough is based on the patient's failure of intent—that she really doesn't *want* to change. Here, too, the helper's failure to appreciate the great ambivalence associated with giving up one's pathological or destructive behavior can be devastating to the patient's nascent attempts at asserting a healthier way of being.

Finally, and most powerfully, Linehan addresses the two-way nature of resistance by suggesting that *patients cannot fail in therapy*. This assumption counters the notion that when a patient fails to improve or she drops out of treatment, the failure rests with the patient. Rather, Linehan maintains that the failure actually lies with the therapy and the therapist and is not attributable to lack of motivation on the part of the client. These assumptions acknowledge the complexity of resistance and begin to provide an empathic framework for the professional posture that can aid in the difficult process of engaging self-injurers.

WHAT TO EXPECT WHEN ENGAGING SELF-INJURERS

There are a number of common problems that a frontline professional can encounter in his or her attempts at engaging a self-injurer. Some of these problems are associated with the general ambivalence and resistance most people experience while struggling to decide whether they want to embark on the journey toward *real* change in their lives. My own clinical experience has taught me that in most cases, at least initially, people come to therapy not to change but to make the pain go away. When they realize that the reduction of pain may require them to take some action or to be different in some fashion, some are frightened off from the process, while others find the resources to move forward and engage in the difficult work that is psychotherapy. These are struggles that are common to most human beings, and I have learned to trust that when people are ready and the supports are in place, many are able to muster the courage to engage in the work. Other problems that are encountered in working with self-injurers, however, are unique to this population and challenge helpers in distinctive ways. The following section highlights some of the problems that may be encountered in working specifically with self-injurers.

The Reluctance of the Self-Injurer to Self-Disclose

One of the most confusing client reactions that helpers encounter is an individual's refusal of help when offered, even when that person has sought it out. This apparent refusal of help can be a common occurrence with self-injurers. The simple fact that an adolescent has been referred to the school counselor by a teacher does not necessarily mean that the individual will want to talk about her behavior. Conterio and Lader (1998) remind the helper that to expect a person to begin to openly talk about a highly emotionally charged subject, particularly when the individual feels a great deal of shame, is unrealistic. Accepting the difficulty the individual has in beginning to disclose and dialogue about her behavior is the first step in "adopting a stance of helpful empathy" (p. 162). Rather than fire questions at the person in the attempt to make her talk (which will invariably put her on the defensive), the helper can be most effective if he or she focuses on communicating the fundamental message of concern and an openness to talk about the behavior if the person so desires. Further, if the self-injurer would prefer to talk with someone else, the helper should encourage that option and facilitate the connection.

The helper may understandably experience a sense of urgency in gathering all of the information immediately while attempting a first contact with a self-injurer, but it is important to keep in mind that the process of engagement, let alone that of healing, takes time. What can be most helpful to injurers at this stage is simply for the helper to communicate her understanding that what may be going on with the injurer is difficult, that she imagines that there must be areas of the injurer's life that are painful, and that the situation the injurer is in now may be scary (Conterio & Lader, 1998). Communicating these basic messages can be the starting point of establishing a connection that can lead to greater engagement. To whatever extent possible, the helper should allow the subtext of her communication to be that the control of the situation is in the hands of the injurer (Deiter et al., 2000) but that the helper is concerned, wants to know more about what is going on, and wants to help.

Extreme Forms of Relating

As noted previously, individuals who self-injure often have a history of instability in their relationships, and their own styles of relating can fluctuate significantly. In encounters with self-injurers, it is reasonable to expect such fluctuations in the helper's attempts at engagement. Linehan (1993a) labels the two extreme styles of client relating as the "butterfly" and the "attached." At one end of the spectrum are those who, like butterflies, float in and out of contact with the helper. Their interpersonal energy may be dispersed in several significant relationships, and, although they may have articulated some desire for help, they may disengage from the helper as they focus on those other relationships. These individuals have very high dropout rates once they initiate therapy. On the other hand, the "attached" individuals may so completely bind themselves to the helper by wanting to spend more time with her or by becoming particularly needy in her absence that it feels impossible to meet their needs. The intensity, inconsistency, and volatility of these relational styles can become a great source of frustration for the frontline professional and can wear on her own motivation to stay engaged.

Challenging Affective States

Closely associated with the extreme interpersonal functioning just described is the probability of experiencing and having to respond to and contain the self-injurer's challenging affective states. As discussed in Chapter 4, many individuals who self-injure have failed to develop those internal self-soothing mechanisms that would allow for the functional regulation of their own affect. Bateman and Fonagy (2004) describe the variety of feelings that can emerge in the context of the helping relationship. They suggest that these feelings can include aggression, envy, idealization, love, hate, contempt, and sexual attraction. They explain, for example, that the attempt to engage an injurer may activate feelings of distrust, rejection, or victimization, and the individual may respond in a verbally aggressive manner or in passive-aggressive ways by refusing to cooperate. In other cases, the helper may experience the effects of destructive envy when the client attacks or rejects precisely that which was asked for and believed to be helpful (e.g., the client may ask for an additional appointment and then not show up)—actions that appear to make little intuitive sense. Or, in other cases, the helper may come to be idealized by the client so that he or she is believed to possess extraordinary powers to be nurturing or to provide perfect parenting. This idealization can be particularly dangerous if it taps into the helper's own grandiosity or into his or her own fantasies about rescuing clients. The idealization, however, can easily but dramatically turn into intense devaluation when the helper responds in a way other than what is expected by the client.

Similarly, helpers can experience undulating swings in attachment on the part of self-injurers, ranging from love to hate and including the many nuanced variations that lie in between. Bateman and Fonagy (2004) note that hate and contempt serve to protect self-esteem and can emerge when some action or change is imminent. In these situations, the helper's efforts are dismissed, and the client may become particularly hurtful to that helper. On the other end of the love-hate continuum is the client's experience of powerful feelings of love for the helper. However, what is problematic in that case is the fact that these clients typically have great difficulty distinguishing between love and other feelings, such as dependency, need, and sexual desire. As an attachment begins to form with a helper, the client may become more destabilized and actually increase her self-injurious enactments because of the growing realization that this helping relationship matters.

Bateman and Fonagy (2004) provide helpful practical guidelines in managing these challenging affective states. Some of the more salient ones for the purposes of the present discussion are listed here:

- Give priority to discussing challenging affect states, and on these occasions help the client label and attribute the affect to a specific interpersonal situation.
- Help the client to recognize how the affect is interfering with her personal and interpersonal functioning.
- Be alert to aggression against you as a helper as an indicator of anxiety and threatened instability of the self.
- Do not react to personal aggression, for example, by being aggressive in response.
- Ensure that the communication is not disrupted, and keep the dialogue open.

- Do not be disheartened by apparent relapse and re-emergence of earlier ways of relating.
- Help the client understand her process of rejecting that which is helpful to her, without inducing excessive self-criticism or guilt.
- Recognize the defensive aspects of idealization.
- Continue to try to engage the client in dialogue, even when she may be distancing you.
- Be honest with the client about your own feelings regarding your experience of her negative affect and aggression.
- Be aware that, as the relationship intensifies, problems within your relationship with the client will also increase.
- Be alert to your countertransferential reactions, which are inevitable. (Adapted and modified from Bateman & Fonagy, 2004, pp. 234–252)

Issues of Impulse Control

Frontline responders can also expect problems with impulse control, that is, individuals may continue to injure themselves throughout your encounters and attempts to engage them. Impulsive acts usually take place during times of emotional arousal (Bateman & Fonagy, 2004), and the attempt at engaging self-injurers around their behavior may catalyze such arousal. Particularly when attachment issues are triggered in relationships (including ones established with a helper), the fear of real or imagined abandonment can increase anxiety to the point of igniting the impulse to self-injure. Of course, the helper who has multiple contacts with the injurer needs to have, at some point, completed a thorough assessment to distinguish self-injury patterns from suicidality (a process that is reviewed in the following chapter) in order that the appropriate interventions may be utilized. Bateman and Fonagy (2004) advise that it is helpful to work with the client collaboratively on the best way for the helper to engage the client in times that may be emotionally arousing and that may increase the likelihood of self-injury. It is also recommended that the helper communicate to the injurer that "his actions are understandable given his feelings immediately prior to the act of self-[injury], his current inability to deal with these feelings, and his past experiences" (p. 232).

Behaviors Disruptive to Others in the Self-Injurer's Setting

It is also reasonable to expect that, in some cases, self-injurers may be disruptive. It is not uncommon for a student's self-injuring behavior to affect others in her school: classmates, concerned friends, or teachers may fear not knowing how to deal with students who self-injure. Likewise, a student living on a college campus with roommates may injure herself in her room and may be discovered by her roommates, thus creating concern and a highly emotionally charged living situation. Student life in the residence halls can also be disrupted when an injurer needs to be transported to the emergency room to receive care for her wounds. In those situations in which the self-injurer's school or living community is disrupted, collateral traumatization can occur in the individuals who are exposed to the self-injurious behaviors. For example, a former patient of a colleague initiated treatment because of her symptoms of depression and anxiety, which developed in response to repeated exposure to her roommate wiping blood off her arms when she walked into the dorm room. The situation was eventually resolved when the residential life staff granted her request to move out of her room. These situations require that frontline responders be attentive to the collateral effects that self-injurers may have on other people, and they must be prepared to make counseling available to those affected individuals, as well. More is said in Chapter 9 about creating an environment of care that addresses the needs of the multiple parties involved.

Finally, one can also expect in some situations that a self-injurer may engage in behavior commonly know as *staff splitting*. "Splitting" is understood to be the dynamic wherein an individual behaves in such a way that she creates conflict among a number of individuals who may be trying to help her. Typically, the individuals may be pitted against each other by the client who subtly conveys one message to one individual and a contradictory one to others. The communication is typically around matters that directly impact attempts at providing help for the individual. For example, an adolescent in school may enlist the help of a trusted teacher to be her advocate. When the student's counselor sets appropriate limits for that student, the teacher may feel that the counselor is being unreasonably harsh and may respond accordingly, inadvertently undermining the work of the counselor. The reverse may also be the case when the student requests permission from a counselor or adminis-trator to be excused from certain activities or classes and the teacher feels that her colleagues are being complicit in the student's "manipulation." In these cases, the people trying to help are split into "good" and "bad" helpers—those who care about the student and are trying to help and those who get in the way of what's best for the student. The end result is staff tension and conflict, often leading to working at cross-purposes.

Linehan (1993a), however, cautions that the responsibility for "staff splitting" ought not to be placed squarely on the shoulders of the client—after all, it may be the nature of these clients to be inclined to give mixed messages. Rather, a "split staff" may speak to a lack of communication and lack of a coordinated approach to helping that exists within the organization. If teachers, administrators, and counselors have effective systems in place that foster communication and encourage a unified plan of action for a particular student, then students will have difficulty "splitting" them, because the helpers are informed, on board with a game plan, and operate as an effective team (more is said about developing staff teamwork in Chapter 9).

ESTABLISHING AND MAINTAINING APPROPRIATE BOUNDARIES

I feel used/manipulated/abused and at the same time feel responsible for her feelings of rejection.... She has hooked me into thinking love/friendship will heal her, as if there is nothing wrong with her, but that it is all of the people in her life who are the problem. Then I come up with fatherly friendship, and her control begins. She tells me in different ways, that I am different than the others. And just when I am basking in "good objectivity," she really begins to control me by telling me that I'm just like the rest, I don't care: "I see you looking at your watch. I know you want to leave. I know you have a life out there. It will be a long night. You don't care. Nobody cares."

(Gabbard & Wilkinson, 1994, p. 1)

As noted in Chapter 4, people who self-injure often have difficulties in knowing how to soothe themselves when psychologically distressed. Not only do they struggle to muster internal resources that can comfort them in times of trouble, but they also lack the skills to effectively ask others for help and to receive the help when it is offered. As a result, they may approach helpers in ways that challenge the helpers' personal and professional limits and that may set the stage for helper burnout. The task of determining, communicating, and maintaining firm but not inflexible boundaries is fundamental both to effectively engaging these individuals and to inoculating the helper against the possibility of burnout.

Creating structure by establishing reasonable boundaries is one of the most important first steps in engaging individuals who self-injure (Bateman & Fonagy, 2004; Connors, 2000; Ivanoff et al., 2001; Linehan, 1993a). Bateman and Fonagy (2004) maintain that creating a structure that is neither intrusive nor inattentive is an essential component of establishing a framework for engagement. They note that structure provides the external consistency, coherence, and predictability that communicate a sense of relational safety for self-injurers, who often have been victims of unreliable, inconsistent, and fragmented interpersonal environments. It is not simply a matter of establishing what form the helping relationship will take and how it will work in practical terms; it is also the creation of a "state of mind" that both individuals in the helping relationship will share and use as the context for their interactions. In other words, the external structure created by the helper through the relationship provides guidelines for relating and, as such, creates stability for the client. It is hoped that the external structure (and the resulting stability) imposed by the helping relationship will eventually be internalized by the client and will provide the structure for inner stability and comfort for her. Setting structure and maintaining boundaries helps to contain the self-injurer's often-chaotic feeling states and can serve to temper and tame the interpersonal enactments that may ensue. To this point, Connors (2000) comments, "Central to the task of consciously managing our boundaries with clients is our capacity to contain two seemingly contradictory elements: to be consistent and dependable *and* flexible enough to sort and respond to each situation. This means that we hold the frame steady *and* we try to meet the client where he is" (p. 188). Rather than thinking about the idea of boundaries from an adversarial or oppositional perspective, Connors suggests that there may be a more helpful alternative. She posits that boundaries may, in fact, be more of a "place of joining" between helper and client than a place of guarded territoriality and self-protection.

Furthermore, Linehan (1993a) argues that boundaries are actually set in the context of the interpersonal space *between* the client and the helper. That is, the challenge of creating effective structure is that of balancing the interpersonal style (and specific behaviors) of the particular client and what the helper is willing to tolerate. Helpers often conceptualize the notion of "boundaries" by suggesting that there is a definitively "correct" and a definitively "incorrect" place where limits are to be set. Rather, Linehan suggests, that "boundary setting is a social function; thus, there are no context-free, correct boundaries" (p. 135). Boundaries emerge out of the dialectic between the client's interpersonal functioning and the helper's personal limits. Areas subject to discussion include demands for additional time and attention, as when a student would prefer to spend a class period in the counselor's office rather than in class; acts that infringe on the helper's personal space or a client's overly familiar manner of interacting with the helper; or demands for solutions to problems that may be unrealistic or beyond the scope of what the helper can offer (e.g., a self-injuring college student asks the counseling center psychologist to intervene with her roommates in ways that may be inappropriate).

If we accept Linehan's position on boundaries, then the manner of identifying and establishing them is always an *in-between* process. That is, boundaries are constantly managed and renegotiated by *both* parties, and, while the client can often push the limits of those boundaries, the helper, too, can contribute to their crossing or violation; for example, in their attempt to engage the self-injurer, helpers may become overly concerned and, perhaps, become intrusive and disrespectful. Helpers also violate boundaries when, experiencing moments of confusion, helplessness, or manipulation, they disengage, withdraw, or even retaliate with their own passive-aggressive enactments—forgetting appointments, not returning phone calls, speaking in a derogatory way to the client, or even breaking confidentiality. These behaviors all contribute to destabilizing the emerging relationship, which is so crucial to therapeutically engaging the self-injurer.

When we, as helpers, fail to maintain consistency, constancy, and coherence, we weaken and undermine our ability to keep the client stably engaged, because we are, in essence, replaying the instability of past relationships in her life. This is not to suggest that as human beings we will not make mistakes or be less than perfectly attuned to these clients; we surely will. The issue is less about making mistakes than it is about what we do when we make mistakes that may violate the client's boundary or be deleterious to maintaining structure. As Bateman and Fonagy (2004) state, "Structure starts with information" (p. 186); that is, not only should the setting of boundaries be openly discussed and their rationale explained, but also mistakes on the part of the helper that work against the maintenance of structure should be nondefensively owned and discussed with the client. Engagement around these kinds of mistakes provides information to the client that allows her to retain a sense of control, and it implicitly communicates to the client the helper's trustworthiness and transparency in the helping relationship.

Because boundaries need to be both firm and appropriately tailored to the needs of the specific situation, the challenge of discerning and maintaining them can be formidable. Connors (2000) offers a number of questions to assist the helper while navigating the continuous process of boundary setting:

1. What are my fundamental boundaries with clients?
2. Do these make sense with this client? If not, why not?
3. Why do I want to change this particular boundary?
4. Can I think of two colleagues I can discuss this with? What do or would they think?
5. Is my changing a basic boundary or limit in the interest of the client in the short run? In the long run?
6. What are the potential risks? What are the potential benefits? How do I decide if it's too risky?
7. How does the client feel about it? What do I know about how my client perceives safety? Will this change create any sense of danger?

8. How do I feel about it? What are my gut reactions and what are my limits in making a change? (p. 189)

In most cases, questions such as these can assist helpers in recentering their focus on the actual short- and long-term goals of their interventions. Reflecting upon these questions can also help them sort through some of the often-conflicting feelings they may experience about their clients and about clients' encroachment on the limits that have been previously established.

AVOIDING UNHELPFUL RESPONSES AND DEVELOPING A POSTURE OF CARE

One must realize that the patient has arrived at his perceptual world over years of employing the best judgment of which he is capable. It is a world deserving of our respect; we cannot ask him to relinquish it at all readily and to embrace gratefully the view of "reality" we offer him.

Harold Searles (1979)

Given the complexity of the engagement process, the resistances raised by the self-injurer (and the helper) to that process, and the various situations that may arise throughout, knowing the best way to respond in the moment may be difficult. The starting point for discerning the best course of action, as pointed out earlier, begins with listening to the client, being attentive to the relational context of your interaction, setting appropriate boundaries and creating structure, and then responding genuinely about your experience from a firm but flexible posture. Meeting the individual where he or she is begins to create the conditions that will educate the helper about what response may be most effective and beneficial to the client at any given moment. There are some responses, however, that are unhelpful to the process of engaging the self-injurer and establishing a useful working alliance.

Unhelpful Responses

Linehan (1993a) observes that there are a number of primarily helper-related factors that may interfere with helpers' effective responses to people who self-injure. These include life stress at home and work; lack of sleep or illness; excessive time demands; insecurity about one's skills; the self-injurer's seeming failure to engage or lack of progress; "blaming the victim" attitudes; actual or attempted violations of one's boundaries; fear that the self-injurer will commit suicide; fear of being sued; and unrealistic expectations of the client. She further notes that the most common and debilitating factor that interferes with making contact with the client and remaining engaged is the helper's "inability to tolerate a [client's] communication of suffering in the present. Attempts to ameliorate patient suffering often lead to reinforcements of dysfunctional behaviors, which, rather than reducing suffering, actually increase it in the long run" (p. 138). These and other factors can elicit a host of unhelpful responses that actually work to distance the self-injurer, rather than bring about connection. What follows is a discussion of ways to avoid some of the more common unhelpful responses.

Do Not Demand That the Self-Injurious Behavior Stop

The first and perhaps the most problematic response to a self-injurer is to try to *make* her stop the behavior. Efforts to demand that she stop her destructive behavior or to cajole her or convince her to do so will usually backfire. While it may be a natural instinctive response to try to get someone to stop intentionally wounding herself, the effort is likely to create a powerful battle of wills. The injurer is again hearing what others may have told her or may feel that she's not being heard or understood or that she is being spoken *at* instead of being respectfully considered. This may be reminiscent of her experience in her home, in which she may have felt or continue to feel invalidated or emotionally neglected. When the helper imposes his or her desire for the client to get better, the ensuing power struggle creates an impasse in the relationship that ultimately diminishes the helper's leverage in helping the client to get help. Connors (2000) comments that "either due to lack of training or lack of awareness, or because we really want to help someone—we use power unfairly and take responsibility for things that aren't ours to manage. Or, conversely, in an effort to respect the clients' power, we may abandon clients to their struggles and pain by *not* using our power or taking responsibility in ways that can help the client more effectively heal or change" (p. 150).

Do Not Rescue or "Do For" the Client What She Might Need to Do for Herself

The attempt to rescue or "do for" the self-injurer those things related to her care that she has it in her power to do diminishes the sense of control she may feel over her life and over her desire to change her behavior. The work of engagement is about establishing some connection that can give life to a real collaboration and help the client retain a sense of control in her life (Connors, 2000). Both the explicit and the implicit message that ought to be communicated by the helper may be something to the effect of "I am concerned; I want to be of help to you and will be here for you; I want to understand what's going on in your life and help to keep you safe; I would like for *you* to help me to understand how best I can help you; but ultimately I want to work *together with* you, and I want you to know that much of the control in what we do is yours" (Conterio & Lader, 1998). Obviously, there are implications for clients who are minors in terms of informing parents and taking other appropriate legal and ethical actions, the details of which are discussed further in the next chapter. However, the attitude and the subtext of the message about concern and the wish to be helpful while, at the same time, leaving in the client's hands as much control as possible over the shape that help may take should be communicated to minors, as well.

Do Not Respond From a Reactive Place of Shock, Fear, or Revulsion

Feelings of shock, fear, anxiety, confusion, and revulsion are quite common among helpers confronted with individuals who self-injure—they are normal human reactions to abnormal and disturbing behaviors. The problem is that when we respond from these feelings, we can more easily react in extreme and unhelpful ways toward the client. When we are overwhelmed with such feelings, the likelihood of our missing the client's needs and focusing on reactions that relieve our own anxiety and fear is heightened dramatically. In these cases, we run the risk of communicating to the client that "I am not able to tolerate you and your behavior and that your pain is too great for me," which, of course, reinjures the individual, and reactivates the deep feeling of shame, and confirms the belief that "no one is there for me." Rather, as Farber (2000) suggests, for the helper to tell the client that he understands her self-injury "to be saying something that she cannot say in words immediately takes her behavior out of the realm of craziness into the realm of communication" (p. 364). This can relieve the client's own self-critical judgments and begin to reduce her shame, which, in turn, allows her to be more open to connection.

Do Not Attribute Self-Injury to "Manipulation" and Respond in Kind

As has been discussed throughout this book, self-injury evokes powerful countertransferential feelings. The ambivalence in a self-injurer's meta-communication—asking for help and yet not accepting it or not complying with the helper's suggestions or agreed-upon plan—creates the impression that the injurer is less than serious about receiving help and following through appropriately. The helper then may feel used, disrespected, or manipulated and may convert his own hurt into aggressive or otherwise unhelpful responses to the injurer. The helper may read the injurer's actions as a personal affront to himself and to his ability to help. He may respond with frustration, anger, dismissiveness, sarcasm, or even vengeance and manipulativeness of his own. It is important to remain present to the notion that "manipulation" is ultimately a word that describes how people may work to have their needs met. Unfortunately, some people, like self-injurers, have difficulty meeting their needs in open and direct ways. Their life experience has taught them that they aren't allowed to have needs. Further, if they become aware of what those needs may be, they have learned that to ask directly that those needs be met is to be treated with disregard, rejection, or anger. The word "manipulation" has come to have a pejorative connotation; in actuality, it simply describes an individual's attempt at working to have her needs met, albeit in ways that come across as indirect and, perhaps, suspicious. However, because the methods employed are veiled, helpers usually feel out of control, deceived, and violated. Understanding that self-injurers may not even be aware of the nature of their needs, let alone how to engage others in a healthy way to have those needs met, may assist helpers in not taking their "manipulativeness" personally. Appreciation of this perspective may be useful in helping contain the responder's feelings of being used and avoiding the inclination to respond in self-protective and distancing ways.

On the Posture of Helpfulness and the Qualities of the Effective Helper

It is more important for the clinician to understand people than to master specific treatment techniques.

Nancy McWilliams (1999, p. 9)

What I give him is permission to be.

Carl Rogers (in Agassi, 1999)

A posture of helpfulness is more about an attitude and a state of mind than about knowing exactly the "right" thing to say or do. Fundamentally, it entails a willingness to examine oneself honestly and to be in touch with one's own issues, fears, competencies, and limitations. It entails coming to an understanding of one's personal boundaries in one's work, being willing to face the ever-shifting question of "Where do I end and the other begins?" and coming to terms with one's powerlessness in making others be other than who they are, even in the face of the most ardent desire to help. We must become comfortable with ambiguity, paradox, and the opposing pull of the contradictions we experience in our clients. Carl Rogers (1961, pp. 50–56) offers a series of questions that I have found helpful in this process of self-examination and in discerning how I bring myself to the encounter with my clients. They are presented in an adapted and modified form as points of departure for reflecting on our own ongoing development as helpers:

- Can I *be* in some way that will be perceived by the other person as trustworthy, dependable, and consistent in some deep sense?
- Have I come to realize that being trustworthy demands not that I be *rigidly* consistent but that I be *dependably real*?
- Can I be expressive as a person such that what I am will be communicated unambiguously?
- Can I let myself experience positive attitudes toward this other person—attitudes of warmth, caring, liking, interest, respect?
- Can I be strong enough as a person to be separate from the other? Can I be a sturdy respecter of my own feelings, my own needs, as well as his? Can I own and, if need be, express my own feelings as something belonging to me and separate from his feelings? Am I strong enough in my own separateness that I will not be downcast by his depression, frightened by his fear, or engulfed by his dependency? Is my inner self hardy enough to realize that I am not destroyed by his anger, taken over by his need for dependency, or enslaved by his love but that I exist separate from him with feelings and rights of my own?
- Am I secure enough within myself to permit him his separateness? Can I permit him to be what he is—honest or deceitful, infantile or adult, despairing or overconfident? Can I give him the freedom to be?
- Can I let myself enter fully into the world of his feelings and personal meanings and see these as he does? Can I step into his private world so completely that I lose all desire to evaluate and judge it?
- Can I receive him as he is, and can I communicate this attitude?
- Can I act with sufficient sensitivity in the relationship that my behavior will not be perceived as a threat?
- Can I meet this other individual who is in the process of *becoming*, or will I be bound to his past or my past?

These questions can be a starting point in the process of reflecting on what personal qualities, attributes, and struggles we may bring to the encounter with our clients. With the greater self-understanding that may come with this kind of reflection, we decrease the likelihood that we may be inappropriately reactive, fearful, or unhelpful with the difficult-to-engage individuals whom we encounter.

Linehan (1993a) adds to our understanding of the personal factors and characteristics that may be helpful in engaging individuals who self-injure. She observes that the attitude and interpersonal position a helper takes in relationship to his client must focus on balancing the client's "capabilities and deficiencies, flexibly synthesizing acceptance and nurturing strategies with change demanding strategies in a clear and centered manner. [And,] exhortations to change must be integrated with infinite patience" (p. 108). The helper's attitude and posture must communicate an acceptance and a validation of who the client is *in the present moment* (acknowledging her pain and conveying to the injurer that her life as it is being lived is difficult and perhaps unbearable), on the one hand, and that she is the one responsible for beginning to solve her problems, on the other. And, what must also be communicated is that *the helper* will help her in that process. In the end, the foundation of this stance is based on the ability to maintain a balance between *acceptance* versus *change*.

This posture of care is further buttressed, according to Linehan (1993a), by the helper's ability to balance the stance of *unwavering centeredness* versus *compassionate flexibility*. By "unwavering centeredness," she refers to the quality of believing in oneself and in the client and having the ability to maintain a sense of "calmness in the middle of chaos. . . . It requires a certain clarity of mind with respect to what the patient needs in the long run, as well as an ability to tolerate the intensity and pain experienced by the [client] without flinching in the short run" (p. 110). In contradistinction to the notion of "unwavering centeredness" is the posture of *compassionate flexibility*, which suggests a posture on the part of the helper of responsiveness, adaptability, and creativity commensurate with the real needs of the client, including the ability to modify and reestablish boundaries, as needed.

The final tension to be negotiated is between what Linehan terms *nurturing* versus *benevolent demanding*. The "nurturing" end of the continuum suggests providing support, sensitivity, and compassion in responding to and assisting the individual in ways that he or she has requested. *Benevolent demanding*, on the other hand, recognizes that situations may arise that require one to be firm or even tough in insisting upon greater self-care on the part of the client. Linehan (1993a) summarizes this dialectical tension as pushing the client "forward with one hand while supporting her with the other" (p. 112).

The ability to tolerate this tension of opposites in creating a posture of helpfulness implies that the helper possesses certain qualities and skills. For example, as noted previously, it is important for helpers to be particularly attentive, responsive, and present when working with individuals who self-injure

(Bateman & Fonagy, 2004; Connors, 2000). Further, they should be compassionate, consistent, and patient, and their belief in the ability of the client to get better should be more powerful than their client's despair and sense of inefficacy (Linehan, 1993a). In addition, the helper's interest in and commitment to the client must outweigh the helper's own fears and the possibility of failing to be helpful (Farber, 2000). By being able to tolerate and contain the client's inconsistent affective states, the helper creates a firm structure in which trust can begin to develop; by not giving up on clients despite their attempts to push her away, the helper lays the groundwork for effective engagement and can accompany the injurer compassionately to the next phase of her recovery.

SUMMARY AND CONCLUSION

Engaging and making connections with self-injuring individuals is a challenging undertaking. Their history of unstable relationships, their inability to self-regulate emotional states, their belief that others do not care about their well-being, and their ambivalence about letting go of self-injurious behaviors that are soothing makes their willingness to trust others and to accept help highly tenuous. The helper's task of engaging the self-injurer is further complicated by the primitive and disturbing nature of the behaviors themselves, which function to distance others and evoke powerful feelings that may be difficult to tolerate. The effective helper understands that the starting point for engagement is making contact with the individual *behind* the behavior and recognizing the suffering that underscores the injurer's self-destructive acts. In doing so, the helper is, in essence, fulfilling the role of compassionate witness for the suffering human being. Presence, attentiveness, responsiveness, firm but flexibly drawn boundaries, a tolerance for taking paradoxical stances, and a belief that one's ability to be helpful is greater than the client's resistance are some of the essential ingredients in the makeup of the effective helper. Further, an honest appraisal and recognition of the helper's own countertransferential feelings and attitudes are an ethical requirement for working with these individuals.

In the next chapter, we turn to exploring how the helper can operationalize these attitudes and qualities in practical ways while triaging and assessing self-injurers and throughout the dispositional decision-making process leading to referral or other appropriate next steps.

CHAPTER 7

Assessing Self-Injury and the Self-Injurious Adolescent

Pay attention not only to the words *but also to the* speaker.

David Shapiro (1999, p. 58)

All truths are easy to understand once they are discovered; the point is to discover them.

Galileo Galilei (in Giovagnoli, 1999, p. 138)

Technique follows understanding.

Rollo May (1958, p. 77)

The effective assessment of self-injuring individuals, as underscored in the previous chapter, begins by being attentive to and making contact with the *person* behind the injurious behavior and meeting that person where he or she is. The importance of the helper's demeanor in this process cannot be overemphasized, as the work of later treatment builds on the relational groundwork developed in early encounters with those who are willing to listen and who are responsive, reliable, validating, and trustworthy. The helper should also work to become aware of any negative feelings that may be inherent in the subtext of her communication. She should take note, for example, to what extent might she come across as critical, judgmental, controlling, or authoritarian in her encounters with the self-injurer. Being aware of these potentially distancing sentiments can avert the possibility of missing a valuable opportunity for connection. It is imperative to remain cognizant of the fact that many self-injurers have histories of relational trauma, and, therefore, to fail to create a positive interpersonal context for assessment can inadvertently reactivate the person's traumatic experience. By maintaining the delicate balance of being present, compassionate, and empathic while also being knowledgeable, direct, and firm, the helper implicitly builds safety and trust and begins to create the relational structure within which to conduct a comprehensive assessment. While the helper may have information from collateral sources (e.g., the self-injurer's friends, parents, teachers, roommates), this information cannot take the place of firsthand details obtained from the self-injurer herself. Without direct information from the client, it becomes difficult to ascertain the scope and depth of the problem, which makes the planning of the next steps more complicated than it might otherwise be.

This chapter provides a framework for the process of conducting a comprehensive assessment of individuals who self-injure. It considers the broad goals of an initial appraisal, outlines general principles to be considered in structuring the actual assessment, presents an overview of the content areas to be assessed, and provides guidelines for effectively gathering information from the client. Issues related to the referral process are considered, and the use of self-injury assessment instruments is briefly discussed. Table 7.1 summarizes the central components of the assessment process in the form of a checklist, *The Self-Injury Assessment Checklist (SIAC)*. The SIAC can be used by the frontline professional as a guide to conceptualizing and carrying out the complex task of assessing the self-injuring individual. The following sections of this chapter discuss the rationale behind the assessment process, as well as providing added details about the items on the checklist.

TABLE 7.1   Self-Injury Assessment Checklist (SIAC)

Containment

Assess:

☐ If the situation is a crisis

☐ If the individual is in immediate danger

☐ If medical attention is required

☐ If other members of the community have been exposed to the SI and need attention

☐ If others need to be immediately notified (e.g., parents, administrators, residential life staff)

Engagement

Recommended demeanor for the frontline responder in assessing the self-injurer:

☐ Present with a "respectful curiosity"; be dispassionate, nonjudgmental, compassionate, firm, knowledgeable about self-injury, confident, hopeful

☐ Communicate interest and develop a collaborative, conversational style

☐ Help client decide to what extent to discuss SI further

Assessment

☐ Distinguish between a suicide attempt and self-injury

Assess the following domains:

Behavioral

☐ Nature, extent, and severity of the injury (inspect wounds if appropriate)

☐ Conditions under which self-injury occurs

☐ Client's awareness of antecedent events

☐ Reactions and effects of aftermath of self-injury

☐ Presence of other situational, physical, or sexual risk-taking behavior

Affective

☐ Client's awareness of feeling states prior, during, and post-SI episode

☐ Current feelings present (e.g., anger, fear of abandonment, helplessness)

☐ Presence of dissociative sequelea around the self-injury

☐ Times and situations in which client experienced positive feelings

Cognitive

☐ Automatic thoughts that lead to self-injury

☐ Core beliefs about self, body image, and relationships

☐ Beliefs about gender identity and sexual orientation

☐ Beliefs about personal assets and resources to cope with distress

Biological

☐ Presence of other comorbid conditions (e.g., depression, trauma-related symptoms, eating disorders)

☐ Presence of substance use; if so, whether acute or chronic

☐ Whether client is on prescribed medication and if compliant

☐ Presence of medical complications due to SI currently or in the past

Environmental

☐ Quality of client's significant relationships

☐ Emotional climate of client's family environment

☐ Cultural background of the client and the client's family

☐ Quality of social supports

☐ History of abuse and neglect

☐ Social nature of client's self-injury social reinforcers for the behavior (e.g., communicates about behavior with others, receives nurturance)

☐ Functional impact of SI on client's life (e.g., school, work, other people)

☐ Treatment history (positive and negative elements)

Planning Next Steps

☐ Involve the client in the planning of next steps; help client retain sense of control over situation

☐ Inform appropriate individuals to be involved in client's care (on a need-to-know basis only)

☐ Assist client in making connections between seeming disparate parts of his or her life

☐ Assist client in identifying other options for coping with distress

☐ Help client understand the benefits of speaking with a mental health professional; educate client about the referral process

☐ Empower client and communicate hope

☐ Make the referral

From D'Onofrio, A. A. (2007). *Adolescent self-injury: A comprehensive guide for counselors and health care professionals.* New York: Springer Publishing Company LLC. © Springer Publishing Company LLC. Reprint permission granted to the purchaser of this book for personal use only and with proper credit to the author.

MAKING FIRST CONTACT

The basic movement of the life of dialogue is the turning towards the other.

Martin Buber (1947/1955, p. 22)

First contact with an individual who self-injures can happen in a variety of settings and under different circumstances. A teacher may come to you as the counselor or school nurse and inform you that she suspects a particular student of cutting and is concerned: Can you speak to her? A parent calls you with the same concern and asks you to intervene with her daughter. A college student's roommate or Resident Assistant (RA) comes to you as a counseling center staff member and asks you to see a student who "cuts herself almost every weekend." A young woman presents at the emergency room (ER) at your hospital because the cuts she has made on her arms are too deep and she needs help stopping the blood flow. Or, perhaps in the best-case scenario, a self-injurer herself comes to you for help as she feels her life to be spiraling out of control and asks for help. These are only a few examples of the circumstances and situations in which frontline professionals may encounter a self-injurer and where their work of engaging and assessing the individual begins.

The last example cited, in which the individual actually comes to the responder for help, is perhaps the most straightforward in that the self-injurer is the one who takes the initiative and seeks help. It is usually easier to work with someone who asks directly for assistance than with someone for whom another person has asked for help. In the cases where the professional's help is unsolicited, one may feel extremely awkward in even broaching the topic of self-injury with the client. How does one offer help when it may not be wanted? How does one inform the individual that others are concerned about her and about her behavior in a way that doesn't put the self-injurer on the defensive and lose the possibility for further contact? How does one appropriately offer more help than is requested, for example, in the case of a self-injurer who presents to the hospital ER simply for wound care? How does the nurse or physician engage the individual about the feelings behind the behavior and begin to plant the seeds for deeper exploration and movement toward better self-care? Engagement and facilitating treatment in these cases become much more complicated and require greater subtlety and sophistication from the helper, as well as a broad understanding of the larger issues involved in these scenarios. Regardless of the setting and the specific situation, however, the primary task of the frontline responder remains the same. Whether in a school or medical facility or on the college campus, the work of the health care professional can be summarized by the fourfold process that often occurs simultaneously and in overlapping and redundant ways. The principal tasks during initial encounters can be summarized as (1) containment, (2) engagement, (3) assessment, and (4) planning next steps. A brief overview of each task is presented in the next sections, followed by an in-depth discussion of the constituent elements that make up a comprehensive assessment of self-injuring individuals.

Containment

Obviously, the first area of concern is the self-injuring individual's safety. Is the situation to which you are asked to respond a crisis? Is the individual in immediate danger? Has she recently self-injured, and is she bleeding, in pain, or otherwise hurt at the present time and in need of immediate medical attention? The containment function of the frontline responder consists precisely of containing the situation so that it does not escalate into a larger crisis. You may be asked to intervene by a self-injurer or by someone close to her directly following an instance of the behavior, and you may need to mobilize quickly (but calmly) to contain the situation so that it does not escalate. The first step is to provide immediate, empathic, calm attention to the injurer as soon as the incident occurs. Engaging her in a nonjudgmental way and encouraging her to talk with you about what has gone on and to begin to ventilate some of her feelings are essential first steps (Shepperd & McAllister, 2003). Clearly, connecting the individual to immediate medical care, should it be required, is also of the highest priority. It is important to note, however, that if medical attention is required, it should be provided with the utmost discretion so that the privacy of the self-injurer can be respectfully maintained.

In other cases, the containing function may also require managing the response and reactions of others. If, for example, a self-injuring incident occurs during the school day, care should be taken to minimize the involvement of other students, as well as other nonessential school personnel. The student should be escorted to an appropriate private location where she can receive the assistance she needs. The helper may also need to be attentive to other students who may have been exposed to the incident in some way and address their concerns and fears as to avoid a spread of alarm or panic. This, of course, should be done only after the needs of the self-injuring individual have been attended to. Situations such as these across settings speak to the importance of coordinated teamwork where some team members are deployed to deal with the crisis with the individual in need, while others attend to the larger community that may have been affected. More is said about team coordination in Chapter 9.

Engagement

Engagement is the overarching process of making contact with the individual throughout the course of the responder's encounters with her. In addition to communicating the attitudes of concern, nonjudgmental acceptance, compassion, and firmness, all of which have been discussed at length in the previous chapter, Walsh (2006) recommends that the initial response be informal and dispassionate—that one be neither overly solicitous and nurturing nor judgmental or condemning. He uses the phrase "respectful curiosity" to capture the essence of the responder's demeanor toward a self-injurer. He notes that "Curiosity conveys an attitude of wanting to know more about a problem rather than wanting the problem to go away quickly. To be helpful, curiosity has to be tempered and respectful. Interest that comes across as prurient or thrill seeking is aversive (or too reinforcing) for most self-injurers" (p. 77). He further suggests that using the client's own language regarding self-injury can be particularly helpful in the engagement process. Using the client's words communicates a sense of respect that fuels the alliance, and the resulting experience of being understood by the helper can be very empowering for the client. Walsh cautions, however, that using the client's language is ill advised when the client has a tendency to minimize the severity of the harm inflicted to the body or when the language is "ultrasubjective" or borders on the delusional. The point behind the use of the client's language is to avoid overly clinical or pathologizing terminology. At the same time, the client's words ought to be avoided when they communicate something other than the reality of the situation or where the self-injurer's perceptions and facts are clearly distorted.

Engaging Self-Injurers Who Have Been Referred by Others

In my work as consulting psychologist in the secondary school setting, I have often had a teacher, coach, or administrator inform me that he suspects that a student is cutting or that the student has actually confided in him about self-injuring and then ask if I will meet with that student. I find that directly approaching students with whom I have little or no relationship is an ineffective strategy of engaging them around self-injury. Rather, I attempt to enlist the assistance of the referring adult to engage the student and either encourage her to come speak with me or suggest that, if the student prefers, the trusted adult be present during the initial meeting. In these situations, I offer suggestions to and even coach the referring adult on some of the language that can be used with the student about making arrangements to meet with me or another counselor.

A sample script I may suggest to the referring adult might go something like this: "I'm glad you've told me about some of these things going on in your life. It sounds like things get so overwhelming for you sometimes that you don't know what to do. Sometimes it gets so bad that you even take it out on yourself. I'm concerned and want to help you, but I'm not sure how to best do that right now. Maybe we can meet with one of the counselors for some guidance. Is there anyone in the counseling department you have a good relationship with or whom you think you can talk to about what's going on? If you like, I can come with you for support. What do you think? Should we make an appointment?" It is important to communicate to the referring individual that his stance toward the self-injurer ought to be one of empathic yet firm guidance, moving the person toward speaking with a mental health professional. Providing the referral source with concrete guidelines for making the referral effectively can relieve much of the referral source's anxiety about feeling ill equipped to personally help the self-injuring student.

As the person responding to a scenario in which it is clear that a crisis does *not* exist, the helper's first task is to communicate interest in the individual. Using the "respectful curiosity" approach presented earlier, you can begin to lay the foundation for a working alliance by communicating, in a nonpossessive, dispassionate way, the simple message "I'm interested in you and want to know more about you." As this communication is accepted by the client, the work begins to shift to helping her decide how much she would now like to discuss her self-injury, as well as other issues in her life that may cause her distress. Again, the importance of the demeanor and the approach of the helper cannot be overemphasized. The more the client comes to trust you as the helper, the more leverage you have to actually *be* helpful. One of the questions I generally ask my clients, regardless of the presenting problem, is whether they have ever spoken to a counselor or therapist before about their difficulties. If they have, my follow-up question concerns what they liked or disliked about the experience or about the counselor and whether they found the experience helpful. The answer to these questions is worth listening to, because clients will generally speak honestly about their experience. They will say things like "I didn't like her because she was too intrusive and controlling," or "she was nice, but didn't say much and made me do all the talking," or "We just didn't click; he always gave me advice and told me what to do. He didn't seem to be interested in hearing what I had to say or really cared." An angry 15-year-old young man who was recently brought in by his mother after having been to three other therapists whom he would not return to see responded to my question about what went wrong by stating, "They all think I'm the problem. No one seems to want to understand that my mother and father hate each other and since their divorce they put me in the middle of their fights. I'm not the problem. I just want to be left alone. They're the ones who need to be fixed." The mere act of acknowledging his perspective on the situation and not identifying him as the sole patient within the family system opened the doors for him to want to return and engage in the process. And he did. Clients will tell us, if we ask, how they want us to be with them, and listening to and considering their perspective can offer us information vital to the task of alliance building.

To this end, Connors (2000) provides sample comments and questions that can be helpful in one's initial encounters with self-injurers in the process of developing trust. The first group of suggested interventions listed here are targeted at communicating interest in the individual and wanting to know more about the self-injurious behaviors. The second set of questions is designed to assist the helper explore the extent to which the client may want to further discuss her self-injurious behaviors and the role they play in her life. A number of the questions she suggests are listed here:

Comments or Questions That Communicate Interest
- I am glad you told me about what you do to your body. Are you feeling okay about having told me?
- I noticed the scars on your arms. I hope it's okay to say that. I am interested in knowing about them if you want to tell me.
- Can you tell me about the times when you hurt yourself?
- I am glad you told me that. If you want to tell me more, or feel like saying more sometime in the future, I am interested in hearing about it.

Questions to Help the Client Decide to What Extent She Wants to Discuss Her Self-Injury
- Do you feel it would be helpful to talk more about your cutting?

- Would you like to talk more about this with me? I'm willing to hear if you want to tell me more.
- Do you have a sense of how your self-injury works for you? Would it help to learn more about it?
- Sometimes talking about how you hurt yourself can be useful. What do you think? (Adapted and modified from Connors, 2000, pp. 372–373)

Because of the shame clients might feel about their self-injury or because they may fear the consequences of disclosing their behavior to a mental health professional, they may be reluctant to volunteer much information initially. It is incumbent upon the helper, therefore, to open the door by further inquiry about their behaviors and to take an active role in encouraging (but not forcing) the client to say more (Farber, 2000). Being active in a respectful way communicates to the client the helper's willingness to be present, to engage with her, and begins to communicate implicitly that the helper is interested in her, is knowledgeable about self-injury, and can "handle" hearing about it.

Assessment

The most important function of the initial encounter is to gather relevant information so that the helper can effectively assess the self-injurer's behaviors, affective state, intentions, and risk factors in order to take appropriate action, if necessary. Elements of this assessment on the frontlines can take place both indirectly (e.g., obtaining information from people close to the self-injurer) and in direct and structured ways, such as through an assessment interview with the client. The goal of the assessment is to gather as much information as possible about the individual in different areas of functioning so that one has a complete snapshot of the person's life, assets, and liabilities at that particular point in time. This information is subsequently used to determine the acuity of the client's situation, the level of risk present, the immediate actions to be taken, and the possible next steps to be considered and planned. Obviously, the more complete the information, the better informed the responder's interventions, referrals, and treatment decisions can be. A comprehensive overview of the assessment process, as well as a description of the domains to be assessed, are presented in detail later in this chapter.

Planning Next Steps

The final task of the frontline responder in his initial encounters with self-injurers is to begin to plan the next steps in their care. Working from the clinical philosophy that treatment disposition or issues of termination ought to begin with the first encounter, I find it most helpful to begin to think about appropriate next steps from the outset of my contact with my client. This does not foreclose the possibility of altering or modifying those plans as new information surfaces. However, by thinking in terms of planning the next practical steps, one can begin to outline the arc of the client's care, which can facilitate the often difficult referral process. Things to consider during this process include: What are the client's immediate first aid needs, if any? Who should be informed about what's going on? Do the client's parents need to be informed immediately? Do school administrators need to be informed? Is the person currently at high risk and not safe being alone or remaining in the school or college residence hall? If so, what are my next action steps? Is the client open to engaging in ongoing counseling? If so, to whom can I refer her?

Of course, the helper's attention ought not to be focused on "what's next" to the point of being distracted or disengaged from listening and "meeting" the individual where he or she is. Rather, the planning of the future course of action emerges *precisely* out of the careful listening and information gathering that occurs while engaging the self-injurer and is the result of actually involving her in developing the plan of action. Returning as much control of the process to the client is fundamental to ensuring "buy-in" and ownership of the decisions made. While it may feel counterintuitive to give some control back to someone who appears out of control, collaboratively enlisting the individual around her own self-care helps the client to regain a greater sense of control over her life and move toward safety (Deiter et al., 2000).

CONDUCTING A COMPREHENSIVE ASSESSMENT

I consciously thought of small ways to involve Tiffany in her own care. When she ended encounters, I respected the decision. When she aided in her self-care, I encouraged it. I also understood that kindness, and a willingness to listen, may well have prompted Tiffany to reveal a powerful story which may or may not be true. Regardless of its veracity, Tiffany was talking and that, I reasoned, was a sign of therapeutic progress.

C. Shepperd (in Shepperd & McAllister, 2003, p. 446)

Given the increased prevalence of self-injury in recent years within the adolescent population (Muehlenkamp & Gutierrez, 2004; Whitlock, Eckenrode, et al., 2006), it is recommended that a simple inquiry about self-injury be included as a routine matter in any initial assessment of adolescents (Simeon & Favazza, 2001). Health care professionals are trained to always inquire about depression and suicidality but rarely ask direct questions regarding self-injury. Suicide attempts and self-injurious behaviors can become conflated within the assessment process, and, when this occurs, there is a strong possibility of misdiagnosis, which can have serious consequences for therapeutic intervention and treatment planning. It is imperative that the responder assess for self-injury in a way that distinguishes that act from a suicide attempt. For example, a simple and direct question such as "Have you ever cut or otherwise hurt yourself even if you weren't feeling suicidal?" may begin to elicit information about self-injurious behavior that would not otherwise emerge. If the client acknowledges that he engages in such behaviors, then a detailed history of the behaviors as well as other relevant information related to self-injury should be obtained. A detailed framework for distinguishing suicidality from self-injury is presented later in the chapter in order to provide the reader with a conceptual structure that can inform this part of the assessment.

A comprehensive assessment of self-injury is complex and time consuming and should be conducted in a casual, conversational style that feels comfortable for the frontline responder and does not come across as forced, rehearsed, or overly clinical. There is no absolute right or wrong way to conduct this kind of assessment. While it is important for the interviewer to obtain specific information, the manner, pace, and sequence must be dictated by the rhythm and tone of the dialogue created with the client. To the extent possible, the client should be made to feel at ease; the purpose and process of the interview or encounter should be made clear to her; she should be asked for permission to broach certain topics (e.g., is it okay if I ask you some questions about ...); and, if she declines, the responder can explore what makes talking about those areas difficult. Most important, the client should be treated respectfully at all times. Again, the experience should be collaborative and conversational, rather than like an interrogation. Helpers must operate within their own styles of engagement and develop an approach that is comfortable for them and that best suits their personal style.

The overview presented in this chapter offers general guidelines for conceptualizing and structuring the assessment process. The guidelines are organized according to five distinct content domains that need to be considered to ensure the thoroughness of the evaluation. While the process itself should be fluid and responsive to the client, the helper must not overlook the importance of gathering the information associated with each of the domains.

Assessing the Nature, Function, and Severity of the Self-Injurious Behaviors

Given that self-injurers may not always volunteer information about their injurious behavior or may minimize its severity, it is important that the frontline responder take an active role in soliciting information in a compassionate yet direct and assertive manner, communicating throughout a sense of competence and confidence about the subject matter. Some clients may feel relief at having been asked directly about self-injury, and, once the matter is out in the open, it may become easier to discuss it openly (Farber, 2000). Walsh (2006) suggests that a comprehensive assessment could be organized around the following domains of influence and functioning: the behavioral, the affective, the cognitive, the biological, and the environmental. Evaluating the client's life situation from each of these different perspectives can help to identify the breadth and depth of the individual's personal dynamics and interpersonal functioning, as well as her assets and liabilities, which, in turn, can inform the choice of intervention and future treatment planning.

The section that follows provides examples of the kinds of questions that can be asked within each of the assessment domains to elicit specific relevant information from the client. The assessment questions are both drawn from my own professional experience and adapted from a number of other sources, including Farber (2000), Simeon and Favazza (2001), and Walsh (2006). The reader is reminded that the information noted here explores the self-injurer's current state and her self-injury, as well as her developmental history. It is probably unrealistic to believe that *all* of the information can be obtained in one sitting (particularly in a time of crisis), although, clearly, the more information gathered, the better. The helper must use his or her best clinical judgment and must be attentive to the cues offered by the client as to how in-depth and thorough the assessment can be during any given encounter. The helper should first gather information about the specifics related to the current problem and behavior and rule out suicidality and other high-risk conditions that may be present; then, as appropriate, he can gather other information that completes the assessment.

The Behavioral Domain
- What is the nature and extent of the wounding?
- What is the primary area of the body that is injured? Are there multiple areas?
- What are the instruments that are used? Are they sharp? Dull? Sanitized?
- Are the cuts shallow or deep? (Depending upon the areas in which the injuries are made, it may also be appropriate to inspect the wounds to assess severity. Of course, this ought to be done within the confines of one's professional expertise.)
- When and where and under what conditions does the individual self-injure? When alone? With others? Does she have a regular routine or ritual around the self-injury?

- What was the age of onset, and what has been the course of the present behavior?
- How much time typically lapses between instances of the self-injurious behavior? Is it intermittent or continuous?
- What is the total time per day spent on the behavior?
- What are the reactions from others and the aftermath of the self-injurious behavior for the individual? In the short run? The long run? Is there relief? Shame? Does the individual feel nurtured by the attention received after the behavior?

The Affective Domain

- Is there an awareness of particular feeling states associated with self-injury? Is there awareness of the feelings that lead to the individual's impulsive urge to self-injure?
- What are the feeling states experienced by the individual before and after the behavior?
- Are there feelings or signs of anger? If yes, who might be the focus of that anger?
- Does the individual feel hopeless and helpless?
- What led to or was responsible for those feeling states?
- Under what circumstances do those feelings usually arise?
- Does the individual experience an altered state of consciousness during the act? Does she dissociate? Is there amnesia about the act? (For example, does the client sometimes feel as if she's standing outside herself watching herself self-injure, as if she were not quite there or it were happening to someone else?)
- What, if anything, besides self-injury helps the client cope or manage those feelings?
- Does the client ever feel good? If so, under what conditions or circumstances does this happen?

The Cognitive Domain

- What are the automatic thoughts associated with the chain of events that lead to self-injury? Is there dichotomous thinking? Does the individual feel that she has options, or is there a sense that she feels trapped in her situation, with no way out? (For example, does the client feel that she *has* to self-injure, that she has no choice? That this is the *only* way for her to feel better?)
- What are her core beliefs about herself, her relationships, and her ability to manage her life? Is there a poor self-concept? A sense of perfectionism?

- Is the individual highly critical and judgmental toward herself? Does she dislike or even "hate" herself?
- What are the self-injurer's beliefs about her body? Are there distorted body image issues present?
- Does the individual have a history of serious illness or surgeries?
- Are there struggles with gender identity or sexual orientation issues?
- How do these core beliefs fuel the self-injurer's urge to wound her body?
- Is there suicidal ideation? Has there been in the past? Actual attempts?
- What is the self-injurer's attitude and stance toward her behavior? Is it even seen as a problem? If so, is it obscured by other, more pressing problems in the person's life? Is there shame? Embarrassment? Self-hatred? Is there a wish to stop? Has she tried to stop? Has the attempt to stop ever been successful? For how long? How has she been able to stop the behavior? If not, is there awareness of what has gotten in the way?
- Does the individual believe she has any assets that help her cope with her situation and behavior? Are there signs of resilience? Of hope?
- Does the individual currently feel motivated to reduce her self-injury? If yes, what is the motivation?

The Biological/Psychiatric Domain
- Might the individual have particular biochemical or neurological vulnerabilities?
- Does she suffer from other comorbid conditions, such as depression, anxiety, substance abuse, an eating disorder, borderline personality disorder, bipolar disorder, impulsivity, conduct disorder, or oppositional disorder, that point to difficulties in her ability to self-regulate? Does she self-injure in conjunction with other behaviors (e.g., a bulimic episode)?
- Is there drug or alcohol use? If yes, how does it affect the individual's functioning? Under what circumstances is the substance used? Is the use a problem? If so, is the problem acute or chronic? Is the individual addicted? Does the individual self-injure while using alcohol or other drugs? If yes, how does the alcohol and drug use affect the nature and the severity of the self-injury?
- Is the individual on prescribed medication? Is she compliant?
- Does she experience an analgesic effect from the behavior, and might that be potentiating an addictive biological consequence? Is there an irresistible impulse to self-injure? Is there pain or numbing after the behavior?

- Have there been any medical complications because of the behavior (e.g., infections, scars, fractures)? How does the individual feel about these complications? (Note: Scars and other noticeable wounds can be a motivation for change. Some clients report embarrassment at having to "explain" them to others.)

The Environmental Domain

- What is the nature and extent of the individual's social and family support?
- What is the client's cultural background? What is the family's cultural background? How does culture play a part in the client's behavior (e.g., inhibit verbal expression of distress, discourage psychological explanations for behavior, create acculturation stress, create bicultural strain, expose the client to racial bias, discourage help-seeking behavior outside the family)?
- What is the nature of the individual's relationship with her parents or guardians? What is the family's emotional climate?
- What are the individual's environmental stressors? Are the parents together or divorced? Is there appropriate adult supervision?
- Is there substance abuse or violence in the home? Is there a history of self-injury in the family?
- Does the individual have a history of physical, sexual, or psychological abuse or assault? Neglect? If so, what are the circumstances around these issues? Does the client come from or is she currently in a family structure that is invalidating? Overly punitive? Overly protective?
- Does the individual communicate with others about her self-injury? If yes, with whom? With family members? How do they respond (e.g., do they minimize, become upset, angry, punitive, nurturing, helpful)?
- What is the impact of self-injury on the person's functional relationships to school, work, and other people?
- Does the individual's environment somehow reinforce her self-injury? What are the contributions to the behavior by her peer group and her inner circle of friends? Do they collude? Participate? Confront the client? Is self-injury a means to receive nurturance or social status within the client's peer group?
- What is the treatment history of the individual? What has helped reduce her behavior, if anything, and what has made it worse?
- Are there any environmental factors that can be used as leverage for the self-injurer's care (e.g., participation in cocurricular activities, travel without parents, permission to remain in the residence hall)? Are there trusted adults that are able to help?

Clearly, the information sought by these questions is extensive, and an assessment of this magnitude takes some time. An in-depth assessment of the myriad cultural factors that may be salient for a particular client requires an even greater investment of time but must be undertaken to ensure the delivery of a multiculturally competent assessment (Grieger, in press; Grieger & Ponterotto, 1995; Paniagua, 1998, 2001). As noted previously, the most helpful approach is for the helper to be conversational, flexible, and collaborative, rather than sounding as if he were conducting a legalistic cross-examination. The interviewer also needs to be skillful in reframing and seeing connections in the information that the client provides. Helping the client begin to make connections among behavior, thoughts, and feelings can perhaps reorient the client to begin to think differently about her behavior (Farber, 2000) and can be an effective way of keeping the person engaged. When we are able to reframe material clients share with us and present it back to them in a way that links the seemingly disparate parts of their lives, and when those connections resonate deep within them, then our clients begin to feel hopeful. Most people who are enduring difficult times find that hope begins to surface when they feel understood, and for many self-injurers, feeling understood is a foreign experience, which makes it all the more powerful. By helping them make these connections, we capture their attention and offer them the possibility that, perhaps for the first time, there may be some more *enduring* relief to their pain. We communicate to them that perhaps we have some insights into their problems that they may not have and that *we* may actually be able to help.

Furthermore, it is recommended that the helper be attentive to the self-injurer's subjective experience and attitude toward her behavior throughout the encounter. Being attentive to the client's relationship with and attachment to her self-injurious behavior can provide important clues to her possible resistance, her willingness to engage with the helper, and her motivation to participate in her self-care. For example, does she ignore the seriousness of her behavior and neglect her self-care? Is she attached to being a victim or patient? Does she maintain her behavior in order to elicit care from others or experience a sense of connection to others as a result of her injuries (Farber, 2000)? Does she find comfort in the response of others? Has the behavior become the centerpiece of her identity? On the other hand, does she feel shame? Self-hatred? Does she see her behavior as a problem or as an indispensable part of her life? How does her cultural background affect her behavior? Her willingness to seek help? And, perhaps most important, does she want to stop? Her own attitude toward her behavior becomes a touchstone for the responder in orienting herself toward the self-injurer. It provides information that helps the helper decide how to best engage the individual and determine what the realistic goals and possibilities are for the assessment, in particular, and, for future encounters with this client, in general. In some instances, the work becomes about helping the client understand that she suffers and that there is hope—that people can learn to deal with pain, conflict, and fear in ways other than self-injury. Helping someone begin to accept the reality that a problem actually *exists* is the beginning of change. In fact, it *is* change! As Linehan (1993a) observes, "The paradoxical notion here is that therapeutic change can only occur in the context of acceptance of what is; however, 'acceptance of what is' is itself change" (p. 99). In short, assisting our clients to acknowledge "what is" constitutes a significant breakthrough in and of itself.

Distinguishing Self-Injury From Suicidality

Assessing individuals who self-injure is a challenge for many reasons, not the least of which is the concern that the individual may be suicidal and that her behavior may, in fact, be a bona fide suicidal gesture. Individuals who have little experience in working with self-injurers may understandably assume that there is suicidal intent because of the very nature of the act. The fear that suicidality engenders can significantly impair the helper's ability to be effective in engaging, assessing, and providing care to the self-injurer. While a suicide assessment is critical to ensure the safety of the individual, to overemphasize it in the assessment process can be counterproductive, as it may work against keeping the individual engaged. It may evoke anger at the all-too-familiar feeling of being misunderstood and ineffectively listened to. Sheena (in Smith et al., 1999) expresses precisely this frustration:

> Each time I'd go to … [the ER] with my cuts it would be the same questions. Did you do this yourself? Did anyone force you to do it? Was anyone with you when you did it? What did you use? Were you trying to kill yourself? I got sick of telling them—I did it myself, no one except myself forced me to do it. I alone, I used a razor blade and OF COURSE I WASN'T TRYING TO KILL MYSELF … I WAS TRYING TO MAKE MYSELF FEEL ALIVE. (p. 37)

To keep the focus of an assessment on the topic of suicide sometimes says less about the client and more about the fear and anxiety of the helper who, understandably, wants to ensure beyond all doubt that this person intends to live. Unfortunately, when this happens, the ensuing interventions are geared toward treating someone who is suicidal, not someone who self-injures—which may represent two very different diagnostic profiles and may warrant different treatment strategies. Nevertheless, making this distinction actually poses a significant challenge for the frontline responder, particularly at the current time, when a great deal of emphasis is being placed on suicide

prevention in high schools and on the college campus (see The Jed Foundation, 2006). Further, the empirical literature does suggest an overlap between
these diagnostic categories. Therefore, in order to help the frontline responder
to make these important diagnostic distinctions between suicidality and
self-injury, we turn to examining some of the central phenomenological differences between the two conditions.

Self-injury and the attempt to end one's life through suicide are, for the
most part, distinctly different phenomena. In fact, self-injury is usually
counterintentional to suicide—the suicidal individual wants to end life, while
the self-injurer engages in the behavior to self-heal or feel alive, rather than
to die (Clarke & Whittaker, 1998; Connors, 2000; Conterio & Lader, 1998;
Farber, 2000; McAllister, 2003; Walsh, 2006; Walsh & Rosen, 1988). The
intent underlying the behavior is often different, if not diametrically opposed.
For example, a recent study of self-reported reasons for engaging in suicide
attempts and in nonsuicidal self-injury suggests that while participants in both
groups expressed the intent to relieve negative emotions, the self-reported
intentions of the nonsuicidal self-injury group were to express anger, to pun-
ish oneself, to generate normal feelings, and to distract oneself. The suicide
attempters, on the other hand, indicated that the intent of their behavior was to
make others feel "better off" (Brown et al., 2002). At the same time, while there
is usually a clear difference in intent and purpose between suicidal acts and
self-injury, the two are *not* mutually exclusive and can coexist in the individual
simultaneously (McAllister, 2003; Muehlenkamp & Gutierrez, 2004). Some
research has noted that as many as 28% to 41% of self-injurers have reported
coexisting suicidal ideation (Favazza, 1996; Pattison & Kahan, 1983). Other
researchers cite data indicating that individuals who chronically self-injure are
18 times more likely to eventually commit suicide than the general population
(McAllister, 2003) and that self-injury can be the best predictor of subsequent
suicide (Farber, 2000). On the other hand, in the most extensive study conducted of college students to date (N = 2,875), 17% (N = 490) reported having practiced self-injury *without* the intent to die (Whitlock, Eckenrode, et al.,
2006). Of all self-injurers, however, more than a third (34.2%) reported having considered or attempted suicide in the past, and 64.3% reported elevated
levels of distress in the preceding 30 days. Another study of self-injuring
adolescents (N = 390 high school students) failed to find significant differences
in suicide ideation and depressive symptoms between the self-injury group
and the suicide-attempt group (Muehlenkamp & Gutierrez, 2004). These in-
vestigators noted that the results of their study add to the already mixed results
in the extant research literature on the presence of suicidal ideation in self-
injurers and, because suicidal ideation is quite common among adolescents,
it may *not* be a reliable variable in distinguishing suicidality from self-injury.

Nonetheless, the reality remains that some self-injurers may be at a higher risk for suicide than others, and care should be taken to assess those individuals accordingly. For these and other obvious reasons, one of the most important tasks of assessment is to rule out suicidality and to arrive at a reasonable understanding of the intent and level of lethality of the client's self-injurious behaviors so that appropriate action can be taken.

Walsh (2006) offers a series of questions that are particularly helpful in conceptualizing whether an individual's behaviors are suicidal in nature or whether they are simply self-injurious. These questions do not necessarily need to be asked directly of clients but can serve as background conceptual guides for the helper in making this vital distinction during the assessment. Walsh's (2006, pp. 6–23) questions are presented here, followed by brief descriptions of how they would be answered differently by a self-injurer and a potential suicide:

> *What was the expressed and unexpressed intent of the act?*
> The intent of the act is significantly different. For self-injurers, it is to experience relief from their tension, anger, pain, and feelings of deadness. For individuals who attempt suicide, on the other hand, the intent is not to experience temporary relief from pain but to escape it altogether.
>
> *What was the level of physical damage and the potential lethality?*
> In most cases, the level of physical damage and potential lethality for self-injurers is minimal in comparison to that of individuals who attempt suicide. Self-injurers' methods tend, for the most part, to have low levels of lethality, and the wounds are often superficial. There are cases, however, when self-injurers accidentally cut too deeply or too close to major blood vessels. In these cases, the level of lethality is significantly raised, and death can be a consequence. The methods used by those who attempt suicide are often highly lethal (e.g., use of a gun or hanging), and, if the person survives, bodily damage can be severe.
>
> *Is there a chronic, repetitive pattern of self-injurious acts, and are multiple methods used?*
> Self-injurers typically use multiple methods and the behavior is repetitive over time. Again, the repetitive nature illustrates the differential function of the behavior in the individual's life as distinguished from the overt desire to die. Suicide attempts are less frequent (though some people may overdose repeatedly) and often do not vary in methods employed.
>
> *What is the level of psychological pain?*
> For the self-injurer, psychological distress is present and uncomfortable but is often episodic and intermittent. For the suicidal individual, psychic anguish is unbearably intense and persistent. Unlike the self-injurer, who can modulate that pain precisely by the acts of self-injury,

the suicidal individual seeks permanent relief from suffering that is viewed as being unendurable.

Is there constriction of cognition?

Suicidal individuals' conception of their choices is highly constricted. That is, they resort to a binary, dichotomous way of looking at their lives, and when they fail to see a variety of choices, they resort to the belief that suicide is the only way out. Self-injurers, on the other hand, may demonstrate a narrowed view of choices but typically still see that they have options (as limited as they may be) and usually do not operate from an all-or-nothing stance.

Are there feelings of hopelessness and helplessness?

Both self-injurers and suicidal individuals experience feelings of hopelessness and helplessness. The primary difference between the two groups, however, is that self-injurers may experience periods of hope and occasional belief that they may someday be better able to handle their current situation, while suicidal individuals do not.

Was there a decrease in discomfort following the act?

Clearly, with self-injurers there is a great sense of relief after the act. In fact, this self-soothing function makes self-injury such a meaningful behavior to many, and it is why it becomes so difficult to stop. The relief is immediate and is under the control of the individual, who may feel she has little or no control in other areas of her life. For the suicidal person, on the other hand, there is no psychological relief or improvement after the act. If they succeed with the attempt, they die. If not, the pain usually persists unless other significant changes (e.g., treatment) occur.

What is the core problem?

The core problem for the suicidal person is generally some combination of feelings of depression, rage, unendurable pain, loneliness, hopelessness, and isolation. Walsh (2006) notes that "The challenge in assisting suicidal individuals is therefore to identify the primary source of unendurable pain and to reduce it" (p. 16). For the self-injurer, on the other hand, the primary problem entails a combination of body alienation, the experience of intense stress, inadequate self-soothing skills, and peer influence that endorses the behavior. The challenge with these individuals is to help them develop better affect-regulatory skills and coping mechanisms and to deal with the underlying trauma that may have contributed to their distorted body image and self-image. These negative images serve to fuel their self-destructive behavior.

Keeping these questions in mind during the initial assessment will help the interviewer make a clearer distinction between self-injury and suicidality.

The reader is cautioned, however, not to ignore the chronic self-injurer's increased chances of becoming suicidal if the relevant conditions are in place (e.g., hopelessness, unendurable pain, and the desire to permanently end it). While a self-injurer and a suicidal individual generally present very differently and can be distinguished rather easily by the criteria described, an assessment of suicidality must take place in order to establish the client's current suicidal ideation and intent (Simeon & Favazza, 2001). It is extremely helpful for the responder, particularly if this is the first contact with the individual, to have a sense whether the individual feels suicidal in the moment or has been in the past. Standard suicide assessment questions can be used here: Have you ever thought about ending your life? Do you feel like that now? Have you ever tried? Do you have a plan now? The means at your disposal? If there was a time you wanted to kill yourself but stopped, what changed your mind? If, after asking some of these questions, the helper is clear that the individual is not imminently suicidal, then the responder should move away from using suicide-related language. It is important that suicidality not be *the* focus of one's assessment, as this will miss the core issues of self-injurers and communicate to them that you, like others, don't understand them.

Since lethality is not limited to simply suicidal intent or action but can occur when self-injury is potentiated by other variables, the assessment of ongoing risk factors is warranted in all situations. It is to that phase of the assessment process that we now turn.

Assessing for Other Risk Factors

Because a strong relationship exists between self-injury and risk-taking activities, the responder should also be attentive during the assessment for other behaviors that reflect poor self-care or actually increase the level of lethality of one's self-destructive actions (Farber, 2000; Walsh, 2006). Risk-taking behaviors can include activities along a broad spectrum. Walsh (2006) notes that, for example, alcohol and drug abuse, eating-disordered behavior, having sex with strangers, walking in high-speed traffic or alone in a dangerous part of town all increase risk for direct or indirect harm to the individual. He recommends that a thorough assessment of other questionable behaviors also be completed in order to better gauge the individual's "at risk" status. Again, sensitivity and care should be taken in eliciting this information, as a self-injurer may be reluctant to disclose the extent of the risk taking, out of a sense of shame or the fear of being judged and rebuked. The importance of having established an alliance and of approaching the individual respectfully and nonjudgmentally cannot be overestimated in helping to bring to light the nature and extent of their risk-taking behavior.

Assessing for Substance Use

While the literature on the comorbidity of self-injury and substance use is still scant, this is nonetheless a critical factor to be considered in the assessment of any adolescent, particularly one who engages in other self-destructive behavior. Substances have a psychological function like that of self-injury: they alter and regulate mood. They are a means to reduce states of tension and to artificially modify the functioning of one's nervous system to bring about a desired effect in mood change. As such, they can enhance or potentiate the effects of self-injury and may raise the level of risk for the individual. We know that alcohol use, in particular, is part and parcel of adolescent culture. Binge drinking on college campuses is particularly problematic and is often thought of by some college students as a normative activity in college. For some students, uncontrolled substance use can severely distort their judgment about high-risk behaviors, especially when combined with a disposition that may already be oriented toward self-destructiveness. For these individuals, the risk for serious harm is increased significantly. It is imperative, therefore, that both the acuity and the chronicity of an individual's substance use be assessed. Some individuals may suffer from an actual addiction to substances and may require substance abuse treatment outright. Others, because of their acute episodes of substance use (which includes binge drinking, use of other illicit substances, abuse of prescribed medication, or any combination of these), also have an increased vulnerability to serious harm.

While little research exists regarding the interaction of substance abuse and self-injury, clinical anecdotal evidence suggests that the use of substances can exacerbate the problems of self-injurers. The example given earlier of the college student who returned from a campus party intoxicated secondary to having broken up with her boyfriend, cut herself too deeply, and was found bleeding while passed out on the campus grounds unambiguously illustrates the role substances can play in elevating the lethality of self-injury. Clearly, the combination of feeling rejected, using alcohol to cope with the situation, and then engaging in self-injury created a powerful confluence of factors that placed her at very high risk. Understanding how substances (whether legal, prescribed, or illicit) are used by self-injurers is essential in accurately assessing the potential level of lethality of their self-injurious behavior.

Assessing for Eating-Disordered Behavior

Assessing an individual's eating-disordered patterns provides another view of the extent of their self-destructive disposition. As discussed in Part I of this book, there is a high degree of comorbidity between self-injury and eating disorders. Some argue that the two phenomena are very similar in their dynamics and have similar subjective psychological functions (Farber, 2000; Levitt et al., 2004). Exploring the level of severity of eating issues can provide valuable information about the individual's self-image, her view of her body, and the extent to which she may attack her body through starving or purging. Questions to guide this part of the assessment for self-injurers can be the standard ones used for conducting an eating disorder assessment. Examples include: Do you frequently think about or obsess about food? About body image? Do you starve yourself or severely restrict food (i.e., have anorexic tendencies)? Has there been significant weight loss recently? Do you induce vomiting (i.e., have bulimic tendencies)? Use laxatives or diuretics? What is the frequency of your binging and purging? Is your binging out of control? Do you overexercise? Having information around these eating-related and body-image issues can provide an important perspective on the client's attitude toward her body and how she may inflict violence upon it. With this additional information in hand, the helper is better equipped to determine if the individual has a comorbid eating disorder that requires treatment and the level of care that would be most appropriate for this particular individual.

Assessing for Situational, Physical, and Sexual Risk Taking

Finally, Walsh (2006) recommends that the level of risk taking be examined in other areas of the self-injurer's life. Do the individuals place themselves in situations that increase the likelihood that harm will befall them? Do they take unnecessary physical risks? Are they thrill seekers? Do they do things like stand on the edge of a roof or walk on train tracks? Do they take risks sexually? Do they have unprotected sex? Do they have sex with strangers? The taking of risks in other areas of one's life speaks to a more general theme of self-destructive tendencies that are symptomatic of deeper pain and distress. Walsh (2006) observes that the overall goal "is to assess the person's self-destructiveness in all its manifestations. The presence of these major forms of indirect self-harm points to the client being in significant distress and lacking important coping skills. Both should be targeted in treatment" (p. 27). Piecing together these important sources of information regarding indirect self-harm helps to complete the diagnostic picture of the self-injurer and allows for more appropriate dispositions to be made.

Assessment Instruments

While there are many assessment instruments that measure other specific forms of self-destructiveness (e.g., suicidal ideation, eating disorders), there are relatively few that assess for self-injury directly (Sansone & Sansone, 2004). Recently, however, there has been a push to develop tools to assess various components of self-injury (Juzwin, 2004). Sansone and Sansone (2004) provide brief descriptions of nine different instruments that assess levels of self-harm. Some assess across the spectrum of self-destructive behaviors, ranging from eating disorders to self-injury to suicidality. Others simply assess self-injurious behavior. Juzwin (2004) describes another, more recently developed instrument whose items assess a wide array of issues, including self-injury, eating disorders, high-risk behaviors, history of abuse and trauma, and suicide attempts. Some of these instruments are self-report inventories, and others are clinician rating forms that can help guide the assessment process. These 10 assessment tools are listed in Table 7.2 as a resource for the reader.

The use of formal assessment instruments in the evaluation of self-injury must, however, be considered with caution. While a formal assessment tool can provide valuable information across domains quickly, its careless or insensitive use can be deleterious to establishing rapport, making it more difficult to gather complete and accurate information from the client. The clinician rating forms can be helpful in guiding the interviewer in systematically assessing the several domains of self-harm. But, again, the responder is cautioned against using those tools in an overly structured, question-and-answer approach. If the assessment feels too clinical to adolescent self-injurers, they may give you incomplete information, be deceptive about the information that is provided, or shut down entirely. Even worse is asking a self-injurer in a very early stage of contact

TABLE 7.2   List of Instruments That Assess Self-Injury

Chronic Self-Destructiveness Scale (CSDS)	Kelly et al. (1985)
Harkavy Asnis Suicide Survey (HASS-II)	Friedman & Asnis (1989)
Impulsive and Self-Harm Questionnaire	Rossotto (1997)
Self-Harm Behavior Survey	Favazza (1986); Favazza & Conterio (1988)
Self-Harm Inventory (SHI)	Sansone, Wiederman, & Sansone (1998)
Self-Injurious Behavior Questionnaire (SIB-Q)	Schroeder, Rojahn,& Reese (1997)
Self-Injury Questionnaire (SIQ)	Vanderlinden & Vandereycken (1997)
Self-Injury Self-Report Inventory (SISRI)	Juzwin (2004)
Self-Injury Survey	Simpson, Zlotnick, Begin, Costello, & Pearlstein (1994)
Timed Self-Injurious Behavior Scale	Brasic et al. (1997)

Compiled from Juzwin (2004) and Sansone and Sansone (2004).

to sit and fill out a self-report inventory. If she is in pain or feels unattended to or rejected, being given a questionnaire about what she is feeling can only confirm her sense of invalidation: "My counselor doesn't even bother to talk with me but instead makes me fill out questionnaires that tell him how crazy I am." Juzwin (2004) speaks precisely to these dynamics when he explains:

> The use of a self-report instrument such as the SISRI always carries with it a number of limitations. Since it is a self-report measure, the patient's motivation, honesty, insight, current mental state, degree of openness, and ability to answer questions may limit the reliability of the information reported. Many of our patients have refused to fill out the inventory for various reasons, and consequently the assessment process was limited. Other patients found the amount of direct inquiry about so many SI behaviors to be somewhat provocative. That is, they reacted to being asked questions about their SI. (pp. 116–117)

Knowledge of the phenomenon of self-injury—understanding its etiology, course, associated features and risks and the variety of intervention strategies that are helpful—creates a solid foundation for the comprehensive assessment of adolescents who may self-injure. Paper-and-pencil assessment tools have some utility in helping to clarify diagnostic particulars or guide clinicians in their multidimensional assessment, but they ought to be used at the appropriate time, in the appropriate setting, with the appropriate individual. To simply hand someone a self-report inventory about self-injury early in the client-helper relationship misses the opportunity to engage the individual and to be attentive to the complex interpersonal dynamics characteristic of this population.

Making Referrals

The final step of the assessment process is to develop an initial plan of action to determine whether a direct referral of the self-injurer is warranted. For example, if the nature of the self-injury is clearly superficial (e.g., a light scratch on the arm made by a paper clip that did not break the skin), and the assessment determines that there is no sufficient cause to refer, the responder may engage in short-term counseling to address the concerns that brought the client to his attention. On the other hand, should an assessment identify the client as someone who is in significant distress, then a referral to a therapist for ongoing treatment is probably a reasonable course of action. While the following chapter delves explicitly into the nature and course of the long-term treatment process, at this point it is appropriate to impress upon the reader the importance of being attentive to the referral process itself. For example, ensuring that the clinician to whom the individual is being referred is knowledgeable about self-injury and that there is a goodness of fit between the clinician and client is crucial. The frontline responder is in the best position to direct the self-injurer's attention to possibilities beyond those she is currently aware of. To encourage engagement and follow-through on the part of the injurer requires both a skillfulness at building an alliance sufficient to create leverage with the individual and the persistence to remain engaged despite the client's resistance. There are some concrete steps, however, that a frontline responder can take that can facilitate the referral process.

First, the responder should have identified clinicians in the community who are especially knowledgeable about the treatment of self-injury and possess the skills to be successful. A self-injurer should not simply be referred to just any competent therapist, regardless of how skilled he or she may be generally. As emphasized throughout this book, this phenomenon is complex, and its treatment must necessarily address different, but often simultaneously occurring, dynamics. The clinician must understand that the work of treating self-injurers is not about simply stopping the behavior. Rather, the skilled clinician will understand that treatment involves the dynamics of unspoken (and perhaps unfelt) pain. It often includes the treatment of long-standing acute or complex relational trauma, as well as a host of comorbid conditions, such as eating disorders, depression, dissociative states, and features of a number of personality disorders. To send the client to someone who fails to understand the confluence of these interwoven factors and who is not competent to address this complexity sets the therapy (and the self-injurer) up for failure and reconfirms for the client that others do not (and cannot) understand her.

As essential as knowledge and skill level are, the personality and character of the clinician are as, if not more, important. By this I mean that, by taking on a self-injurer as a patient, the clinician understands the level of commitment that effective treatment demands. Self-injurers are difficult patients. Their past traumas bring to the therapy difficulty with trusting, connecting, and receiving help. These dynamics can precipitate the occasional roller-coaster ride in treatment, as can the client's conflict, fear of abandonment, and acting out against the self. For example, because therapy is an experience of intimacy and attachment in which one's dependency needs become easily activated, self-injurers, because of their self-other boundary difficulties and interpersonal turbulence, may actually engage in self-injurious behavior when the therapy is *working*. That is, the experience of closeness, nurturance, care, and hope derived from a strong connection with a therapist can trigger self-injurers' abandonment fears, to which they respond with destructive, self-sabotaging behaviors (Farber, 2000). The clinician who fails to understand this dynamic and is unable to maintain the treatment frame in spite of these occurrences runs the risk of blaming the patient, disengaging from the work, or personalizing the patient's response and acting out in turn.

Further, the clinician needs to understand that working with this population may also require greater flexibility and availability than are offered to other patients. Extra sessions or even phone consultations may be needed (Linehan, 1993a). For one who can make him- or herself available only for weekly sessions while expecting no surprises in the interim, the outcome may be less than satisfactory. In addition, the effective clinician is aware of the possibility of vicarious traumatization in working with this population (Connors, 2000) and therefore uses collegial supervision when needed and attends to his or her own self-care. The characteristics of the effective helper presented in Chapter 6 are essential for the clinician to engage in (and endure) the long-term work that is often necessary to help self-injurers.

Finally, the frontline responder must ensure that the client does not fall through the proverbial cracks, which can happen in many ways during the process of referring the individual outside one's organization or agency. Simply giving the client or her parents a therapist's name and number is not the optimal way to make effective referrals. Prior to giving out a therapist's name, the responder should consult with the therapist to see whether she has availability and whether or not she is willing to take this particular case at this time. To give an already hesitant individual, who may be wary of others being able to help, a referral to a therapist who is not available or who refuses to take on the case creates another hurdle to connecting the self-injurer to treatment. In sum, there is an art to making referrals. The frontline responder must be knowledgeable about and believe in the ability of the clinician to help the client and must be able to communicate this confidence to the self-injurer. The effective responder then follows up to ensure that the connection is made between client and clinician, and, if problems occur, doggedly perseveres in helping the client connect to someone else.

SUMMARY AND CONCLUSION

This chapter provided basic guiding principles for conducting a comprehensive assessment of self-injurers and their behavior. It identified the primary tasks of the overall process as including: *containment, engagement, assessment,* and *planning next steps* and offered practical examples of the kinds of questions that can be used to elicit the desired information. The chapter also discussed some of the characteristics that distinguish between acts that are bona fide failed suicide attempts and those that are purely self-injurious in nature. The chapter concluded with an examination of other risk factors that may elevate the level of lethality of self-injury, offered a listing of formal assessment instruments to assist in the evaluation of self-injurers, and commented on the vital role played by the frontline responder in the referral process.

Now that the assessment process has been explored, we turn in the next chapter to an overview and discussion of the myriad components of treating self-injurers, both in the short and the long-term. General treatment goals are discussed in the context of the various therapies and treatment modalities often used in the care of self-injurers, and issues related to hospitalization, the use of medication, and long-term follow-up care are also addressed.

CHAPTER 8

From Self-Injury to Health: An Overview of the Treatment Process

What one has to negotiate some sort of alliance with is the patient's practice of self-cure, which is rigidly established by the time he reaches us. To treat this practice of self-cure merely as a resistance is to fail to acknowledge its true value for the person of the patient. . . . What, however, is most difficult to resolve and cure is the patient's practice of self-cure. To cure a cure is the paradox that faces us in these patients.

Masud Khan (in Yates, 2004, p. 63)

One of the frequent obstacles to therapy is that the patient conceives of the process of getting well as getting rid of something within himself.

Andras Angyal (1965, p. 104)

Throughout this book, I have suggested that self-injury is a complex and multidetermined phenomenon and that treating individuals who engage in these behaviors is extraordinarily complicated and challenging. Understanding the meaning of one's self-destructive acts and making contact with the person behind the behavior serves as the starting point for engaging these individuals in the multilayered, intricate, and often taxing therapeutic work that leads to recovery. The long-term effort is not simply about ending the self-injurious behavior—a primary goal, of course. It is also about addressing the secondary layer of treatment that deals with the forces that continue to fuel and sustain the behavior. A comprehensive approach to treatment entails developing a two-pronged approach that, on one hand, focuses on symptom reduction and eventual elimination (i.e., the self-injury), and on the other

sses the underlying suffering from which the self-injury emanates. We
that the behavior does not occur in a vacuum but emerges out of a complex developmental history that may have been laced with early attachment
difficulties, relational trauma, and neglectful or invalidating environments, all
of which synergistically resulted in impairments across primary domains of
development. As illustrated in Chapter 5, because of their exposure to complex trauma, many self-injurers suffer developmental impairments in the areas
of attachment, biology, affect regulation, ability to maintain consistent states
of consciousness (i.e., they tend to dissociate), behavioral control, cognition,
and self-concept. For treatment to focus only on the behavior of self-injury
misses the complexity of the phenomenon and ultimately fails to address the
core issues that fuel the acts. Effective treatment of self-injury is, therefore,
always a bi-level endeavor: the first level, the more obvious target of intervention, is to help the self-injurer reduce her overt destruction of the body
through her injurious acts; the second is to help the individual transform
the pain that she knows at the visceral, bodily level into thoughts and feelings that she can articulate through words. The clinical work is about helping
self-injurers become reflective about their internal experience—to begin to
identify and put the inchoate inner turmoil they feel into thoughts—and then
begin to find words so that their voice can speak out loud what heretofore
they have only acted out upon their bodies.

Conterio and Lader (1998) state the primary goal of treatment simply: to help
self-injurers think and behave in developmentally age-appropriate ways. The approach of their treatment program, *S.A.F.E. Alternatives*, the first short-term program devoted exclusively to the treatment of self-injury (www.selfinjury.com),
is to "serve as a crash course in realism, a rare exposure to a life in which people
are not constantly subjected to abuse and denigration, and where their thoughts
and opinions matter" (pp. 224–225). They see the goal of treatment as helping
clients to move away from a victim stance and to come to understand that they
can have real power and control in their lives, in that they can actually *choose*
healthier alternatives to self-injury. The healing process for these clients involves
learning how to not reactively turn to self-injury as a means to cope with, communicate about, or regain control over distressing events in their lives. Healing
is about learning how to take responsibility for their behavior and to cultivate
new ways to ease their pain and suffering. The work is about learning to move
away from the "quick fix" and toward tolerating other ways of self-soothing. It is
about learning how to slow down, how to be present to oneself, how to resist the
urge to act upon the body, how to learn to *think* and *reflect* about their internal
experience, and how to problem-solve in a nondestructive fashion. The challenge is not about getting rid of what one feels; rather, it is about learning how

to embrace it, tolerate it, and integrate it. It is about transforming feelings into words, thereby diffusing their intensity and power.

The bi-level treatment goals of reducing self-injury and addressing the more deeply ingrained psychological pain that fuels the behavior typically occur simultaneously and are often synergistically bound as the treatment progresses. That is, as the self-injurious behavior is reduced, the client is forced to turn inward and deal with her history and suffering in a new way. As the underlying trauma is understood, reframed, and integrated, it comes to be expressed more through words than through action, and the client can therefore more squarely face her internal life. The goals are achieved through treatment that is structured, yet flexible. It must be supportive, yet have clear limits and boundaries; it must help clients become reflective about their feelings and relationships while helping them learn new, concrete skills in living (Conterio & Lader, 1998; Linehan, 1993a); it must accept them as they are, yet challenge them to their better selves. Although clinicians may use different language to describe the treatment objectives for self-injurers (usually as a function of their respective theoretical orientation), the list that follows provides a generic summary of the core treatment goals to be considered in the care of self-injurers, which has been culled from the literature (e.g., Bateman & Fonagy, 2004; Conterio & Lader, 1998; Connors, 2000; Farber, 2000; Favazza, 1996; Guralnik & Simeon, 2001; Ivanoff et al., 2001; Levitt, 2004; Linehan, 1993a; McCabe & Marcus, 2004; Sansone, Levitt, & Sansone, 2004a; Walsh, 2006). The goals toward which treatment should be directed include helping the client to:

- track and recognize the patterns of her self-injury (e.g., antecedent events, feelings, thoughts)
- develop alternative soothing behaviors
- identify and understand her underlying psychological dynamics of the behavior
- enhance her interpersonal, emotion regulation, and distress tolerance skills
- observe, be attentive to, and reflect upon her internal states and develop a language to articulate that experience

These goals are usually achieved through multiple means that include individual psychotherapy, group therapy, family therapy, skills training groups or activities, journaling exercises, and possibly other forms of artistic expression. The ultimate aim of these activities is to resuscitate those developmentally impaired parts of the self and to create the conditions that will realign those parts with normative developmental patterns.

While the scope of this book does not allow for an in-depth exploration of the efficacy of various treatment modalities, it is nonetheless helpful for frontline responders to have some sense of the long-term treatment arc so that they can be better informed as they assist their clients in the recovery process. To this end, this chapter outlines the key clinical domains that ought to be considered throughout treatment and examines ancillary issues such as hospitalization, the efficacy of medication, and family treatment. The presentation that follows is intended to be atheoretical in nature, as effective treatment is less about theoretical orientation and more about the understanding of the person and the characteristics of the pathology. It is about being aware of the specific target goals to be pursued, as well as having a clear sense of the appropriate demeanor and therapeutic attitude—one that communicates support and presence while setting and maintaining the structure necessary for treatment (Conterio & Lader, 1998). With this said, the theoretical model that most explicitly addresses the issues inherent in the treatment of self-injury as part of its general theoretical position is Dialectical Behavior Therapy (Linehan, 1993a, 1993b). Further, adherence to its manualized approach has been demonstrated to be effective in the treatment of self-injurious behavior (see Ivanoff et al., 2001; Linehan, 1993a, 1993b; McCabe & Marcus, 2004). While including elements from different treatment modalities, the overview that follows is organized not by what a particular theory may propose but around the practical goal of redressing the various developmental impairments suffered by clients as a result of their relational histories and exposure to environments that may have been invalidating and traumatic. Ultimately, effective treatment of self-injury is that which assists clients to develop healthier attachments to others and enhances their interpersonal skills. It also helps them to better understand and regulate their affect, to acquire replacement coping behaviors that will substitute for self-injury, to restructure their distorted thinking about their identity and body image, and to develop a more coherent, bounded sense of self. It is to the specific processes by which these changes occur that we now turn our attention.

DEVELOPMENTALLY RESPONSIVE TREATMENT

We know what we are, but know not what we may be.

William Shakespeare, *Hamlet, IV, v.*

Why does anyone go into treatment? The conscious wish is to be rid of suffering ... and the unconscious wish is to be known and remembered by another.

Sharon Farber (2000, p. 363)

In Part I of this book, I outlined a number of the developmental antecedents that may create the psychological conditions for individuals to develop a propensity to engage in self-injury. In Chapter 3, for example, I suggested that the exposure to trauma in both its acute, shocking form and its more complexly chronic and perhaps more subtly invalidating manifestation serves as a foundation for derailing normative development in children across a host of critical domains of functioning. This was followed in Chapter 4 by a detailed discussion of the specific developmental effects that can result in the loss of core capacities for self-regulation and interpersonal relatedness. The cumulative impairment resulting from the exposure to trauma was proposed to be wide-ranging and included disruptions in areas such as affect regulation, attachment patterns, information processing, self-soothing, feelings of competence, body image, and self-esteem, to list a few. The experience of early trauma can lead to adaptational problems that disrupt the ability to manage interpersonal relationships and create stability in one's life, both as an adolescent and as an adult (Cook et al., 2005; Ford, 2005; Saxe, Ellis, Folger, Hansen, & Sorkin, 2005; Spinazzola et al., 2005; van der Kolk, 2005).

The primary focus of the long-term care of self-injurers, therefore, is the treatment of the effects of the relational trauma to which these individuals have been exposed earlier in their lives (Connors, 2000; Conterio & Lader, 1998; Farber, 2000; Walsh, 2006). Their experience of being invalidated and disconfirmed, of having key psychological and emotional needs neglected, has created a developmental chasm in their ability to tolerate the inner groundlessness they feel, contain their angst, and bind their suffering in nondestructive ways. It is this trauma that must be remembered and worked through (Bateman & Fonagy, 2004; Farber, 2000; Walsh, 2006). Van der Kolk's (2005) proposal for the treatment of complexly traumatized children can serve as a paradigm for conceptualizing trauma work with self-injurers. He asserts that treatment should "focus on three primary areas: establishing safety and competence, dealing with traumatic re-enactments, and integration and mastery of the body and mind" (p. 407). The starting point for treatment is creating a sense of safety in which the self-injurer can learn to divert her energy from being interpersonally reactive (i.e., from having to be constantly aroused in the fight/flight/freeze response) toward making real interpersonal contact. Also, when feeling safe, the client can direct her focus inward. Without safety, the individual cannot focus on the self in a playful, imaginative, and, ultimately, nondefensive way that allows her reflective function to develop. Through the experience of safety, one can let down one's psychological guard and make room for the emergence of an observing ego—that is, a state of the self that can dispassionately observe oneself in one's own skin and give attention to one's inner world of feelings. With a greater capacity for thought and reflection related to one's history and inner experience, one can then begin to be more self-contained and better tolerate being separate from others. It is the development of this ability that, in the end, allows self-injurers to more effectively curtail the reenactment of their past pain (Bateman & Fonagy, 2004; Fonagy et al., 2002).

Because the experience of chronic trauma becomes imprinted on the core of one's psychological makeup, treatment must actively help the individual to understand the cycle of trauma and its subsequent repetition upon the self. The work here is about remembering and reconstructing the trauma of one's life. Specifically, this means helping clients understand that their cycle of trauma reenactment evolved out of the need to survive—to protect oneself from further harm, to defend oneself against pain, to preserve one's relationships and self-esteem, and to maintain some semblance of hope and control in their lives (Bateman & Fonagy, 2004). This work proceeds by helping clients bring to consciousness the pain which they know only at the level and "language" of the body, but not through thoughts and words. An informed psychotherapy helps to process and metabolize the anger that is misdirected at the self and allows the client to "grieve what he never had in his life, what he once had but lost, what might have been but was not and was never to be, and what happened to him that should not have happened" (Farber, 2000, p. 463). Through the awareness of old patterns and attention to their playing out in the present (particularly as enacted with the therapist), through grieving the wounds and deprivations of childhood, and through the experience of the therapist's affirmation and presence, the self-injurer can slowly begin to relinquish those old, destructive patterns and to replace them with healthier, more mature ways of relating (Farber, 2000).

Finally, work with complexly traumatized individuals involves helping them to integrate the parts of themselves that have been split apart because of the terror experienced in the trauma and the hypervigilance required to survive. As children, these individuals "shut down" as a means of self-protection and avoided engagement and exploration of themselves and their surroundings; their energy was directed at fortifying themselves against harm and not at carefree play and imaginative exploration. Treatment involves reawakening these individuals' curiosity and hope in the possibility of developing multiple competencies and mastery over the seemingly disconnected parts of their lives. It involves helping them to make new connections among their experiences, emotions, and physical reactions and to step back and "look at" their trauma without repeating it and re-experiencing it in full (van der Kolk, 2005). Cook and colleagues (2005) extend this treatment overview by providing a further elaboration of the core intervention targets associated with the treatment of complex trauma. Their summary is provided in Table 8.1.

TABLE 8.1 Six Core Components of Complex Trauma Intervention

1. **Safety:**
   The installation and enhancement of internal and environmental safety.

2. **Self-regulation:**
   Enhancement of the capacity to modulate arousal and restore equilibrium following dysregulation across domains of affect, behavior, physiology, cognition (including redirection of dissociative states of consciousness), interpersonal relatedness and self-attribution.

3. **Self-reflective information processing:**
   Development of the ability to effectively engage attentional processes and executive functioning in the service of construction of self-narratives, reflection on past and present experience, anticipation and planning, and decision making.

4. **Traumatic experiences integration:**
   The transformation, incorporation, or resolution of traumatic memories, reminders and associated psychiatric sequelae into nondebilitating, productive, and fulfilling existence through such therapeutic strategies as meaning-making, traumatic memory containment or processing, remembrance and mourning of the traumatic loss, symptom management and development of coping skills, and cultivation of present-oriented thinking and behavior.

5. **Relational engagement:**
   The repair, restoration or creation of effective working models of attachment, and the application of these models to current interpersonal relationships, including the therapeutic alliance, with emphasis on development of such critical interpersonal skills as assertiveness, cooperation, perspective-taking, boundaries and limit-setting, reciprocity, social empathy, and the capacity for physical and emotional intimacy.

6. **Positive affect enhancement:**
   The enhancement of self-worth, esteem and positive self-appraisal through the cultivation of personal creativity, imagination, future orientation, achievement, competence, mastery-seeking, community-building and the capacity to experience pleasure.

Cook et al. (2005). Complex trauma in children and adolescents. *Psychiatric Annals, 35,* 390–398. © SLACK Incorporated. Reprinted with permission.

Keeping these broader treatment goals in mind, we now turn to examining how these goals are specifically operationalized vis-à-vis the domains of functional impairment created by the exposure to the trauma. The following discussion addresses the repair of deficiencies in the areas of attachment and interpersonal relationships, affect tolerance and regulation, behavioral dyscontrol, distorted cognitions, and biological disequilibrium.

Therapeutic Attachment, Affect Regulation, and the Development of a Reflective Self

To be is to mean something to someone else.

Andras Angyal (1965, p. 18)

Psychotherapy must remain an obstinate attempt of two people to recover the wholeness of being human through the relationship between them.

R. D. Laing (1967, p. 32)

The core of our work is just this: cultivating a loving, valuing attitude that supports the client's own healing process. And this is not insubstantial.... When we join with a client, allowing ourselves to be moved by and to bring compassionate witness to another person's pain, something real happens. Clients may or may not comment, or even focus, on what is happening between us. The relationship may simply be a steady part of the background, creating enough safety and substance to contain the work.

Robin Connors (2000, p. 141)

We again return to the theme of the centrality of relationship in the healing process for self-injurers. As intimated throughout this book, the nature, shape, and structure of the therapeutic relationship constitute the critical elements in the treatment of self-injurers (Bateman & Fonagy, 2004; Connors, 2000; Farber, 2000; Fonagy et al., 2002; Guralnik & Simeon, 2001; Levitt, 2004; Linehan, 1993a; McCabe & Marcus, 2004). How one relates to the client and the quality of the alliance established is as important as what is actually said or done in therapy, if not more so. Without the context of safety, trust, respect, and connection, little enduring work can take place. Because the core issues of these individuals are grounded in problems of attachment and relating, effective treatment for self-injurers begins with the therapeutic alliance. As discussed in Chapter 3, the exposure to early trauma significantly impacts one's ability to attach in healthy ways to others. When one's relationship with a caregiver is the very source of the trauma, one's ability to attach well is severely compromised. The insecure and disorganized attachment patterns that develop in these individuals take erratic, unstable, and volatile forms in later relationships (Cook et al., 2005). As a result, self-injurers who are victims of trauma start out at a considerable disadvantage. They lack the ability to engage and attach to others in healthy ways, and it is this primary attribute that colors their presentation within the therapeutic encounter. Farber (2000) comments precisely on this dynamic when she notes:

> Before the patient can come to care for himself and develop a reflective mind, he must feel cared for and protected and know that his well-being is foremost in the therapist's mind. To create the capacity for reflective thought, a working relationship must be established in which the patient feels a sense of security and safety that over time can come to change the encoded attachments in the brain. Because expression of emotions is so concrete, impulsive, body focused, and destructive, treatment should aim at helping these patients develop a capacity for taming their aggression and impulsiveness, altering a negative body image, and developing a greater capacity for self-care, affect tolerance, and containment, and a greater ability to use words symbolically. (p. 361)

Effective treatment of self-injurers, therefore, begins with the therapist's acute awareness of this dynamic and with a consciously focused attentiveness to the nature and structure of the therapeutic alliance. Farber (2000) notes further that "The therapeutic relationship should be a safe haven. The therapist holds and contains the patient, like a 'second skin,' until the patient's experience of herself is sufficiently intact and cohesive so that she can live within her own skin" (p. 367). The therapist is reliable, dependable, and ready to listen to the patient's story and personal perspective and to respond in a caring, nonshaming, and compassionate way. It is the experience of being understood by the therapist that generates a feeling of safety and security in the client, which, in turn, facilitates psychological exploration at greater depths. Bateman and Fonagy (2004) add, "Only when a patient feels sure that a therapist can listen from his point of view is it possible for the patient to be 'ready to listen' to the therapist's standpoint" (p. 169). The therapeutic relationship becomes the corrective emotional experience that can grow to be the new paradigm for other ways of being in relationship with others.

How, then, does a therapist forge a therapeutic alliance—a bond of emotional communication and a system of affect regulation—with individuals who have defective attachment patterns and who lack a well-developed reflective capacity? First, therapists need to focus on issues of demeanor and engagement, the characteristics of which have been described at length in Chapter 6. Briefly, therapists must possess sufficient stability of self and interpersonal strength to tolerate the instability and affective volatility of self-injuring individuals. They must be sufficiently proficient at balancing the polar tensions of support and compassion with singularity of purpose and firmness. They must be willing to listen to and be receptive to the client as he or she is, to honor the meaning of the self-injurious behavior, and to communicate that understanding to the client. At the same time, they must set limits and boundaries that foster an atmosphere of self-care. Therapists working with this population should be aware of the powerful countertransferential reactions that may be evoked by these clients, and they should have in place their own supervision and supports to help them manage their reactions rather than enact them with their clients. The process of engaging self-injurers is very complex and demanding, and the reader is referred back to Chapter 6 for a discussion of the multifaceted dynamics involved.

Above and beyond the initial steps of engagement, however, lie the complexities of developing a relationship with individuals who have difficulty with precisely that task. Bateman and Fonagy (2004) describe this process of relationship building as occurring in the following way:

> The relational alliance is built up gradually through empathy and validation, reliability, and readiness to listen. Hope in hostility, assurance in affect storms, and the very basic quality of being human are also necessary if a relational alliance is to survive the vicissitudes of treatment. The therapist needs continually to remain calm and to maintain hope especially when being relentlessly criticized or denigrated by the patient. Affect storms can rapidly undermine a working alliance and leave a therapist feeling unappreciated, misunderstood, and hurt. (p. 167)

This therapeutic constancy that allows the alliance to develop does not only occur through overt, direct verbal communication on the therapist's part but is also engendered through more subtle unconscious contact. The therapist must communicate to the client that she and the client are "in this" together, that she is committed to staying engaged in the work and will be there to help the client "fight the good fight" against her struggles. This being *for* the client is ultimately communicated not through words but through the clinician's therapeutic posture and personal way of being. That is, as Schore (2003b) notes, the therapeutic attachment with the client is fostered not only by the words the therapist speaks but also by the subtle communication achieved through tone of voice, facial expressions, physical gestures, tempo in movement, and other nonverbal means. The goal is to communicate attunement in diverse yet natural human ways and on multiple levels. In a sense, the attachment that occurs in therapy is facilitated in a way similar to that used by the attuned caregiver to create and communicate to the infant safety, nurturance, and care—all transmitted to the infant without the use of words, as infants do not yet understand the meaning of words. What they do understand (or rather experience), however, is the caregiver's mood, warmth, engagement, and responsiveness—all of which communicate volumes to the infant about connection and care. When infants experience the sort of nonverbal communication from their caregiver that conveys safety and care, the foundation is set for them to develop secure attachment patterns.

Therapeutic attachment, Schore contends, develops from a similar dynamic between therapist and client—the care is communicated at a deep, primal level and functions as the source for secure attachment in the therapy. Ultimately, it is *this* therapeutic attachment that is responsible for regulating the client's neurophysiology, which, in turn, allows her to access and to modulate her stress regulatory systems and develop her reflective function. In short, it is the therapist's capacity for empathy that promotes attachment and creates the conditions for a strong working alliance. Schore (2003b) suggests that the question is not *what to say* to the client or *what to do* for the client, but rather *how to be with* the client. Effective therapy works not because it is the "talking cure" but because it is a "communicating cure"—communication that is multilayered and that "holds" and "contains" the client in such a way that she can begin to develop her own abilities to regulate her internal world (Fonagy et al., 2002). For self-injurers who may have never had the experience of being understood, "help" that is communicated at this level, while terrifying because of its unfamiliar feel, can also offer hope for real connection and healing.

The therapist who works with self-injurers must be able to tolerate primitive modes of relating and be willing to make his or her psychological self available for the client's use as she experiments with new ways of relating (Bateman & Fonagy, 2004; Connors, 2000; Farber, 2000; Fonagy et al., 2002). Fonagy and colleagues (2002) explain that the negotiation of the client's therapeutic attachment serves as the interpersonal context in which understanding of internal states can become the focus. It is within this interpersonal milieu that the client's inner life can be recognized as intentional and real by the therapist—an experience that the client has historically been deprived of. Through the therapist's acknowledgment, experience, containment, and communication of the client's inner life, the client comes to recognize the reality of her own intentional, real, and valued sense of self through the mirroring of the other—the therapist. This experience can then lead the client to develop the capacity to generate multiple perspectives in interpreting her interpersonal history and to the experience of herself as connected to others, yet separate and real in her own right. In short, what is communicated in this process is the "experience of other human minds having the patient's mind in mind" (Bateman & Fonagy, 2004, p. 141).

In other words, the goal of therapy is to help clients "mentalize affectivity," that is, transform inchoate affective experience into thoughts and words. In being able to identify multiple perspectives to one's internal experience and therefore learn to distinguish between one's affective states and reality, the client no longer is compelled to act as if her feelings are an accurate representation of reality. For example, a client may interpret a certain behavior within a significant relationship as a sign that the relationship has been ruptured. However, with a better-developed ability to generate multiple hypotheses about the nature and meaningfulness of that behavior (e.g., a person may not have been attentive to the client not because he was angry with the client but perhaps because he was tired or preoccupied with his own affairs), the client does not have to respond from a catastrophic reactive position. Through interpersonal feedback, particularly about the client's internal affective states and how they manifest themselves in the therapeutic relationship, the client can come to develop a greater introspective capacity that will lead to regulating those heretofore unruly affects. In this way, the client gradually develops new skills in self-regulation by learning how to express, apprehend, and modify her emotional impulses by "mirroring" herself (Fonagy et al., 2002). The therapist's primary task, then, is to

> remain in touch with the patient's mental state, despite the patient's dramatic enactments, to address and challenge the patient's mental capacities by verbalizing internal states, differentiating feelings, breaking down unmanageable anxiety-provoking experiences into simpler, more manageable entities, helping the development of an "as-if" attitude where ideas can begin to be thought about as ideas rather than as reality, yet retaining their links to the internal world. (Fonagy et al., 2002, p. 478)

This work is accomplished in therapy first by focusing the client's attention to her own affective states and, second, by helping her begin to take an "as if" perspective of the therapist's own experience in relation to her. This is specifically achieved, for example, by engaging in such therapeutic activities as:

- continually naming and clarifying feelings (e.g., toward whom are they directed?)
- understanding the immediate precipitant of emotional states within present circumstances
- understanding feelings in the context of previous and present relationships
- expressing feelings appropriately, adequately, and constructively within the context of the relationship
- understanding the likely response of the therapist (or others) to the interactions in question, thus generating multiple perspectives on the internal states of others
- reviewing consequences for both self and others

- generating alternative hypotheses or explanations for interpretations of interpersonal behavior. (Adapted and modified from Bateman & Fonagy, 2004, pp. 222–223)

These tasks are facilitated by the therapist's ability to reflect the client's affective expression in modified form. Specifically, this is done through the therapist's ability to:

- empathize with the client's internal state
- accept what is real for the client
- break down the client's experience into small components, keeping to the interpersonal focus
- explore alternative understanding of the verbalized events and internal experience
- validate the client's accurate perception of experiences while challenging possible distortions or overreactions to those experiences
- focus on translation of behavior into verbal expression as opposed to acting it out. (Adapted and modified from Bateman & Fonagy, 2004, p. 305)

The intensity and intimacy created by this work can be terrifying for self-injurers. Although they long for connection with others and to be in a relationship, they lack both the experience of being in healthy relationships and the belief that they can be safe in relationships and actually have their needs met. Self-injurers experience relationships as highly dangerous—a danger that must be hypervigilantly guarded against (Guralnik & Simeon, 2001). As a result, rather than making the client feel safe, the intimacy that develops in the therapeutic relationship may actually activate the client's fears of abandonment and result in acting out of that fear through self-injury (Bateman & Fonagy, 2004; Farber, 2000). The acting out is a consequence of the powerful attachment the client begins to feel and is a reaction to intolerable closeness. The therapist should remain calm during these "affective storms," help the client identify precursors to the storms, label and clarify feelings, examine consequences, and, above all else, maintain the therapeutic frame (Bateman & Fonagy, 2004). The paradox is that it is precisely the working through and being able to tolerate therapeutic intimacy that allows the client to function more autonomously and to develop more stable interpersonal relationships. The use of the relationship as the primary "intervention" with self-injurers is designed to restructure the meaning and function of the client's self-injurious behavior within the context of "relationship." It is hypothesized that this reorganized interpersonal functioning with the therapist will generalize to other relationships in the self-injurer's life (Guralnik & Simeon, 2001).

Redressing Cognitive Distortions

Nothing is, but believing makes it so.

Catherine Landis (2004, p. 127)

The second area of focus in the treatment of self-injurers is the identification and restructuring of the core beliefs that create the conditions for self-injurious behaviors. Distorted core beliefs function as the cornerstone for the cognitive schemas that are self-reinforcing and that maintain self-injury (Rayner et al., 2005; Walsh, 2006). The cycle of self-injury begins with one's core beliefs about the self (e.g., "I am unlovable," "I deserve punishment," or "No one really cares about me"). These beliefs then produce attitudes and assumptions about who one is and how one should be in relationships with others. Unfortunately, the resulting attitudes and assumptions are also distorted and therefore inevitably create instability and turbulence in the individual's relationships, which eventually serve as a trigger for self-injury. The acting-out behavior then fortifies one's core beliefs (that one is unlovable or deserves punishment), and the cycle is perpetuated. The task in therapy, then, is to collaboratively identify and evaluate these cognitive schemas, to uncover evidence for their veracity or falsehood and, in that process, to modify the thinking patterns that lead to and sustain self-injury (Walsh, 2006). The identification of the *core* schemas that underlie the distorted intermediate thinking patterns leading to dysfunctional behavior often takes place well into the therapeutic process (Beck & Freeman, 1990). That is, the therapist uses data from the client's life—expressed attitudes, rules she uses to live by, as well as her actual behavior—to accumulate evidence for the schemas that support the client's self-concept and resulting presentation. As the distorted beliefs are challenged and refuted, the larger underlying schemas are simultaneously being restructured.

For instance, common faulty cognitions such as "Self-injury is an acceptable way to cope" and "I deserve to be punished" point to particular beliefs that may have arisen out of the individual's dysfunctional family background. The schemas and attitudes that underlie these beliefs are far from the individual's awareness, but they operate as the fertile backdrop for the maintenance of self-injury (Sansone et al., 2004a). The client may say, "There's nothing wrong with cutting. It's just another way to deal with life. After all, my mother takes prescription drugs, my father is an alcoholic, and everyone at school does it." These more accessible attitudes held by the client serve as the starting point for discussion and exploration in therapy. As the client engages in this process, the more pervasive and entrenched core schemas that produce her distorted thinking begin to crystallize and become more clearly identifiable (Sansone et al., 2004a). Young (1999) has described a number of core maladaptive schemas that are often characteristic of individuals who exhibit poor interpersonal functioning. Several of these schemas are particularly common to self-injurers and often emerge in the course of treatment. These schemas are the source for many of the distorted beliefs self-injurers express and function as the glue that holds those beliefs so firmly in place. The core maladaptive schemas that are most often present in self-injurers tend to be schemas of *abandonment/instability* ("I'll always be alone and have to fend for myself"), *defectiveness/shame* ("I am unlovable. No one will ever love me"), *mistrust/abuse* ("People will hurt me and take advantage of me. I can't let them get too close"), *dependence/incompetence* ("I'm incompetent. I need others to take care of me"), *subjugation* ("If I don't do what others want, they'll be angry at me and leave me"), *insufficient self-control/self-discipline* ("I have no self-control. I'm helpless to change"), and *punitiveness* ("I'm a bad person. I deserve to be punished").

The maladaptive cognitive schemas that drive the underlying self-injury are deeply rooted and have become a defining aspect of the self-injurer's personality. Challenging and actually modifying these core beliefs is an arduous undertaking and must be done sensitively and in the context of the therapeutic relationship as discussed earlier (Walsh, 2006). The eventual goals in reworking core beliefs are to decrease dichotomous thinking ("Self-injury is the only option I have"), increase the client's control over her emotions by reframing the antecedent thoughts that lead to those emotions, and, consequently, improve impulse control.

Body Image Work

Alienation from the body, in its many forms, is a common characteristic of self-injurers and a powerful prognostic indicator (Farber, 2000; Walsh, 2006; Walsh and Rosen, 1988). Walsh (2006) points out that core beliefs about one's attractiveness, sexual characteristics, and body integrity (feeling disconnected from or not in control of one's body) are dominant concerns for many self-injurers. Clients may see themselves as ugly and unattractive or react to their emerging physical and sexual development with revulsion. Also, due to surgery or illness or to the trauma of physical or sexual abuse, they have come to think of the body as the repository of pain. This alienated relationship that identifies the body as separate from the self and, in a sense, other and foreign from who one is sets the stage for the body to be seen as the enemy and therefore as open to attack. Walsh (2006) maintains that providing body image work—examining and restructuring beliefs about the body—is central to the treatment of self-injury. Helping the client identify and engage in activities that enhance beliefs and attitudes about body image is paramount in the recovery process.

Behavioral Interventions

The therapist creates a context of validating rather than blaming the patient, and within that context the therapist blocks or extinguishes bad behaviors, drags good behaviors out of the patient, and figures out a way to make the good behaviors so reinforcing that the patient continues the good ones and stops the bad ones.

Marsha Linehan (1993a, p. 97)

Self-injury can be seen as a problem-solving strategy that may offer tempo-rary emotional relief for the client but is essentially ineffective at providing a long-term solution. The problem is that, because of the client's developmental history, effective coping, affect-regulating, and self-soothing strategies have not been adequately learned. Therefore, to ask a self-injurer to discontinue a behavior (as destructive as it may be) without helping her develop other ways of regulating herself is likely to be unproductive and an impediment to the treatment. At the same time, self-injury is a self-destructive act and cannot be ignored. Linehan (1993a) asserts that targeting the behavior itself must remain a high priority in the treatment. She supports her position by noting that (1) self-injurious behavior is the best predictor of subsequent suicide; (2) self-injury is clearly self-destructive; it cannot be undone—it leaves scars and damages the body—and can lead to accidental death; (3) self-injury is incompatible with the overarching goals of therapy, which is to engage in better self-care as opposed to self-harm; and (4) "it is quite difficult for the therapist to communicate caring for a patient if the therapist does not react to the patient's harming herself" (p. 127). Communicating that self-injury is not an acceptable behavior is, according to Linehan, the "quintessential com-munication of compassion and caring." The behavior itself must be addressed and kept in the foreground of the treatment.

To this end, some clinicians insist on having the client sign no-harm con-tracts, because ultimately they see self-injury as a choice over which the indi-vidual has ultimate control (Conterio & Lader, 1998; Sansone et al., 2004a). In these cases, continuing treatment is contingent on the individual's stopping the behavior. Others contend that, for chronic self-injurers, contracting is *unlikely* to be helpful and that cognitive restructuring and replacement skills training are required for the behavior to desist (Walsh, 2006). Both positions, howev-er, maintain that the core of the problem lies in the individual's not knowing other ways to self-soothe and to regulate her affect. Therefore, an important part of the treatment is to assist self-injurers in learning other behaviors that can help them cope and self-soothe. New behaviors, of course, cannot be self-destructive and should help individuals begin to divorce themselves from self-injury-related affect (Conterio & Lader, 1998; Linehan, 1993a). For example, negative replacement behaviors (e.g., marking one's body with a red marker to represent the wound, snapping a rubber band on the part of the body where one would normally cut) are sometimes suggested to clients as a means of symbolically representing the act of the self-injury without actually causing harm. The objection to these kinds of replacement behaviors is that they maintain the individual's focus on self-injury (and its associated affects) as *the* way to ultimately cope with stress, upset, or emotional turmoil. These replacement behaviors, in a sense, keep the individual entrenched in the "culture" of self-injury and hamper their search for relief and comfort that can be found through other means (Conterio & Lader, 1998).

Less controversial replacement skills include a host of different soothing behaviors that can be generated by the client herself with the assistance of the therapist. Some of these behaviors include mindful breathing and visualization activities (see Walsh, 2006, for a detailed description), writing in a journal, talking to a trusted person, listening to music, performing physical exercise, filling out an impulse control log (see Conterio & Lader, 1998), playing a musical instrument, spending time with one's pet, and reading. Engaging in artistic expression or writing has the added dimension of helping individuals translate their somatic urges and affects into images and words that can begin to articulate and ventilate the internal pain they experience in nondestructive ways. The added benefit of these alternate forms of self-expression is that they can be brought into the therapy session and used as a springboard for deeper exploration.

The other principal behavioral intervention that is helpful in the treatment of self-injury is having the client track and analyze her impulse to self-injure (even if the impulse is not acted upon) or to track the act itself, as well as the environmental, affective, and cognitive conditions surrounding it. This activity can be conducted in various ways; the client can do it alone by completing a Brief Self-Injury Log (see Walsh, 2006) or Impulse Control Log (see Conterio & Lader, 1998), or the helper can conduct a Chain Analysis of the behavior while in session (Linehan, 1993a). These activities help the client identify the antecedent events and the resulting cognitions and affects that led to the impulse to self-injure and also to recognize the negative consequences in the aftermath of the impulse or behavior. Through these concrete activities, the client can better identify the important variables that may trigger and maintain the self-injury, and thus learn to directly target these variables in treatment (Walsh, 2006).

Psychopharmacological Treatment

To date, no medication has been approved for the treatment of self-injury by the U.S. Food and Drug Administration, and research on the efficacy of medication on curtailing or eliminating self-injurious behavior has been scant (Favazza, 1996, 1998; Grossman & Siever, 2001; Sansone et al., 2004b). The challenge in conducting clinical trials on the psychopharmacological treatment of self-injury involves a number of factors, including the heterogeneity of diagnostic and phenomenological issues associated with self-injury and the preponderance of comorbid conditions. Most self-injurers also suffer from a number of other neuropsychological disorders ranging from depression and anxiety to eating disorders and dissociative and personality disorders. Isolating the neurobiological foundations of self-injury is a complicated task and one that has received little direct attention to date. There are a few studies, however, that highlight the benefits of the various classes of medication in addressing some of the prominent symptoms of self-injury (e.g., impulsivity, aggression, dissociation), but experts note that the use of medication should be considered carefully and primarily as an adjunct to psychotherapeutic interventions (Favazza, 1996; Grossman & Siever, 2001; Sansone et al., 2004b). Medication alone cannot adequately remediate the multiple developmental deficiencies (i.e., attachment difficulties, affect dysregulation, self-soothing skill deficits) that have resulted from the exposure to trauma that is characteristic of the experience of many self-injurers. What appropriate medication can do, however, is lessen the intensity and power of certain symptoms so that more favorable conditions for psychotherapy can be created and the stage can be set for longer-term characterological and behavioral changes (Grossman & Siever, 2001).

Because no single medication or class of medications has been consistently and powerfully shown to be effective in the management of self-injury, prescribing clinicians must carefully consider the unique situation of the individual under his or her care (Sansone et al., 2004b). Medication should target those symptoms that interfere with general functioning and those that activate or maintain the self-destructive behavior. For example, the newer class of antidepressant medication, *Selective Serotonin Reuptake Inhibitors (SSRIs)*—(i.e., fluoxetine [Prozac], sertraline [Zoloft], citalopram [Celexa], escitalopram [Lexapro], paroxetine [Paxil], and fluvoxamine [Luvox]) has been typically recommended as the first line of biological treatment as it targets many of the focal symptoms of self-injury, such as impulsivity, depression, worry, anxiety, irritability, and aggression. This class of medication is relatively safe, generally has few side effects, and therefore can serve as an initial pharmacological intervention for self-injurers (Sansone et al., 2004b).

The effects of *SSRIs,* however, may be short lived in some cases, and therefore other medication may need to be considered (Favazza, 1998; Grossman & Siever, 2001). Mood stabilizers and anticonvulsants (e.g., valproate [Depakote] and carbamazepine [Tegretol]), usually prescribed for the treatment of bipolar disorder, have been shown to decrease behavioral dyscontrol and aggression and improve impulse control (Sansone et al., 2004b). Lithium, also a mood stabilizer, has a calming effect on patients, reduces both manic and depressive symptoms, and has also been shown to reduce aggression and impulsivity. Unfortunately, it has many side effects, requires intense monitoring of blood levels, and can be lethal (Grossman & Siever, 2001; Sansone et al., 2004b).

Antipsychotic medication (neuroleptics) have also been shown to reduce aggression, anxiety, and impulsivity, but there is a reluctance to prescribe them for nonpsychotic individuals, as their side effects have been very serious. With the newer atypical antipsychotics (e.g., risperidone [Risperdal], olanzapine [Zyprexa], and quetiapine [Seroquel]), however, clinicians are revisiting their use with diverse clinical populations. Substantive clinical trials targeted at the treatment of self-injury, however, have yet to be conducted, and, therefore, their use with self-injury clients must be considered with caution (Sansone et al., 2004b). Other classes of medication (e.g., opioid blockers, benzodiazepines, atypical and tricyclic antidepressants) all target some of the symptoms associated with self-injury, but clear evidence as to their efficacy does not exist, and thus they must also be considered with caution (Grossman & Siever, 2001). Medication should be tailored to the specific individual patient given his or her specific symptoms and overall clinical profile. The costs and benefits of targeting specific symptoms in the hope of affecting the target behavior of self-injury must always be weighed carefully. See Sansone, Levitt, and Sansone (2004b) for a recommended prescribing strategy for self-injury across classes of medication.

Sansone, Levitt, and Sansone (2004b) suggest that the use of medication in the treatment of self-injury is a complicated issue because of the dynamics of the phenomenon itself. Because of the provocative personality traits of some self-injurers—that is, they use both splitting and crisis behavior to engage others—medication may be seen by these individuals as a cure to their problems at the expense of more intensive psychotherapy. The authors caution that the prescriber and the therapist (if different) must work closely in order to avoid the possibility of being split. They further advise that clinicians take care not to align with the client's impulsivity around medication use and that they accordingly take a conservative approach to prescribing. Despite these concerns, they maintain that "most [self-injury] patients will modestly benefit from intervention with medications" (p. 255).

Family, Group, and Other Environmental Treatment Issues

Pain is real when you get other people to believe in it. If no one believes in it but you, your pain is madness or hysteria.

Naomi Wolf (2002)

As we have seen, self-injury does not develop in a vacuum but results from the interplay of a constellation of factors that include the individual's own biological vulnerabilities and both positive and negative environmental influences on his or her psychological development. Self-injury often has multiple triggers, usually of an interpersonal nature. Sufferers are familiar, and have become comfortable, with their erratic and frequent volatile relationships with family members and with peers. While self-injurers may have learned dysfunctional attachment and relating styles from already dysfunctional family systems, their current self-destructiveness has nevertheless contributed to the further deterioration of their relationships with family members and with peers. As a result, comprehensive treatment of self-injury must also address the family and peer relational systems in two important ways. First, they must be assessed in terms of how they may trigger self-destructive behaviors in the client and reinforce and maintain them. Second, consideration must be given to whether and how those systems may be transformed to create a more stable environment that provides structure for the self-injurer and supports recovery and health.

Family Treatment

Family treatment is essential for the long-term recovery of adolescent self-injurers, yet it is a very complicated matter. As seasoned clinicians who work with children and adolescents know all too well, family pathology often emerges through the identified patient (usually a child) within the family system. Also, the relational experience of self-injurers within their families is often far from supportive and validating. As we have seen, some experience the severe trauma of sexual or physical abuse within their own family units, and others are victims of neglect or more subtly complex trauma. Both kinds of trauma lead to severe impairment in development for the individual. A particular family's way of communicating and relating may be characterized by an undertone of control, hostility, and discomfirmation that may be out of the conscious awareness of family members. Nevertheless, it creates toxicity in the family environment that fuels destructive behavior in some or all of the individuals involved, particularly in those who are most vulnerable.

These kinds of issues complicate the task of engaging family members in the treatment of their self-injuring adolescent. In some cases, the family dysfunction may be so severe (for example, abuse may have occurred and be ongoing, or there may be other pathology, such as substance abuse) that to enlist family members' help in the treatment may be futile. In these cases, the safety of the client becomes paramount, and the removal of the adolescent from the toxicity of the family environment may be the most appropriate intervention. Removal from the family may also have an immediate impact on the reduction of the individual's self-injurious behavior (Walsh, 2006).

In cases where the family is relatively stable and is genuinely concerned and wants to help, treatment involves (1) enlisting the family in providing further information about the adolescent client that can be helpful in assessment, diagnosis, and treatment; (2) educating the family about self-injury and about how each family members' own dynamics may trigger, contribute to, or maintain the behavior; and (3) working with the family on redressing its larger dysfunction so that a more stable environment can be created that meets the recovery needs of the client (Costin, 2004; Walsh, 2006). This latter task also enlists family members as "skills practice allies" (Walsh, 2006) that can monitor, reinforce, and support the client's new interpersonal skills development that will replace the existing dysfunctional ones.

More specifically, family members can provide clinicians with additional information that may either corroborate or disconfirm the client's self-report. They can assist in filling in the gaps so that a more thorough and accurate diagnostic picture can be formulated by the clinician. Family members also need to be educated about such issues as what constitutes the differing levels of severity of the self-injurious behavior, how to distinguish it from suicide attempts, and how to assist the client when the behavior reaches a crisis point. Family members should also be helped to explore their own roles in sustaining the adolescent's behavior and to determine how their behaviors and styles of communication and discipline contribute to invalidating the client and activating her dysfunctional response to the stressful situation. They can be educated on how to respond to the client's provocative and injurious activities and on how to set the appropriate boundaries to help contain the client's affective storms and acting-out behavior. Parents can be educated to not respond in extreme ways—resorting to anger, guilt, or punishment to compel the individual to change her behavior. Rather, they can be taught how to respond with greater affective neutrality and how to tap into their adolescent's own understanding of herself in order to learn what may be helpful for her. Teaching the family members to ask the adolescent direct questions about how to respond can be quite helpful. For example, they can ask the injurer, "In the future, when something is really bothering you or you are feeling really stressed out, how would you like us to respond?" or "What should we avoid doing at all costs?" or "Is there anything missing from our relationship that would, if it were present, make a difference?" (Selekman, 2006). Questions such as these demonstrate involvement and care and communicate to the adolescent that the parents, too, have a role in this and are willing to look at themselves and change. I find that adolescents generally do not expect perfection from their parents. Rather, their hope is simply that their parents can admit and own their own shortcomings and not place the blame solely on the shoulders of their child. Children can forgive their parents for being human and flawed. What is harder to forgive, however, is parents who fail to acknowledge their own imperfections and defensively identify their child as the one with the problem. The simple act of asking the self-injurer what she thinks would be helpful validates her right to have her own thoughts and opinions and suggests, perhaps for the first time, that her family is willing to listen to her and make room for her inner life.

In addition to the dynamic family issues noted earlier, the effective helper also considers issues of culture when intervening with the family system. What are the implications of the family's cultural values for how the parents are informed of the client's self-injurious behavior? Or, for how they are enlisted to assist in the client's care? Are they open to discussing private family matters with outsiders? Are they psychologically minded? Are their methods of dealing with family difficulties different from those practiced in the dominant culture? Might their methods also be effective in dealing with the self-injurer's problems? And, if not, how are they to be engaged in the treatment process? Being attentive to and properly addressing these kinds of issues can have significant implications for the level of support the client receives from her family and for her course of treatment. For a review of multicultural considerations in family treatment see Grieger (in press) and Sue and Sue (2003).

Finally, family treatment can help transform dysfunctional patterns of communication into more supportive and empathic ones that will set the stage for healthier patterns of attachment within the family and, eventually, within other relationships. The presence and active involvement of the family can help the self-injurer to be attentive to triggers and can encourage the practice of appropriate coping skills in response to those triggers (Walsh, 2006). Actually practicing some of those newly learned coping skills with the client serves the multiple functions of being involved in the adolescents' treatment, creating the external structure that can help the individual to better contain her internal distress, and, most important, compassionately communicating to the client that she is not alone on the journey of recovery.

Treatment of the families of self-injurers is multidimensional and complex, yet essential to the recovery of adolescent self-injurers. Costin (2004) emphasizes the importance of working with the significant people in clients' lives and helping them to establish healthier attachments so that the client can learn new, healthier ways of relating. She summarizes the central tasks of this work as follows:

> The therapist must correct any dysfunctions occurring in the various relationships [in the family], for this may be where the underlying causal issues have partly developed or at least sustained. Family and significant others need to be educated about … self-harm symptoms, and particularly the patient's unique embodiment of them. Significant others need help in learning how to respond appropriately to the various situations they will encounter and what they might do that either sabotages the patient's progress or supports it. Serious conflicts between family members must be addressed. Parents may need to learn how to solve conflicts between themselves and how to nurture each other, which will then enable them to better nurture their child. Other problems may include faulty organizational structure in the family, miscommunication about expectations, and psychiatric difficulties among family members, all of which must be pointed out and corrected. (pp. 209–210)

Helping the family restructure and heal itself creates the foundation for greater safety for family members to be themselves and have a voice. When this happens, adolescents find that they have less need to act out their distress in destructive ways, and they can then learn to manage themselves through more appropriate means.

Group Treatment

Group therapy can be a powerful adjunct to individual psychotherapy for self-injurers in a number of ways. First, as all groups do, group therapy for self-injurers allows participants the opportunity to experiment with new ways of relating and connecting with others in a safe environment. Members can engage in developing mutual problem-solving strategies, give and receive support, and demystify the secrecy and the experience of aloneness often felt by self-injurers (Sansone et al., 2004a). However, group therapy for self-injurers can be a very precarious undertaking and must be conducted and managed with great caution. Issues of participant selection related to motivation, ability to function in group process, the presence of comorbid conditions, and the degree of chronicity and severity of the self-injurious behavior must be carefully considered. As is discussed in greater detail in the next chapter, one of the primary problems with the adolescent cohort around self-injury is the phenomenon of contagion (Sansone et al., 2004a; Walsh, 2006; Walsh & Rosen, 1988). In the close, intimate space of group therapy centered on the unifying common characteristic of self-injury, competition for attention, nurturance, and status within the group can easily develop. Individuals may compete with one another in terms of the frequency and severity of their self-injury; for example, if a member feels neglected in the group, he may turn to injuring himself in order to receive the interest and care of the group. Group members can also learn other ways to self-injure from one another if the focus of the group becomes graphic and titillating. The group therapist must be highly skilled in managing the multileveled interactions that occur in group treatment and must remain vigilant to the emergence of potentially disruptive dynamics to the process and to the possibility of contagion.

Hospitalization and Residential Treatment

When confronted with individuals who do physical harm to their bodies as self-injurers do, clinicians often feel compelled to question whether the individual needs to be hospitalized. Clearly, this is a reasonable question, and if the individual's life is in danger or her ultimate safety cannot be assured, hospitalization can certainly be the appropriate intervention. It is important to keep in mind, however, that hospitalizing a self-injurer must be distinguished from treating the self-injurer. Conterio and Lader (1998) maintain that "most self-injurers can be treated without hospitalization. While the most severe cases ... can benefit from the structured environment of a clinical setting, most self-injurers—people who continue to function in their lives while engaging in the behavior—can learn to abstain from self-harm on an outpatient basis" (p. 238). They note that hospitalization may be appropriate when the behavior becomes so frequent and so potentially lethal that the client's safety is seriously compromised or when the behavior becomes so disruptive in the person's life and in therapy that no work can be effectively accomplished.

In most other cases, however, hospitalization may not be appropriate for a number of reasons. First, in some instances, clinicians may have such powerful countertransferential reactions to the behavior and experience such anxiety around their helplessness to have the behavior stop that the decision to hospitalize the client is made more to assuage their own concern than for the benefit of the client (Farber, 2000). Second, inpatient psychiatric units are rarely the kinds of therapeutic milieus that are appropriate for treating self-injury. The staff is usually poorly trained to work with this population; they tend to be authoritarian in their treatment approach and may respond punitively to clients' self-destructiveness (Conterio & Lader, 1998). The staff's lack of understanding and sensitivity actually recreate the oppressive conditions that communicate invalidation to the self-injurers. As a result, the potential for large scale reenactments between patients and staff that lead to self-injury may, in fact, be increased (Connors, 2000).

In other cases, the individual's behavior may be so out of control (but not assessed to be highly lethal) and his general functioning in school and at home so impaired that his parents are no longer able to provide care for him. In this case, residential treatment may be an appropriate option. Or, if the structure in the home is so dysfunctional or chaotic that it is to the adolescent's benefit that he be removed from the home, residential care may also be appropriate. Of course, the kind and quality of setting selected is of great consequence to the care provided and to the individual's recovery process. Needless to say, the facility should not simply be one that "warehouses" adolescents with behavior problems; rather, it should have demonstrated expertise in providing treatment to self-injurers.

THE INTANGIBLES OF TREATMENT

We are healed of a suffering only by experiencing it to the full.

Marcel Proust (in Strong, 1998)

The treatment of self-injurers is a lengthy and painstaking process that requires multileveled interventions and a therapeutic constancy that firmly holds the client so that she can rummage through, discover, and experiment with her inner life. Within the context of a respectful therapeutic relationship, the client can learn to trust the therapist enough to bring the reality of the pain she carries into the consulting room. She can then begin to reexperience it by the hard work of transforming her pain into thoughts and words. As this suffering is contained by the safety of the therapist's "holding" of the client, the individual can come to discover (or perhaps recreate) her real self, which has been splintered off and buried. As a result, the client can gradually come to "accept that feelings can safely be felt and ideas safely be thought about. There is a gradual shift to experience the internal world as separate and qualitatively different from external reality" (Fonagy et al., 2002, p. 432). This, in turn, allows the individual to not be overwhelmed by the external threats that were previously experienced as coextensive with the self. This shift allows her to more effectively tolerate her own anxiety and distress and, in turn, to think about and speak about these feelings, rather than act on them in self-destructive ways. With this psychological movement, one can begin to find anew one's identity and, in doing so, one can begin to "experience oneself as a person, thinking one's thoughts and feeling one's feelings" (Odgen in Farber, 2000, p. 89). In a sense, the skin that was once cut and punctured is now restored as the boundary between the inner and the outer world. The client comes to understand that she has the right to her own thoughts and feelings and that others, in their separateness, also have their own thoughts and feelings that matter. The experience of this separateness, however, does not preclude the possibility of connecting and relating to others (Farber, 2000). It is the therapist's empathic communication and presence, her unwavering commitment to the process, and the constancy of her powerful communication of her belief in the possibility of health over the client's despair that ultimately serve as the active ingredients of the treatment.

The variable omitted from the nature of the transformative process just discussed is the stance of the client toward her illness and her desire to get better. Without a motivated client who genuinely wants to get better, change will not occur (Conterio & Lader, 1998; Sansone et al., 2004a). For the therapist to take responsibility for *making* the client stop her self-injury or change in other ways is misguided and is ultimately a setup for failure. The more that the client comes to understand that she has choices as to how she behaves in her life, the more empowered she will be, and the more control she will ultimately have over her feelings and behaviors. At the end of the day, we, as therapists, cannot save our patients from their own pain and suffering. Our ability to *be with* them in their pain better allows them to experience it in full. In most cases, the best we can do is to communicate to our clients that, although we may *not* be able to stop them from harming themselves, weJ certainly will be there and work with them to reduce the need to do it (Bateman & Fonagy, 2004). We must be willing to battle through their ambivalence toward health and be ready when they finally resolve to let go of their suffering and decide to heal. When we are attendant and responsive to this choice, we share in what Shengold describes as "the privilege of assisting in the psychological rebirth of a soul" (in Farber, 2000, p. 495).

SUMMARY AND CONCLUSION

While providing a comprehensive discussion of the treatment of self-injury is beyond the scope of this book, this chapter presented an overview of the key treatment issues in order for frontline responders to be better informed about the longer-term recovery process. This chapter discussed the treatment considerations aimed at addressing the developmental deficiencies across key domains of functioning that are often typical of self-injuring individuals. Treatment goals targeted at redressing difficulties in affect regulation, attachment and relationship instability, cognitive distortions, and behavioral dyscontrol were discussed, as were psychopharmacological interventions and the criteria for decisions on whether to hospitalize a self-injurer or place her in residential care. Effective treatment of self-injury ultimately entails assisting clients to transform their felt experience and distress into thoughts and words, rather than enacting them in self-destructive ways. As they are able to restructure their distorted core beliefs and develop alternative self-soothing skills, self-injurers become better able to tolerate their own feelings and their separateness from others. They can then learn to develop less destructive modes of being in their relationships with their families, friends, and with themselves.

Having concluded Part II of this book, we now turn, in the next chapter, to examining the role of the frontline responder in creating an extended network of care to facilitate recovery for the self-injurers in their educational settings and within their peer networks. Issues related to consultation with parents, teachers, and school administrators are discussed, along with the ancillary but nonetheless important concern about preventing contagion in the school setting. The chapter also includes specific recommendations about mental health and safety policy and provides guidelines for the development of protocols for managing self-injury in the school and on the college campus.

PART III

Creating Pathways to Care

We don't accomplish anything alone ... and whatever happens is the result of the whole tapestry of one's life and all the weavings of individual threads from one to another that creates something.

Sandra Day O'Connor (in Combs & Fox, 2004, p. 17)

Genuine responsibility exists only where there is real responding.

Martin Buber (1955, p. 16)

CHAPTER 9

Managing Self-Injury in the School and on the College Campus

The nice thing about teamwork is that you always have others on your side.

Margaret Carty (in McGuire & Duff, 2005, p. 63)

With the explosion of self-injury in schools and on college campuses in recent years, frontline responders—(counselors, social workers, nurses, psychologists, administrators, student affairs personnel, and others in these settings)—are challenged to rethink their traditional ways of doing business and to rework their institutional approaches to providing care. The primitive, shocking, and florid nature of self-injury has made health care professionals in educational settings take note of their unpreparedness to address this new epidemic and has highlighted the urgent need to develop new tactics for prevention, identification, and treatment of the phenomenon. Despite the fact that the primary mission of schools and colleges is to educate students and *not* to serve as de facto mental health facilities, the reality remains that, increasingly, some students come to school with serious mental health problems. Some of these problems, like self-injury, suggest that the student is in significant psychological distress and requires immediate attention. The educational setting, unfortunately, is functioning more and more as the place where these individuals are first assessed and directed toward treatment. Further, professionals in these settings have the added responsibility of being attentive to the collateral effects of an individual's problems on the larger living and learning environment. The self-injurious behavior of a particular individual, for example, not only places that individual at risk but can also affect others close to him or her (i.e., friends and roommates) and can be highly disruptive to these people's lives. It is therefore incumbent on health care and administrative professionals to increase their awareness about how self-injury plays out in their particular setting. They must also develop institutional protocols for assessing and intervening, at both the individual and the systems levels, in order to respond effectively to self-injurious behavior.

This chapter presents an overview of the broader issues involved in addressing self-injury in educational settings. Specifically, organizational and systems issues that play a role in the prevention, assessment, and intervention of self-injury are discussed. Some of the questions that are addressed include: What is the role of the frontline responder in engaging parents, teachers, administrators, and peers in the care of the self-injurer? How does one create a "network of care" that supports the recovery of the individual? How does the frontline responder manage and curtail contagion of self-injury in the school or in the residence halls? How does one take a leadership role in educating colleagues and creating teamwork in one's setting so that institutional protocols to effectively deal with distressed students can be developed? And, finally, what are some of the important elements to consider in crafting and establishing those protocols, and what resources are needed to do so successfully? The direct initial response to the self-injurer is only one component of the frontline professional's role in the school or on the college campus. Equally important is the leadership role that the professional must take in educating others in the community regarding the relevant issues involved, as well as in actively creating linkages among the various stakeholders in order to build fluid and effective pathways to care.

SELF-INJURERS' PATHWAYS TO CARE

In her qualitative study of self-injurers, Conte (2004) identified a number of informal and formal pathways that participants used to receive help. Informal pathways that led to the decrease in their self-injury included being able to turn to supportive friends and family, making a promise to stop the behavior to someone with whom the self-injurer was in a caring relationship, and breaking away from the people, places, and things that formerly triggered self-injury. More formally, the respondents received care through one or more of the following avenues: high school counseling services, college and university counseling services, and the broader mental health system, including psychotherapy in the community, hospitalization, medication, or some combination of these. Those participants who eventually decided to seek professional help reported their self-injury first to a high school mental health professional, which, in turn, set the stage for their receiving further treatment.

These findings are consistent with other studies that similarly suggest that school mental health professionals are the primary frontline responders. Typically, they are the first adults to whom many adolescents choose to disclose their problems, and they can have significant leverage in securing appropriate care (American Academy of Pediatrics, 2004; Borders & Drury, 1992; Crespi & Hughes, 2003; Paternite, 2005; Roberts-Dobie, 2005). In addition to delivering direct service, mental health professionals in these settings facilitate care for their clients by enlisting and mobilizing resources of the school or college environment. That is, because they are the resident experts in adolescent development and in matters of psychological health and distress, they are in the best position to take a leadership role in creating a collaborative network that involves students, parents, teachers, administrators, student services personnel, and support staff in order to maximize care for their students (American School Counselor Association, 2003; Pumariega & Vance, 1999; Weist, Ambrose, & Lewis, 2006).

The increased prevalence of adolescent self-injury has brought to the fore some of the policy gaps that exist in educational settings that fail to provide clear protocols for staff in helping students who are in distress and who may engage in self-destructive behaviors such as self-injury. In many cases, rather than following stated protocols that direct intervention strategies, frontline professionals are learning to intervene with self-injurers by trial and error and by drawing on their own experience to respond to the self-injurers they encounter. As noted in Chapter 1, inadequate training about self-injury, coupled with the lack of institutional support in responding to this population, greatly contributes to responders' sense of incompetence in managing these clients. This sense of incompetence affects one's confidence in one's abilities as a helper and leads the helper to disengage from his clients. Therefore, it is critical that institutions build teams, provide training, and develop policies and procedures that govern interventions in order to assist frontline professionals to function more effectively in their roles.

Roberts-Dobie (2005) recently conducted a comprehensive study of 443 school counselors randomly selected from the membership of the American School Counselor Association that sheds light on counselors' knowledge of self-injury, intervention strategies, and beliefs about resources needed to improve their work with this population. First, a large percentage of respondents believed that they were the most appropriate contact person in the school to respond to self-injury (75.39%) and the most likely to actually be contacted about a self-injuring student (76.74%). Almost all of the respondents had heard of self-injury (98.41%); 6% rated themselves "highly knowledgeable" in working with self-injurers; 74% rated themselves as "moderately knowledgeable"; and 20% rated themselves as "not very knowledgeable." Most (81%) respondents indicated that they had worked with a self-injurer, but only

17% felt "highly confident" in working with this population. Additionally, the study showed inconsistency in the primary methods of assistance provided to self-injurers. The most common method identified by experienced counselors (those who reported having worked with at least one self-injurer) was providing individual counseling (91%); this was followed by contacting a parent or guardian (88%) and referring to a psychiatrist (81%). The least common methods endorsed by these counselors were referring to the school nurse (18%) and providing group counseling (13%). Results also indicated that the interventions of experienced counselors differed significantly from those of inexperienced ones (those who had never worked with a self-injurer). For example, while only 18% of experienced counselors said they would contact the school nurse, 58% of inexperienced counselors said they would take this step. Also, experienced counselors reported that they would refer the self-injuring student to the school principal, while only 18% of inexperienced counselors said they would proceed that way.

Only a small number of respondents (23%) reported the existence of a written policy or protocol to guide them in dealing with self-injury within their institution. Respondents did report, however, that institutional policies did exist regarding other serious health concerns: suicide attempt (90%), alcohol use (87%), physical or sexual abuse (98%), sexual harassment (95%), or presence of weapons on school grounds (99%). Roberts-Dobie (2005) observes that formal policies not only help raise awareness of the training and intervention issues and help to coordinate appropriate care to self-injuring students but also convey what schools deem important and what will receive priority in terms of budget decisions and staff development. The general findings of this study suggest that, while counselors see themselves as the appropriate professional at the school to work with self-injurers, they also suggest that greater training, coordination, and institutional guidance and support are needed to sustain their work with this challenging population.

Health care professionals in the higher education community are finding themselves in similar circumstances with the increase of the incidence of self-injury taking place on campus (Whitlock, Eckenrode, et al., 2006). As college and university administrators have become more aware of the broad mental health problems that place students at high risk, there has been a concomitant recognition of the need to develop specific policies and protocols for managing acutely distressed and potentially suicidal students (Jed Foundation, 2006). Having safety and crisis management protocols in place speaks directly to the many overlapping practical, ethical, and legal issues that are part and parcel of addressing the psychological and emotional needs of students on the college campus.

Unlike working with a minor in the school, intervening with a distressed college student can involve another layer of complexity. College students are usually no longer minors. They may be living independently from their parents and, as adults, are responsible for their own care. Difficult questions arise in these situations. For example, should a representative of the college contact the student's parents or guardians if she is simply self-injuring and is not an imminent suicidal threat? What if the student objects to having her parents or guardians contacted? Policy about confidentiality in these instances must be clearly articulated so that the appropriate individuals may be informed of the student's situation and enlisted to assist in providing care. The issue of confidentiality also comes into play in deciding what other members of the college or university staff should be informed of the student's condition. Should the residence hall staff be informed? The student's professors? The provision of appropriate care may necessitate that others in the community be informed, and the rationale for these decisions should be clearly articulated in the policies and response protocols that are developed. Without clear policy statements and action protocols for responding to students who are in distress, institutions of higher education may not only fail to respond adequately to the mental health needs of their students but may also expose themselves to legal action for failing to implement best practices in the provision of mental health services.

CORE COMPONENTS OF RESPONSE PROTOCOLS FOR SELF-INJURY

No single response protocol can be appropriate for all schools, colleges, or universities. Institutions must develop their own policies on the basis of what established best practices dictate is appropriate for their settings and the available resources. There are, however, some key issues that ought to be considered in developing an institutional policy regarding the management of students who self-injure. This section identifies and briefly discusses those core components and provides some generic guidelines that can be applicable across settings. Guidelines are presented that address protocols for managing self-injury in schools; and a discussion of the central issues to be considered in the process of developing policies and procedures for the college campus community concludes the chapter.

Guidelines for Responding to Students in Distress in Schools

Some of the basic procedures in developing protocols for responding to students who may be in psychological distress and require immediate intervention while at school include:

- Create a mental health crisis team in the school that clearly identifies the key staff members and the roles they play on the team. Members of the team should include the mental health professionals on staff (e.g., counselors, social workers, psychologists), as well as key members of the administration, including the dean of students and the principal or vice-principal. The selection of team members is contingent on the size of the school, as well as on the various roles each individual member typically fills. Determinations can then be made regarding such issues as who assesses the student, who is responsible for contacting parents, who makes decisions about the student's condition and her continued ability to remain in school given her level of distress, and so forth.
- As a team, with consultation from faculty representatives, develop procedural policies around the sequence of steps to be taken in identifying, assessing, and deciding upon a plan of action for a student deemed to be in distress and in need of further attention. Staff members responsible for performing those tasks should be clearly identified.
- In the context of creating a culture of openness and responsiveness to students' needs in the school, develop mechanisms and programs that will help educate both staff and students about the warning signs in individuals who may be in distress, as well as the proper action to be taken to assist those individuals. Policies and action protocols should be disseminated among staff, and the point person(s) to be contacted when a student in need should be made known to all members of the community.
- Finally, it is important that the policies and protocols outline the specific criteria that will be used in making decisions about the student's disposition and under what conditions or circumstances the student will be permitted to remain in or return to school.

Walsh (2006) suggests specifically that when a student presents with instances of suicidal talk or other evidence of suicidal themes (e.g., in their art, poetry, or humor) or any instance of self-injury or other high-risk behaviors (e.g., significant substance abuse; situational, physical, or sexual risk taking; failure to take prescribed medication; or signs of significant or atypical emotional distress or dyscontrol), the individual should be referred to the identified contact person for an assessment. In other cases, the mental health professional may be informed (by teachers, coaches, or friends) that a particular student is in distress without the student's knowledge. In these situations, the responder should approach the student discreetly and begin to engage her around the issues of concern raised by others. In some instances, the reporting individuals may want to remain anonymous. If this is the case, it is important to try to honor that request. At the same time, I have found it help-ful to engage the reporters about the possibility of letting the student know that, because of their concern, they shared information about the student with someone who might be able to help her. While some identified students may initially be angry at this disclosure, I find that they are ultimately grateful that others cared enough to involve professionals who could actually help them.

Once the student is assessed, the mental health professional can deter-mine whether the incident is relatively minor or has been resolved or is seri-ous enough to warrant further intervention (Walsh, 2006). If the latter is the case, the student's parents or guardian should be contacted, and a plan for next steps (which can include outpatient treatment, medication evaluation, or simply ongoing counseling in the school itself) can be developed. The point person at the school can then recontact parents periodically to ensure that there is follow-through on the agreed-upon plan. If the initial assessment of the student suggests that he or she is in serious crisis or imminent risk (e.g., clear evidence of suicidality or a self-injurer who needs immediate medical attention because of her wounds), then the developed protocol for crisis or emergency care should be immediately implemented.

While these general intervention steps may appear simple and straightfor-ward, it takes a highly coordinated effort by professionals working as a team to ensure that the process proceeds smoothly and that the student is appropri-ately cared for. There are a host of ancillary issues that need to be considered and handled with great skill and tact to ensure that the outcome of helping the student secure the most suitable level of treatment is achieved. For example, the process of building an effective continuum of care for self-injurers in a school necessarily involves informing others of the individual's situation and enlisting their assistance, which raises questions regarding the limits of confi-dentiality in these cases. Disclosing a client's information to others raises im-portant ethical and legal issues, and it must be done in well-thought-out and appropriate ways. A school's institutional protocol for dealing with distressed students should provide guidelines for addressing issues of confidentiality and avenues for appropriate disclosure of information. However, the reality is that these issues are rarely clear-cut in school settings, where others (students and faculty) may already be aware of the student's situation.

For example, a student may have been brought to the attention of profes-sionals by her friends or by a teacher in the school. Clearly, these individuals already know of the student's problems, but when they come to the profes-sional for follow-up on how the student is doing, how much information is appropriate to disclose to them about the case? I find that in most situations, these individuals are concerned about how to be with the student—what should they say or not say, and how can they be helpful and supportive? My own approach is to assure them that I have responded to their concern without providing them with any specific details. I then also listen to their concerns and try to alleviate some of their anxiety by coaching them on what they can do or say to the student to be supportive during the process. I also invite them back to speak with me should they have other concerns or questions. Dealing with other members of the community in this respect and addressing their own unease is an important part of the work for mental health professions working in schools.

Working With Parents

A more complicated issue may be informing and engaging parents around their child's problems and need for intervention. Informing a client's parents about the client's self-injurious behavior and involving them in establishing an effective continuum of care is an important part of the response process but one that can be very complicated. While the issue of confidentiality for minors is rather clear-cut in legal terms—parents own the child's privileged communication and therefore have a right to know of their child's disclosures to a mental health professional—it is challenging in practice. As anyone who has worked with children or adolescents and their parents well knows, sometimes the most difficult part of the work is dealing with parents regarding their own dysfunction. Also, given the increasing cultural diversity of student populations on all educational levels, responding to their children's psychological issues and discussing family matters with "outsiders" may not be consonant with some parents' cultural worldview. A parent's response to a call from a school counselor or administrator alerting them to their child's problem can be highly variable. Some come on board immediately and work cooperatively with the school to secure appropriate help for the student. Others may be disengaged or in denial and may minimize the severity of the student's problems. Some may react in an unsupportive, punitive way toward their child and actually make matters worse. And still others may even attack the counselor (the "messenger," as it were) for bringing the problem to their attention (Downing, 1991). It is important to keep in mind that many self-injurers may be emotionally and psychologically disconnected from parents and family, and their home environments may be experienced as hostile and invalidating. A responder must, therefore, be cautious and deliberate in considering how much detailed information to share with parents and how to best involve them in the initial interventions.

Obviously, in working with minors in school, parents or guardians should be contacted immediately after an initial assessment is conducted by the appropriate mental health professional when it has been determined that the student is engaging in self-injurious behavior (Onacki, 2005; Walsh, 2006). Again, as underscored in Chapter 6, it remains imperative that the responder treat the student with respect throughout the engagement and assessment process and in communicating to the client the need and rationale for contacting her parents. Also, as noted in Chapters 7 and 8, it is important for the responder to be acutely attuned to cultural factors that may inform the manner in which family members are made aware of this problem and how it is framed. It is essential to communicate to clients one's respect for their privacy, but at the same time it is important to clearly explain the importance of involving others who may be able to offer help beyond what can be provided at school. The assumption I make in having this conversation with students is that they have disclosed their self-injury to me because they ultimately want help. My work with them is to assist them to understand what that help may look like and what steps we may need to take to ensure that we can best address their problems. Students may be reluctant to involve their parents at first for a number of reasons, not the least of which is the possibility of evoking negative reactions and being punished for their behavior. The fear of one's parents' negative reaction can be a significant obstacle to getting help for self-injury (Conte, 2004), and the responder's job in the process is to frame the issues to both students and parents so that communication between the two can be facilitated. Along these lines, one of the primary goals of mediating a discussion between student and parents is to help them reach some agreement as to what the problems actually are and what needs to be done to address them. Parents need to be educated about the kind and level of distress their child is in, as well as about the nature and course of self-injury. Understanding the problem and coming to some agreement as to its nature and seriousness are vital for the individual's recovery. In fact, studies indicate that when parents and adolescents disagree regarding the adolescent's level of distress, the prognosis for recovery is usually much poorer (Ferdinand, van der Ende, & Verhulst, 2004).

The approach that I have found most helpful in initiating a conversation about contacting parents is to remain respectfully engaged with the student and to place as much control over the process in her hands as possible. I first ask if the student would like to call the parent herself from my office. If she would not, I then ask which parent she would want me to contact, and I engage her in a discussion of what the purpose of the call is, what plan I will recommend to the parent, and what information will be shared with the parent and what will not. If the situation is an emergency, the parent is contacted over the phone immediately and informed of the situation. If the situation is less critical, an in-person conference is scheduled with the parents to discuss the matter. While students may not have a choice as to *whether* a parent will be contacted, they do have some role in and control over the process. By allowing them to retain as much control as possible, I communicate both respect for their autonomy and care for their safety, thus creating the groundwork for the development of a strong working alliance. My experience has been that students feel a sense of relief when someone who understands what their problems are (and how their families may contribute to creating or maintaining those problems) intervenes with the family and takes charge of the situation. Self-injurers can often begin to find hope once the issues are out in the open and another adult hears them and is willing to help. Of course, this help is not always received resistance free. There are cases in which the family system is so dysfunctional that securing treatment for only the student addresses just a part of the problem. In these situations, I look for whatever leverage I can find to mobilize the family to participate. A strategy that has been effective is to identify the student as the patient and to recommend that the parents be involved in the treatment in order to help in the student's recovery. The parents then become included at some level in the initial treatment, and it is hoped that they will participate more fully as the process moves forward.

Working With Teachers and Other School Personnel

In the often close-knit communities in schools, information about particular student incidences or problems usually travels throughout the school unhindered—rumors spread, information is distorted, and uninformed conclusions about students are drawn. Part of the function of the mental health crisis team is to contain information about students in crisis and to stem the spread of incorrect or misleading information to the larger school community. The challenge for team members is to do this without inappropriately disclosing information about the student to others.

The delicate balance that must often be negotiated in these circumstances is between upholding the privacy and confidentiality of the student and nurturing a collaborative relationship with faculty and other school personnel. Teachers or other staff members may be genuinely concerned about a student and may ask for information. While the value of their concern should be acknowledged, it is not necessary to share the student's information with them. Legitimate issues of information sharing do arise when teachers want to know if the student is a danger to herself or to others and how they should manage and respond to the student in the classroom. Often, the teacher's need to know this information is less about trying to pry or be meddlesome than it is about their own anxiety regarding how to manage and respond to the student in the classroom. In these cases, I try to provide a concrete picture of what to expect from students who self-injure in general and offer a number of possible options about what to say and/or courses of actions to follow. This can be done without inappropriately revealing specifics about the individual by instead framing the discussion more in terms of classroom management. I find that most teachers are appreciative of any concrete suggestions that they receive, as they help to relieve their sense of helplessness and their fear that they will lose control of the classroom.

I have also found it effective in helping to curtail inappropriate inquisitiveness about students on the part of school staff to work continuously to establish a culture of professionalism and to attempt to keep the lines of communication open between the mental health staff at the school and the rest of the school community. This is an ongoing task because some degree of tension almost always exists between the teaching faculty and the counseling or guidance department because of their different responsibilities and the work that they do. Teachers sometimes view counselors as interfering with their classroom work, and counselors, in their roles as advocates for students, can sometimes view teachers as insensitive and uncaring. In order to bridge this gap, it is important for mental health professionals working in schools to demystify the work they do and to try to explicitly link their goals to those of the teachers and the larger educational mission of the school. This can be done by providing the faculty with regular updates on the department's work, reviewing with them policies and protocols for identifying students at risk and for making effective referrals, and periodically discussing with them the limits of confidentiality and their concerns around this issue. Engaging faculty members around these concerns and soliciting their input communicates respect for their views and demonstrates a willingness to work collaboratively with them.

Working With Administrators

Another important function of the counselor in schools is to educate administrators about self-injury so that it can be distinguished from suicidality, which may require a different response from the school. Problems arise when administrators, who may be poorly informed about particular mental health issues, react similarly across situations, regardless of the unique circumstances of the incident or the individual. That is, they may collapse into one category all seemingly serious mental health problems identified in students and react in the same fashion to each. The role of the mental health professional in the school setting is to take the lead in helping administrators understand the differences in psychopathology and to provide different options for appropriate courses of action.

Similarly, a student who may be in emotional distress at school may present with a range of behaviors, which may include being emotionally labile and tearful or being disruptive, irritable, angry, and challenging. These oppositional behaviors can be symptoms indicating that the student is anxious, depressed, or traumatized or is otherwise in significant distress. Occasionally, the signs that suggest distress are interpreted primarily through a disciplinary lens and are responded to punitively. We know that self-injurers exhibit significant emotional and behavioral dyscontrol that manifests itself in different ways. In addition to ongoing self-injurious behavior, students may also be emotionally labile (exhibiting significant mood swings), they may have tearful or angry outbursts, and they may also present as oppositional and challenging to authority figures. Administrators should be educated on the clusters of behaviors that may be indicative of emotional distress so that they can refer those individuals for an assessment, rather than deal with them exclusively as disciplinary problems.

Guidelines for Responding to Students in Distress on the College Campus

The recently released document titled *Framework for Developing Institutional Protocols for Acutely Distressed or Suicidal College Students* (Jed Foundation, 2006) offers an outstanding generic template for the central issues to be considered in developing safety, emergency notification, and leave-of-absence and reentry protocols for college campuses. While the role of the frontline professional on the college campus should encompass the triad of activities of *prevention, intervention,* and *postvention,* given the purpose and scope of this book, the following overview will focus on issues related to developing intervention protocols for responding to students in distress (which includes individuals who engage in self-injury).

The Jed Foundation's (2006) framework for developing a safety protocol on the college campus recommends that the following questions be considered in the development of institutional policies:

- How does the institution prepare administrators to identify and intervene with students who may be in distress and at risk for harm or suicide?
  - How are they educated to identify warning signs?
  - How are they trained to intervene and effect a referral for assessment, if required?

- How should the individual be transported to the counseling center? Should she be accompanied?
- What information should the administrator provide to the clinician?
- What emergency response protocols are in place to govern responses in an emergency and when an individual requires immediate medical attention?
- How does the institution prepare other members of the college community (e.g., professors, mental health professionals, roommates, peers) to identify students who may be in distress and at risk for harm?
  - How are they educated to identify warning signs?
  - What are the different responsibilities for different members of the college community?
  - What are appropriate actions to take if the concerned other learns directly or indirectly that a student is in acute distress?
  - Who specifically should be contacted (e.g., counseling center, student affairs, campus security)?
  - How and by whom is the student approached or assessed after a report has been made (e.g., initially by residence life staff, a student affairs administrator, or someone else)?
  - Who has the responsibility for completing the initial assessment (e.g., counseling center staff, a campus psychiatrist, someone in the community)?
- What is the decision-making process when a potentially at-risk student has been identified?
  - What are the roles of the various campus officials? Who takes the lead?
  - What information will be required in order to make informed decisions?
  - If the student has an off-campus mental health practitioner, how is it determined whether to make that person part of the decision-making process?
  - What is the procedure for responding to the student in distress outside standard business hours?
- How is it decided what to do if a student who needs help refuses it?
- What is the decision-making process for determining whether hospitalization is in the best interest of the student?
- What are the mechanisms that will facilitate the process of hospitalization?

- What other intervention or treatment might be appropriate if hospitalization is not indicated?
  - How is that decision made?
- What issues must be addressed if the student is to be allowed to continue residing in the residence halls or to attend classes?
  - How is this determined, and by whom?
- How is a follow-up plan developed with the student?
  - How is the plan implemented and monitored, and by whom?
  - What are the consequences for the student of failing to follow through on the plan?
- How is the threshold for intervention determined if a student shows signs of distress?
- How does the college follow up with those involved with or affected by the distressed student (e.g., friends, roommates, faculty, RAs)?
  - How are those affected identified?
  - Who communicates with them?
  - What, specifically, is offered to them?
- How is it determined whether a voluntary or involuntary leave of absence from school is in the best interest of the student?
  - How is a student's desire to stay in school balanced with the services and support the institution is able to provide?
  - What is the leave and reentry process?
- How is it decided when to notify an emergency contact?
  - Who is permitted to make the contact, and who is responsible for it?
  - What strategies can be used to encourage the reluctant student to allow notification to take place when the school deems notification necessary?
  - How is it determined what information to disclose?
  - How is the need to notify the emergency contact balanced with concerns about potential consequences of notification for the student (e.g., when the parents are part of the problem), and who makes the final determination?
- How does the campus professional engage the emergency contact who may be in denial about the seriousness of the student's mental health issues?
- How does the professional decide whether it is appropriate to notify someone other than the named emergency contact—either voluntarily or involuntarily—during a crisis? (Adapted and modified from The Jed Foundation, 2006, pp. 10–21. Readers who work on the college campus would be well served by reviewing this document in its entirety.)

Although generic, these questions can provide a thorough basis for developing safety protocols for students who may be in distress, suicidal, or both on the college campus and certainly apply to self-injurers who come to the attention of others and may require assistance. Again, it is important to keep in mind that self-injury is different from suicide and that the two should not necessarily be treated identically. Self-injurers, however, can be in great distress, and their behavior can be very dangerous to themselves and disruptive to others in the college environment. College mental health professionals need to educate the community on the phenomenon by developing psychoeducational programming (see DiLazzero, 2003, for a sample program) and through outreach. Self-injurers do not typically seek help on their own on the college campus (Whitlock, Eckenrode, et al., 2006), and, therefore, mechanisms must be created that will better identify these individuals and direct them to established pathways to care.

THE PROBLEM OF CONTAGION

Self-injury can become a highly contagious activity within cohorts (Conterio & Lader, 1998; Farber, 2000; Favazza, 1996; Walsh, 2006; Walsh & Rosen, 1988). Because of the increased prevalence of self-injury among the adolescent population, the "epidemic of disclosure" of celebrities, and the media coverage and Internet Web sites on the topic, adolescents are learning about self-injury (and *how to* self-injure) from a variety of sources. When this flood of information is combined with the pressures of emerging adolescence and its accompanying changes and responsibilities, young people can find themselves vulnerable to engaging in behaviors like self-injury as a way to manage the overwhelming strain they feel around connecting and wanting to fit in with others (Conterio & Lader, 1998).

The powerful interpersonal dimensions of the adolescent peer group appear to provide the fuel for the contagion of self-injury. Farber (2000) likens the phenomenon to that identified in groups of young women suffering from eating disorders. In these cases, Farber observes, "Girls may compete for status by demonstrating that they can starve themselves better than any of their friends, or purge themselves of the most food" (p. 60). Likewise, in pathologically enmeshed peer groups, self-injurers may compete with one another over who has the most cuts, or whose cuts are deepest, or who is in the most psychological pain and therefore requires the most nurturance from the group.

Walsh (2006) reports that episodes of contagion among adolescents have occurred across institutional and treatment settings and explains that they may be motivated by a number of dynamics that include interpersonal factors, the negotiation of peer hierarchies, and the desire for group cohesiveness. He notes that, first of all, there are powerful interpersonal factors that support the contagion of self-injury. Because self-injurers have limited communication skills, self-injury is a way for them to communicate with others in a powerful and intense way. One of my own clients once remarked, "My parents never listened to what I had to say. They finally began to pay attention to me when I started cutting myself." The behavior can emerge as an attempt to change the behavior of others by coercing or punishing them through the self-injury. The self-injurer hopes to bring others closer and to find greater connection; at the same time, the behavior can distance others by its shocking and violent subtext. As Walsh (2006) explains, self-injury can be viewed as an attack on others in the sense of "Look what you've done to me!" saying, in essence, "It's your fault that I cut myself, and you are responsible for my pain." This communication functions to discharge one's rage and aggression at others with the simultaneous coercive intent to change caregivers' or peers' reactions or behavior toward the self-injurer.

Also significant in exacerbating the contagious effects of self-injury are the peer hierarchies and the desire for group cohesiveness that develop within peer groups. "High-status instigators" or those who reach the top of the group "pecking order" can have a powerful influence on the spread of self-injury within the group (Walsh 2006). Walsh and Rosen (1988) explain:

> Members who cut themselves most frequently and severely tend to have the most prominence within the group. They are the center of attention and are seen as most at risk and most in need of protection. Members who are most adept at responding to the crises of others also achieve high status.
>
> Given that high status is important to group members, there is pressure to self-mutilate and pressure to be a savior. These pressures facilitate the contagion phenomenon. When one member self-mutilates, other members need to reassert their place within the hierarchy. They need to demonstrate that they also still self-mutilate and that they are still available to provide empathy and assistance to other members in crisis. (p. 91)

In sum, both group members' vulnerability to self-injury and their ability to be supportive to others who are in distress serve as important criteria for gaining status within the group.

Added to these dynamics is the powerful bond that is created among self-injurers, which bolsters and fortifies group cohesiveness. Self-injurers report feeling connected to other self-injurers in ways that non-self-injurers cannot understand—a phenomenon similar to that described by war veterans who develop intense emotional and psychological connection because of their common experience of combat, an experience that noncombatants cannot possibly understand (Walsh & Rosen, 1988). Walsh (2006) explains:

> When a contagion episode is unfolding, a sense of escalating excitement often develops. People within the group may feel a sense of intimacy and exhilaration that they are unable to achieve through other means. Contagion episodes can be intensely invigorating until the inevitable "crash" happens. Self-injury contagion cannot really provide sustained and stable intimacy within the group. (pp. 239–240)

The example used earlier about one of my own adolescent patients is apropos: she had made a pact with three other self-injurers; they agreed that, while each was attempting to stop her injurious behavior, they would all self-injure in support of and solidarity with the relapsing group member. Another patient reported having a similar pact with "friends" she had met online but had never met in person. In this instance, the level and kind of disclosure—sharing with each the techniques by which they self-injured—and the connections formed around the emotional volatility connected to the behavior created a more powerful bond within these relatively anonymous Internet relationships than any the patient had formed with any other individual she had actually met in her life.

As a result of these and other contagion dynamics, frontline responders in the school or on the college campus have the added responsibility to attend to other vulnerable individuals in the community and to curtail the spread of the behavior. Walsh (2006) recommends three approaches to minimize the risk of contagion in school settings. First, he suggests that, because self-injurers freely and easily talk about their behavior with peers in ways that can be titillating and provocative, encouraging students to limit their communication of self-injury with peers is an important step. Speaking about their feelings and behaviors is an important part of the recovery process, but self-injurers should be encouraged to speak about this to their counselor and other appropriate adults and not to their peers, despite their belief that their peers are supportive of them in their recovery. To encourage them not to speak to peers, the helper can appeal to their "social conscience," asking that they not negatively influence other vulnerable individuals. Second, Walsh (2006) observes that self-injurers can be provocative by showing their scars or wounds to others. This, too, can ignite strong urges in vulnerable individuals and can trigger the spread of self-injury. School officials may need to address this behavior and firmly communicate to self-injurers that wound exhibition is not acceptable in the school community and must stop. Walsh recommends that families be enlisted to help curtail this problem and that disciplinary action be considered, including sending the student home if she continues to be provocative and uncooperative about concealing her wounds. Finally, self-injurers in the school should be engaged individually by school mental health professionals rather than in group modalities. Group work with this population is highly delicate, and the possibility of contagion within the group is high when members become stimulated by speaking about and sharing "war stories" about their behavior. Their disclosures can provide a vicarious thrill for other members and stir them on to engage (or reengage) in self-injury.

In addition to the contagion issues already noted, professionals on the college campus have the added challenge of having less direct day-to-day contact with self-injuring students. Unlike high school students, who are, essentially, a captive audience because they are in the actual school setting for most of the day, college students may live at home or in residence halls, where they have greater privacy and less direct contact with those who may address issues of contagion. Residence hall staff and student affairs personnel must nonetheless remain vigilant to the spread of self-injury among roommates, groups, or subcultural cohorts on campus. While we currently have little research data to document the effect of contagion on the college campus, ample anecdotal evidence exists that some individuals living in close quarters during the college years do experience and participate in the contagious effects of self-harming behaviors, including self-injury and eating-disordered behaviors.

The challenge of curtailing the spread of self-destructive behaviors in the college setting begins with the institution's commitment to developing a culture of wellness. This means educating individuals about the healthy and unhealthy choices they make and creating a supportive professional community that encourages nonblaming communication and teaches nonstigmatizing help-seeking behaviors. Frontline responders in these settings can develop both formal and informal venues for education, such as in-service training for resident advisors regarding self-injury; psychoeducational programming in the residence halls; outreach by counseling center staff to faculty, administrators, and parents; and informal information sessions coordinated by student activities organizations. Other mechanisms and media for information delivery can include classroom presentations, parent orientation programs, online resources, brochures, feature articles in the campus newspapers, and posters and other printed information available in campus wellness centers, health centers, and counseling centers. With education and awareness, we can begin to dismantle the culture of secrecy and shame around self-injury, and caring others can engage and intervene with those who may be caught up in its painful, self-destructive cycle.

ON THE NECESSITY OF TEAMWORK

No individual can singlehandedly create a culture or network of care in any school or college campus. Working with self-injurers and, for that matter, other high-need individuals can be daunting, draining, and overwhelming for all helping professionals. These clients' volatility and emotional instability and the entrenched nature of their problems can evoke a sense of helplessness and despair in those trying to help. Consequently, helpers can experience a malaise in working with self-injurers and accordingly disengage; when this happens, adolescents in need are passed over for care. Given the hazards of this work, frontline responders can be most effective in educational settings when they create partnerships with other professionals in their setting and strive to work well together as a team.

Developing formal teams, being trained together as a team, and using other professionals as resources and for support helps to maintain a sense of competence and confidence in working with difficult client populations (Bateman & Fonagy, 2004). Further, working in teams also increases the potential for diverse points of view to emerge based on members' respective professional experience and background. This richer and more multidimensional perspective can only enhance the quality of care that is provided for distressed students. When teams are clear about policies and procedures and have a clear sense of what the pathways to care are in a particular organization, the guesswork is taken out of the equation and professionals feel less alone in their struggle to deal with challenging clients. The development of policies and protocols that reinforce teamwork and that provide clear and fluid mechanisms to address distressed adolescents is therefore a crucial part of reducing the responder's anxiety, empowering him to take leadership in responding to a situation, and ensuring that optimal care is provided for clients. If the responder is confused, frightened, or unsure about how to handle a situation or intervene with the self-injurer, how much more unsettled will the client who is in need be? Our own uncertainty and anxiety invariably get communicated to our clients despite our maneuvers to conceal our insecurity. Clarity of processes and roles, mutual support, honest appraisal of team members' professional skills, and ongoing communication and willingness to reevaluate team functioning are an indispensable part of creating effective intervention teams and creating the best pathways to care for the self-injuring clients with whom we work.

SUMMARY AND CONCLUSION

This chapter examined the major issues related to managing self-injury in the school and the college setting and proposed guidelines for developing effective pathways to care. The role of the frontline mental health professional in engaging parents, teachers, and school administrators as well as college student life personnel was discussed, and recommendations to facilitate and optimize those interventions were presented. The process for developing specific and comprehensive institutional protocols for dealing with distressed students was described, and specific guidelines in creating those procedural strategies were proposed. The chapter then addressed the issue of contagion of self-injury among groups of adolescents and explored approaches that frontline responders can take to curtail the spread of self-injuring behavior. Finally, the importance of teamwork and support for those who work with highly distressed adolescents like self-injurers was highlighted, and some key guiding principles for building effective mental health teams were suggested.

The epilogue of this book, to which we now turn, comments on the challenges of working with the self-injuring adolescent population and underscores the importance of helper's commitment to self-care. It is argued that helpers *must* attend to their own care in order to effectively sustain their work with this population to prevent professional burnout and to maintain hope in the face of their own occasional doubt. The chapter also speaks to the struggle to find the courage to squarely face the pain of our clients and, in doing so, to communicate to them our commitment, compassion, and trust in their own abilities to be gentler with themselves and thereby to live healthier and more fulfilling lives.

CHAPTER 10

Epilogue: A Voice of Hope in the Face of Suffering

What makes us heroic?—Confronting simultaneously our supreme suffering and our supreme hope.

Friedrich Nietzsche (1974, p. 219)

The recurrent and most significant discovery in analysis is that beneath all the distortions and defenses, resistances and denials, beneath all the fears and inhibitions, and beneath all the tales of victimage and passivity, an affirmative voice can be heard.

Walter Davis (1989, p. 251)

I began this book by noting the challenges frontline responders face in working with adolescents who cut their own skin to speak to us of a pain for which they have no words. I conclude this book by coming full circle to revisit this theme and to highlight both the depth of the suffering we meet in our self-injuring clients and the courage required to speak hope to their often dispirited hearts. Engaging individuals who are so disconnected from others and so alienated from themselves that their bodies have become their enemy *and* their refuge confuses us, scares us, and often renders us helpless. Their self-destructive acts repulse us, throw us off balance, and challenge our most basic instincts to care and to respond. Their behavior seems incomprehensible. We often feel powerless, lacking any control over their seeming senseless and morbid desire to wound themselves. Perhaps we come to believe that "No matter what I do, I can't stop them from hurting themselves. No matter what I do, nothing will ever change. All I feel is frustration and helplessness. Why keep trying?" The irony in all this is that for individuals who feel voiceless and powerless, self-injurers' voices are indeed very powerful. They communicate the profundity of their pain through wounds that loudly capture our attention and piercingly speak to us of their suffering. We see it and feel it, and it occasionally overpowers us.

As I have attempted to illustrate throughout this book, self-injury is a multidetermined phenomenon, and its management and treatment is quite complex. The myriad sociocultural forces that shape our self-understanding, our gender roles and our body images and suggest how we ought to live our lives set the stage for many of the dynamics that play out through self-injury. One's personal vulnerabilities, one's family dysfunction, and the experience of trauma in all its forms, subtle and overt, further enrich the soil out of which self-injury can emerge. However, in the final analysis, self-injury, most specifically, is about disconnection and invalidation. It is about these debilitating sentiments that have been internalized by the sufferers and have been appropriated as their defining identity as human beings. It is precisely this sense of disconnection and invalidation that we helpers encounter in our clients and, if unaware, can easily appropriate for ourselves. Our clients tell us that they feel alone, afraid, and unloved, and, in our attempts to relieve them of their despair, we can make these feelings our own. When we do, we understandably come to doubt ourselves, we recoil in fear, and we abandon the hope that is so necessary to help them heal and to sustain us in the face of their great suffering.

It has been suggested in this book that effective work with self-injurers entails primarily understanding, managing, and working with countertransference. That is, self-injurers' pain is transferred to helpers quite fluidly, and primal feelings are clearly communicated without the use of words. Being left with the weight of self-injurers' anguish, when one is unprepared, becomes overwhelming and burdensome and depletes the helper of energy, compassion, and the desire to be present. In essence, self-injurers induce in us the very reaction that they want least; rather than enlist us to their cause, they, in fact, push us away. Bion (1998) speaks precisely to the painful nature of change when he notes that "Of all the hateful possibilities, growth and maturation are feared and detested most frequently" (p. 53); it is this hatefulness that self-injurers have toward their own healing that we experience so powerfully and that repels us so compellingly.

Understanding this dynamic can liberate frontline responders from its power. The awareness that we can be vicariously traumatized by our work with these clients, that their primitive behavior and affects can threaten our very sense of competence and confidence, and that our compassion can become so strained that our fatigue turns to aggression allows us to better modulate our own feelings and reactions. This awareness further allows us to know the snare of our instinct to rescue and helps us to find solace in the reality that "healing" must not be *imposed* on our clients but cultivated within them. In fact, surrendering the desire to "fix" them and to stop them from their self-injury actually increases our leverage with them and our power to actually help them heal. The effective helper understands that work with these individuals is more about embarking on a long, sometimes rocky journey than about running a sprint. It is about "turning toward" our clients in openness and acceptance and in a spirit that confirms their humanity in spite of their reluctance and protestations. It is about being present to the person obscured by the behavior and listening for and honoring her own self-affirming voice, which may be buried deep within. It is about accepting the unacceptable in her, allowing her to suffer through her legitimate pain, and being unwavering in our faith in the power of human connection.

This is hard work indeed and, certainly, easier said than done. However, this is the challenge that lies before us. If we choose to undertake this challenge, we must remain steadfastly conscious of our own human struggles, limitations, and needs. We must honestly appraise our ability to engage these very difficult to engage clients, educate ourselves in order to increase our competence, and earnestly seek out the support and guidance we need to sustain ourselves in this arduous work. The danger is that we will fall into the same trap of neglecting our own self-care, as our self-injuring clients have learned to do so well. Connors (2000) reminds us that "Just as we encourage our clients to discern what they need to physically and emotionally care for themselves amidst the stresses of everyday life … we need to do the same for ourselves. This includes everything from getting enough sleep to processing difficult feelings that emerge in response to our work with clients. Discovering what sustains and nourishes us takes time and effort" (pp. 360–361). Being committed to our own self-care means that we should look to engage in activities that comfort us and that allow us to recenter in order to bring ourselves to our work in more complete ways.

Holding the pain of others and helping them transform it is difficult work and therefore demands that we be "held" as well. Self-injurers are discon-nected from others, feel voiceless, and have a poorly developed ability to self-soothe in healthy ways. Ironically, these very deficiencies we find in our clients can enlighten our own path to self-care. In order to avoid burnout, we counselors, health care professionals, and other frontline responders must, first and foremost, nurture healthy human connections in our own lives. We must cultivate both personal and professional relationships that will allow us to have our relational needs met—where our own voices can be heard, where we can speak *our* truth, and where we feel understood, mirrored, accepted, and emotionally and psychologically held. We must seek out relationships in which imaginative play is allowed and even encouraged and celebrated. We must seek out relationships that provide us with opportunities for our own soothing and our own care. Knowing how to self-soothe and seek comfort from others when in distress is a skill that we help our clients develop, and it is fundamental to our own well-being and must also be attended to. If we neglect our own care, we place that of our clients in jeopardy, as well.

Finally, our work with self-injurers requires that we have the courage to maintain hope in spite of the hopelessness *they* may feel. It requires courage to appreciate that healing is nonlinear and often abounds with ambiguity. It requires courage to affirm the self-injurer in spite of her resistance, and it requires courage to be gentle with oneself in the face of fear and doubt. In the end, the most valuable gift we helpers can give our self-injuring clients is to listen to their muted voices, endeavor to understand their pain, and stand beside them as they continue on their journey.

Bill of Rights for People
Who Self-Harm

PREAMBLE

An estimated one percent of Americans use physical self-harm as a way of coping with stress; the rate of self-injury in other industrial nations is probably similar. Still, self-injury remains a taboo subject, a behavior that is considered freakish or outlandish and is highly stigmatized by medical professionals and the lay public alike. Self-harm, also called self-injury, self-inflicted violence, or self-mutilation, can be defined as self-inflicted physical harm severe enough to cause tissue damage or leave visible marks that do not fade within a few hours. Acts done for purposes of suicide or for ritual, sexual, or ornamentation purposes are not considered self-injury. This document refers to what is commonly known as moderate or superficial self-injury, particularly repetitive SI; these guidelines do not hold for cases of major self-mutilation (i.e., castration, eye enucleation, or amputation).

Because of the stigma and lack of readily available information about self-harm, people who resort to this method of coping often receive treatment from physicians (particularly in emergency rooms) and mental health professionals that can actually make their lives worse instead of better. Based on hundreds of negative experiences reported by people who self-harm, the following Bill of Rights is an attempt to provide information to medical and mental health personnel. The goal of this project is to enable them to more clearly understand the emotions that underlie self-injury and to respond to self-injurious behavior in a way that protects the patient as well as the practitioner.

The Bill of Rights for Those Who Self-Harm

1. The right to caring, humane medical treatment.
    Self-injurers should receive the same level and quality of care that a person presenting with an identical but accidental injury would receive. Procedures should be done as gently as they would be for others. If stitches are required, local anesthesia should be used. Treatment of accidental injury and self-inflicted injury should be identical.
2. The right to participate fully in decisions about emergency psychiatric treatment (so long as no one's life is in immediate danger).
    When a person presents at the emergency room with a self-inflicted injury, his or her opinion about the need for a psychological assessment should be considered. If the person is not in obvious distress and is not suicidal, he or she should not be subjected to an arduous psych evaluation. Doctors should be trained to assess suicidality/homicidality and should realize that although referral for outpatient follow-up may be advisable, hospitalization for self-injurious behavior alone is rarely warranted.
3. The right to body privacy.
    Visual examinations to determine the extent and frequency of self-inflicted injury should be performed only when absolutely necessary and done in a way that maintains the patient's dignity. Many who SI have been abused; the humiliation of a strip-search is likely to increase the amount and intensity of future self-injury while making the person subject to the searches look for better ways to hide the marks.
4. The right to have the feelings behind the SI validated.
    Self-injury doesn't occur in a vacuum. The person who self-injures usually does so in response to distressing feelings, and those feelings should be recognized and validated. Although the care provider might not understand why a particular situation is extremely upsetting, she or he can at least understand that it *is* distressing and respect the self-injurer's right to be upset about it.
5. The right to disclose to whom they choose only what they choose.
    No care provider should disclose to others that injuries are self-inflicted without obtaining the permission of the person involved. Exceptions can be made in the case of team-based hospital treatment or other medical care providers when the information that the injuries were self-inflicted is essential knowledge for proper medical care. Patients should be notified when others are told about their SI, and, as always, gossiping about any patient is unprofessional.
6. The right to choose what coping mechanisms they will use.
    No person should be forced to choose between self-injury and treatment. Outpatient therapists should never demand that clients sign a

no-harm contract; instead, client and provider should develop a plan for dealing with self-injurious impulses and acts during the treatment. No client should feel they must lie about SI or be kicked out of outpatient therapy. Exceptions to this may be made in hospital or ER treatment, when a contract may be required by hospital legal policies.

7. The right to have care providers who do not allow their feelings about SI to distort the therapy.

Those who work with clients who self-injure should keep their own fear, revulsion, anger, and anxiety out of the therapeutic setting. This is crucial for basic medical care of self-inflicted wounds but holds for therapists as well. A person who is struggling with self-injury has enough baggage without taking on the prejudices and biases of their care providers.

8. The right to have the role SI has played as a coping mechanism validated.

No one should be shamed, admonished, or chastised for having self-injured. Self-injury works as a coping mechanism, sometimes for people who have no other way to cope. They may use SI as a last-ditch effort to avoid suicide. The self-injurer should be taught to honor the positive things that self-injury has done for him/her as well as to recognize that the negatives of SI far outweigh those positives and that it is possible to learn methods of coping that aren't as destructive and life-interfering.

9. The right not to be automatically considered a dangerous person simply because of self-inflicted injury.

No one should be put in restraints or locked in a treatment room in an emergency room solely because his or her injuries are self-inflicted. No one should ever be involuntarily committed simply because of SI; physicians should make the decision to commit based on the presence of psychosis, suicidality, or homicidality.

10. The right to have self-injury regarded as an attempt to communicate, not manipulate.

Most people who hurt themselves are trying to express things they can say in no other way. Although sometimes these attempts to communicate seem manipulative, treating them as manipulation only makes the situation worse. Providers should respect the communicative function of SI and assume it is not manipulative behavior until there is clear evidence to the contrary.

Recommended Further Reading

BOOKS FROM THE POPULAR PRESS

Alderman, T. (1997). *The scarred soul: Understanding and ending self-inflicted violence.* Oakland, CA: New Harbinger Publications, Inc.

Conterio, K., & Lader, W. (1998). *Bodily harm: The breakthrough healing program for self-injurers.* New York: Hyperion.

Levenkron, S. (1998). *Cutting: Understanding and overcoming self-mutilation.* New York: Norton.

Smith, G., Cox, D., & Saradjian, J. (1999). *Women and self-harm: Understanding, coping, and healing from self-mutilation.* New York: Routledge.

Strong, M. (1998). *A bright red scream: Self-mutilation and the language of pain.* New York: Penguin Books.

BOOKS FOR CLINICIANS

Bateman, A., & Fonagy, P. (2004). *Psychotherapy for borderline personality disorder: Mentalization-based treatment.* London: Oxford University Press.

Connors, R. E. (2000). *Self-injury: Psychotherapy with people who engage in self-inflicted violence.* Northvale, NJ: Jason Aronson.

Farber, S. K. (2000). *When the body is the target: Self-harm, pain, and traumatic attachments.* Northvale, NJ: Jason Aronson.

Favazza, A. R. (1996). *Bodies under siege: Self-mutilation in culture and psychiatry* (2nd ed.). Baltimore: Johns Hopkins University Press.

Gabbard, G. O., & Wilkinson, S. M. (2000). *Management of countertransference with borderline patients.* Northvale, NJ: Jason Aronson.

Linehan, M. M. (1993a). *Cognitive-behavioral treatment of borderline personality disorder.* New York: Guilford.

Linehan, M. M. (1993b). *Skills training manual for treating borderline personality disorder.* New York: Guilford.

Walsh, B. (2006). *Treating self-injury: A practical guide.* New York: Guilford.

APPENDIX III

Internet Resources

The Internet is replete with information regarding self-injury. A simple search will yield thousands of Web pages on the topic. Some sites were developed and are maintained by mental health professionals and organizations, and others are not. The information one can find on the Internet can, therefore, be highly variable in accuracy and helpfulness. Some sites are, in fact, graphic and contain material that is provocative and that can serve as a trigger for vulnerable individuals who may be wanting to stop their self-injury. The reader is, therefore, cautioned about the information obtained on the Web and encouraged to be diligent in verifying the reliability of self-injury-related sites and the information presented therein.

A starting point for conducting an Internet search on self-injury and its treatment can begin by visiting the following well-regarded sites:

1. American Self-Harm Information Clearinghouse
   www.selfinjury.org
2. S.A.F.E. Alternatives (Self-Abuse Finally Ends)
   www.selfinjury.com
3. SIARI: Self-Injury and Related Issues
   www.siari.co.uk

References

Adams, J., Rodham, K., & Gavin, J. (2005). Investigating the "self" in deliberate self-harm. *Qualitative Health Research, 15,* 1293–1309.

Adler, P. A., & Adler, P. (2005). Self-injurers as loners: The social organization of solitary deviance. *Deviant Behavior, 26,* 345–378.

Agassi, J. B. (Ed.) (1999). *Martin Buber on psychology and psychotherapy.* Syracuse, NY: Syracuse University Press.

Alderman, T. (1997). *The scarred soul: Understanding and ending self-inflicted violence.* Oakland, CA: New Harbinger Publications.

Alighieri, D. (1950). *The divine comedy* (Carlyle-Wicksteed, Trans.). New York: Random House.

American Academy of Pediatrics. (2004). School-based mental health services. *Pediatrics, 113,* 1839–1845.

American Psychiatric Association. (2000). *Diagnostic and statistical manual of mental disorders IV-TR.* Washington, DC: Author.

American School Counselor Association. (2003). The ASCA national model: A framework for school counselor programs. *Professional School Counseling, 6,* 165–169.

American School Counselor Association. (2004). The role of the professional school counselor. Retrieved January 2, 2006, from http://www.schoolcounselor.org/role.htm.

Andover, M. S., Pepper, C. M., Ryabchenko, K. A., Orrico, E. G., & Gibb., B. E. (2005). Self-mutilation and symptoms of depression, anxiety, and borderline personality disorder. *Suicide and Life-Threatening Behavior, 35,* 581–591.

Angyal, A. (1965). *Neurosis and treatment: A holistic theory.* New York: Wiley.

Austin, L., & Kortum, J. (2004). Self-injury: The secret language of pain for teenagers. *Education, 124,* 517–527.

Bateman, A., & Fonagy, P. (2004). *Psychotherapy for borderline personality disorder: Mentalization-based treatment.* London: Oxford University Press.

Beck, A. T., & Freeman, A. F. (1990). *Cognitive therapy of personality disorders.* New York: Guilford.

Berger, P. L., & Luckman, T. (1967). *The social construction of reality: A treatise on the sociology of knowledge.* New York: Anchor Books.

Berlin, I. (1981). *Karl Marx* (4th ed.). Oxford: Oxford University Press. (Original work published 1939)

Bion, W. (1998). *Attention and interpretaion.* Northvale, NJ: Jason Aronson.

Borders, L. D., & Drury, S. M. (1992). Comprehensive school counseling programs: A review for policymakers and practitioners. *Journal of Counseling and Development, 70,* 487–498.

Bowlby, J. (1969). *Attachment and loss. Vol. 1. Attachment.* New York: Basic Books.

Brasic, J. B., Barnett, J. Y., Ahn, S. C., Nadrich, R. H., Will, M. V., & Clair, A. (1997). Clinical assessment of self-injurious behavior. *Psychological Reports, 80,* 155–160.

Briere, J., & Spinazzola, J. (2005). Phenomenology and psychological assessment of complex posttraumatic states. *Journal of Traumatic Stress, 18,* 401–412.

Brown, M. Z., Comtois, K. A., & Linehan, M. M. (2002). Reasons for suicide attempts and nonsuicidal self-injury in women with borderline personality disorder. *Journal of Abnormal Psychology, 111,* 198–202.

Buber, M. (1955). *Between man and man.* Boston: Beacon Press. (Original work published 1947)

Buber, M. (1958). *I and Thou* (2nd ed.). New York: Charles Scribner's Sons.

Buber, M. (1999). Healing through meeting. In J. B. Agassi (Ed.), *Martin Buber on psychology and psychotherapy* (pp. 17–21). Syracuse, NY: Syracuse University Press.

Bugental, J. F. T. (1987). *The art of the psychotherapist.* New York: Norton.

Carroll, L., & Anderson, R. (2003). Body piercing, tattooing, self-esteem, and body investment in adolescent girls. *Adolescence, 37,* 627–637.

Cicchetti, D., & Toth, S. L. (2005). Child maltreatment. *Annual Review of Clinical Psychology, 1,* 409–438.

Claes, L., Vandereycken, W., & Vertommen, H. (2005). Self-care versus self-harm: Piercing, tattooing, and self-injury in eating disorders. *European Eating Disorders Review, 13,* 11–18.

Clarke, L., & Whittaker, M. (1998). Self-mutilation: Culture, context, and nursing responses. *Journal of Clinical Nursing, 7,* 129–137.

Clay, D. L., Hagglund, D. J., Kashani, J. H., & Frank, R. G. (1996). Sex differences in gender expression, depressed mood, and aggression in children and adolescents. *Journal of Clinical Psychology in Medical Settings, 3,* 79–92.

Combs, D., & Fox, M. (2004). *The way of conflict: Elemental wisdom for resolving disputes and transcending differences.* Novato, CA: New World Library.

Connors, R. E. (2000). *Self-injury: Psychotherapy with people who engage in self-inflicted violence.* Northvale, NJ: Jason Aronson.

Conte, S. A. (2004). Speaking for themselves: A qualitative study of young women who self-injure. *Dissertation Abstracts International Section A: Humanities and Social Sciences, 65*(01), 286A (UMI No. 3119926).

Conterio, K., & Lader, W. (1998). *Bodily harm: The breakthrough healing program for self-injurers.* New York: Hyperion.

Cook, A., Spinazzola, J., Ford, J., Lanktree, C., Blaustein, M., Cloitre, M., et al. (2005). Complex trauma in children and adolescents. *Psychiatric Annals, 35,* 390–398.

Corsini, R., & Wedding, D. (Eds.). (2005). *Current psychotherapies* (7th ed.). Pacific Grove, CA: Brooks/Cole.

Costin, C. (2004). Interventions and strategies for families and friends of the self-harming patient with an eating disorder. In J. L. Levitt, R. A. Sansone, & L. Cohn (Eds.), *Self-harm behavior and eating disorders: Dynamics, assessment, and treatment* (pp. 195–210). New York: Brunner-Routledge.

Crespi, T. D., & Hughes, T. L. (2003). School-based mental health services for adolescents: School psychology in contemporary society. *Journal of Applied School Psychology, 20,* 67–78.

Cushman, P. (1990). Why the self is empty: Toward a historically situated psychology. *American Psychologist, 45,* 599–611.

Davis, W. A. (1989). *Inwardness and existence.* Madison: University of Wisconsin Press.

Deiter, P. J., Nicholls, S. S., & Pearlman, L. A. (2000). Self-injury and self-capacities: Assisting an individual in crisis. *Journal of Clinical Psychology, 56,* 1173–1191.

DiLazzero, D. B. (2003). Addressing self-injury in the college environment: A psychoeducational program. *Dissertation Abstracts International: Section B, 64,* 1486 (UMI No. 3085513).

Dollarhide, C. T., & Saginak, K. A. (2003). *School counseling in the secondary school: A comprehensive process and program.* Boston: Allyn & Bacon.

Downing, J. (1991). Parents' tough beat and the school counselor. *School Counselor, 39,* 91–98.

Edwards, T. M. (1998, November 9). What the cutters feel. *Time, 152,* 93.

Farber, S. K. (2000). *When the body is the target: Self-harm, pain, and traumatic attachments.* Northvale, NJ: Jason Aronson.

Favaro, A., Ferrara, S., & Santonastoso, P. (2004). Impulsive and compulsive self-injurious behavior and eating disorders: An epidemiological study. In J. L. Levitt, R. A. Sansone, & L. Cohn (Eds.), *Self-harm behavior and eating disorders: Dynamics, assessment, and treatment* (pp. 31–43). New York: Brunner-Routledge.

Favazza, A. R. (1986). *Self-harm behavior survey.* Columbia, MI: Author.

Favazza, A. R. (1996) *Bodies under siege: Self-mutilation in culture and psychiatry* (2nd ed.). Baltimore: Johns Hopkins University Press.

Favazza, A. R. (1998). The coming of age of self-mutilation. *The Journal of Nervous and Mental Disease, 186,* 259–268.

Favazza, A. R., & Conterio, K. (1988). The plight of chronic self-mutilators. *Community Mental Health Journal, 24,* 22–30.

Favazza, A. R., & Conterio, K. (1989). Female habitual self-mutilators. *Acta Psychiatrica Scandinavica, 79,* 283–289.

Ferdinand, R. F., van der Ende, J., & Verhulst, F. C. (2004). Parent-adolescent disagreement regarding psychopathology in adolescents from the general population as a risk factor for adverse outcome. *Journal of Abnormal Psychology, 113,* 198–206.

Fonagy, P., Gergely, G., Jurist, E., & Target, M. (2002). *Affect regulation, mentalization, and the development of the self.* New York: Other Press.

Ford, J. D. (2005). Treatment implications of altered affect regulation and information processing following child maltreatment. *Psychiatric Annals, 35,* 410–419.

Frank, J., & Frank, J. (1991). *Persuasion and healing: A comparative study of psychotherapy* (3rd ed.). Baltimore: Johns Hopkins University Press.

Friedman, J. M. H., & Asnis, G. M. (1989). Assessment of suicidal behavior: A new instrument. *Psychiatric Annals, 19,* 382–387.

Froeschle, J., & Moyer, M. (2004). Just cut it out: Legal and ethical challenges in counseling students who self-mutilate. *Professional School Counseling, 7,* 231–235.

Gabbard, G. O. (1996). *Love and hate in the analytic setting.* Lanham, MD: Rowan & Littlefield.

Gabbard, G. O., & Lester, E. P. (1995). *Boundaries and boundary violations in psychoanalysis.* Washington, DC: American Psychiatric Publishing.

Gabbard, G. O., & Wilkinson, S. M. (1994). *The management of countertransference with borderline patients.* Northvale, NJ: Jason Aronson.

Gabbard, G. O., & Wilkinson, S. M. (2000). *Management of countertransference with borderline patients.* Northvale, NJ: Jason Aronson.

Gardner, F. (2001). *Self-harm: A psychotherapeutic approach.* East Sussex, England: Brunner-Routledge.

Giovagnoli, M. (1999). *Angels in the workplace.* San Francisco: Jossey-Bass.

Gratz, K. L. (2001). Measurement of deliberate self-harm: Preliminary data on the deliberate self-harm inventory. *Journal of Psychopathology and Behavioral Assessment, 23,* 253–263.

Gratz, K. L. (2006). Risk factors for deliberate self-harm among female college students: The role and interaction of childhood maltreatment, emotional inexpressivity, and affect intensity/reactivity. *American Journal of Orthopsychiatry, 76,* 238–250.

Grieger, I. (in press). A cultural assessment framework and interview protocol. In L. A. Suzuki, J. G. Ponterotto, & P. J. Meller (Eds.), *Handbook of multicultural assessment: Clinical, psychological, and educational applications* (3rd ed.). San Francisco: Jossey-Bass.

Grieger, I., & Ponterotto, J. G. (1995). A framework for assessment in multicultural counseling. In J. G. Ponterotto, J. M. Casas, L. A. Suzuki, & C. M. Alexander (Eds.), *Handbook of multicultural counseling* (pp. 357–374). Thousand Oaks, CA: Sage.

Grossman, R., & Siever, L. (2001). Impulsive self-injurious behaviors: Neurobiology and psychopharmacology. In D. Simeon and E. Hollander (Eds.), *Self-injurious behaviors: Assessment and treatment* (pp. 117–148). Washington, DC: American Psychiatric Publishing.

Guntrip, H. (1986). My experience of analysis with Fairbairn and Winnicott (how complete a result does psycho-analytic therapy achieve?). In P. Buckley (Ed.), *Essential papers on object relations* (pp. 447–468). New York: New York University Press.

Guralnik, O., & Simeon, D. (2001). Psychodynamic theory and treatment of impulsive self-injurious behavior. In D. Simeon and E. Hollander (Eds.), *Self-injurious behaviors: Assessment and treatment* (pp. 175–197). Washington, DC: American Psychiatric Publishing.

Hawton, K., Hall, S., Simkin, S., Bale, L., Bond, A., Codd, S., et al. (2003). Deliberate self-harm in adolescents: A study of characteristics and trends in Oxford, 1990–2000. *Journal of Child Psychology and Psychiatry, 44,* 1191–1198.

Hodgson, S. (2004). Cutting through the silence: A sociological construction of self-injury. *Sociological Inquiry, 74,* 162–179.

Huband, N., & Tantam, D. (2004). Repeated self-wounding: Women's recollection of pathways to cutting and the value of different interventions. *Psychology and Psychotherapy: Theory, Research, and Practive, 77,* 413–428.

Hund, A. R., & Espelage, D. L. (2005). Childhood sexual abuse, disordered eating, alexithymia, and general distress: A mediation model. *Journal of Counseling Psychology, 52,* 559–573.

Hycner, R. (1991). *Between person and person.* Highland, NY: Gestalt Journal Press.

Ivanoff, A., Linehan, M. M., & Brown, M. (2001). Dialectical behavior therapy for impulsive self-injurious behaviors. In D. Simeon and E. Hollander (Eds.), *Self-injurious behaviors: Assessment and treatment* (pp. 149–173). Washington, DC: American Psychiatric Publishing.

Jed Foundation. (2006). *Framework for developing institutional protocols for the acutely distressed or suicidal college student.* New York: Author.

Juzwin, K. R. (2004). An assessment tool for self-injury: The Self-Injury Self-Report Inventory. In J. L. Levitt, R. A. Sansone, & L. Cohn (Eds.), *Self-harm behavior and eating disorders: Dynamics, assessment, and treatment* (pp. 105–118). New York: Brunner-Routledge.

Kalb, C., & Springen, K. (1998, November 9). An armful of agony. *Newsweek, 132,* 82.

Kegan, R. (1982). *The evolving self: Problem and process in human development.* Cambridge, MA: Harvard University Press.

Kelley, K., Byrne, D., Przybyla, D. P. J., Eberly, C. C., Eberly, B. W., Greendlinger, V., et al. (1985). Chronic self-destructiveness: Conceptualization, measurement, and initial validation of the construct. *Motivation and Emotion, 9,* 135–151.

Kettlewell, C. (1999). *The skin game.* New York: St. Martin's Press.

Khulsa, D. S., & Stauth, C. (1999). *The pain cure.* New York: Warner Books.

Kihlstrom, J. F. (2005). Dissociative disorders. *Annual Review of Clinical Psychology, 1,* 227–253.

Kinniburgh, K. J., Blaustein, M., Spinazzola, J., & van der Kolk, B. A. (2005). Attachment, self-regulation, and competency: A comprehensive intervention framework for children with complex trauma. *Psychiatric Annals, 35,* 424–430.

Koening, L. M., & Carnes, M. (1999). Body piercing: Medical concerns with cutting-edge fashion. *Journal of General Internal Medicine, 14,* 379–385.

Kuhn, T. (1970). *The structure of scientific revolutions* (2nd ed.). Chicago: University of Chicago Press.

Laing, R. D. (1967). *The politics of experience.* New York: Pantheon Books.

Laing, R. D. (1969). *Self and others.* New York: Pantheon Books.

Lambert, M. J., & Ogles, B. M. (2004). The efficacy and effectiveness of psychotherapy. In M. J. Lambert (Ed.), *Bergin and Garfield's handbook of psychotherapy and behavior change* (pp. 139–193). New York: Wiley.

Landis, C. (2004). *Harvest*. New York: St. Martin's Press.

Lehnert, K. L., Overholser, J. C., & Spirito, A. (1994). Internalized and externalized anger in adolescent suicide attempters. *Journal of Adolescent Research, 9*, 105–119.

Levenkron, S. (1998). *Cutting: Understanding and overcoming self-mutilation*. New York: Norton.

Levitt, J. L. (2004). A self-regulatory approach to the treatment of eating disorders and self-injury. In J. L. Levitt, R. A. Sansone, & L. Cohn (Eds.), *Self-harm behavior and eating disorders: Dynamics, assessment, and treatment* (pp. 211–228). New York: Brunner-Routledge.

Levitt, J. L., Sansone, R. A., & Cohn, L. (Eds.) (2004). *Self-harm behavior and eating disorders: Dynamics, assessment, and treatment*. New York: Brunner-Routledge.

Linehan, M. M. (1993a). *Cognitive-behavioral treatment of borderline personality disorder*. New York: Guilford.

Linehan, M. M. (1993b). *Skills training manual for treating borderline personality disorder*. New York: Guilford.

May, R. (1958). Contributions of existential psychotherapy. In R. May, E. Angel, & H. F. Ellenberger (Eds.), *Existence: A new dimension in psychology and psychiatry* (pp. 37–91). New York: Simon and Schuster.

McAllister, M. (2003). Multiple meanings of self-harm: A critical review. *International Journal of Mental Health Nursing, 12*, 177–185.

McAllister, M., Creedy, D., Moyle, W., & Ferrugia, C. (2002). Nurses' attitudes towards clients who self-harm. *Journal of Advanced Nursing, 40*, 578–586.

McAndrews, S., & Warne, T. (2005). Cutting across boundaries: A case study using feminist praxis to understand the meanings of self-harm. *International Journal of Mental Health Nursing, 14*, 172–180.

McCabe, E. B., & Marcus, M. D. (2004). Dialectical behavior therapy strategies in the management of self-harm behavior in patients with eating disorders. In J. L. Levitt, R. A. Sansone, & L. Cohn (Eds.), *Self-harm behavior and eating disorders: Dynamics, assessment, and treatment* (pp. 147–162). New York: Brunner-Routledge.

McGuire, V., & Duff, C. S. (2005). *Conversations about being a teacher*. Thousand Oaks, CA: Sage.

McWilliams, N. (1999). *Psychoanalytic case formulation*. New York: Guilford Press.

Menninger, K. (1938). *Man against himself*. New York: Harcourt Brace World.

Miller, A. (1980). *For your own good: Hidden cruelty in child-rearing and the roots of violence* (Trans. from the German by Hildegarde & Hunter, 1983). New York: Farrar, Straus, & Giroux.

Miller, A. (2005). *The body never lies: The lingering effects of cruel parenting*. New York: Norton.

Millon, T. (1996). *Disorders of personality: DSM-IV and beyond*. New York: Wiley.

Muehlenkamp, J. J. (2005). Self-injurious behavior as a separate clinical syndrome. *American Journal of Orthopsychiatry, 75*, 324–333.

Muehlenkamp, J. J., & Gutierrez, P. M. (2004). An investigation of differences between self-injurious behavior and suicide attempts in a sample of adolescents. *Suicide and Life-Threatening Behavior, 34*, 12–23.

Nasser, M. (2004). Dying to live: Eating disorders and self-harm behaviors in cultural context. In J. L. Levitt, R. A. Sansone, & L. Cohn (Eds.), *Self-harm behavior and eating disorders: Dynamics, assessment, and treatment* (pp. 15–27). New York: Brunner-Routledge.

Nevious, C. W. (2005, April 19). Epidemic that cuts to the bone. *San Francisco Chronicle,* B1.

Nietzsche, F. (1974). *The gay science* (Trans. W. Kaufman). New York: Vintage Books.

Nock, M. K., & Prinstein, M. J. (2004). A functional approach to the assessment of self-mutilative behavior. *Journal of Consulting and Clinical Psychology, 72,* 885–890.

Nock, M. K., & Prinstein, M. J. (2005). Contextual features and behavioral functions of self-mutilation among adolescents. *Journal of Abnormal Psychology, 114,* 140–146.

Onacki, M. (2005). Kids who cut: A protocol for public schools. *Journal of School Health, 75,* 400–401.

Orlinsky, D. E., Ronnestad, M. H., & Willutzki, U. (2004). Fifty years of psychotherapy process-outcome research: Continuity and change. In M. J. Lambert (Ed.), *Bergin and Garfield's handbook of psychotherapy and behavior change* (pp. 307–390). New York: Wiley.

Osuch, E. A., Noll, J. G., & Putnam, F. W. (1999). The motivations for self-injury in psychiatric inpatients. *Psychiatry, 62,* 334–346.

Paivio, S. C., & McCulloch, C. R. (2004). Alexithymia as a mediator between childhood trauma and self-injurious behaviors. *Child Abuse and Neglect, 28,* 339–354.

Paniagua, F. A. (1998). *Assessing and treating culturally diverse clients: A practical guide* (2nd ed.). Thousand Oaks, CA: Sage.

Paniagua, F. A. (2001). *Diagnosis in a multicultural context: A casebook for mental health professionals.* Thousand Oaks, CA: Sage.

Pao, P. (1969). The syndrome of delicate self-cutting. *British Journal of Medical Psychology, 42,* 195–206.

Paternite, C. E. (2005). School-based mental health programs and services: Overview and introduction to the special issue. *Journal of Abnormal Child Psychology, 33,* 657–663.

Pattison, E. M., & Kahan, J. (1983). The deliberate self-harm syndrome. *American Journal of Psychiatry, 140,* 867–872.

Piran, N., & Cormier, H. C. (2005). The social construction of women and disordered eating patterns. *Journal of Counseling Psychology, 52,* 549–558.

Pumariega, A. J., & Vance, H. R. (1999). School-based mental health services: The foundation of systems of care for children's mental health. *Psychology in the Schools, 36,* 371–378.

Rayner, G. A., Allen, S. L., & Johnson, M. (2005). Countertransference and self-injury: A cognitive behavioural cycle. *Journal of Advanced Nursing, 50,* 12–19.

Rayner, G., & Warner, S. (2003). Self-harming behavior: From lay perceptions to clinical practice. *Counselling Psychology Quarterly, 16,* 305–329.

Roberts-Dobie, S. (2005). Self-injury in the schools: School counselors' perspectives. *Dissertation Abstracts International, 65(7-B),* 3416 (UMI No. 3138482).

Rogers, C. R. (1961). *On becoming a person.* Boston: Houghton Mifflin.

Ross, S., & Heath, N. (2002). A study of the frequency of self-mutilation in a community sample of adolescents. *Journal of Youth and Adolescence, 1,* 67–77.

Rossotto, E. (1997). Bulimia nervosa with and without substance use disorders: A comparative study. *Dissertation Abstracts International: Section B, 58,* 4469.

Sansone, R. A., & Levitt, J. L. (2002). Self-harm behaviors among those with eating disorders: An overview. *Eating Disorders, 10,* 205–213.

Sansone, R. A., & Levitt, J. L. (2004). The prevalence of self-harm behavior in those with eating disorders. In J. L. Levitt, R. A. Sansone, & L. Cohn (Eds.), *Self-harm behavior and eating disorders: Dynamics, assessment, and treatment* (pp. 3–14). New York: Brunner-Routledge.

Sansone, R. A., Levitt, J. L., & Sansone, L. A. (2004a). An overview of psychotherapy strategies for the management of self-harm behavior. In J. L. Levitt, R. A. Sansone, & L. Cohn (Eds.), *Self-harm behavior and eating disorders: Dynamics, assessment, and treatment* (pp. 121–134). New York: Brunner-Routledge.

Sansone, R. A., Levitt, J. L., & Sansone, L. A. (2004b). Psychotropic medications, self-harm behavior, and eating disorders. In J. L. Levitt, R. A. Sansone, & L. Cohn (Eds.), *Self-harm behavior and eating disorders: Dynamics, assessment, and treatment* (pp. 245–258). New York: Brunner-Routledge.

Sansone, R. A., & Sansone, L. A. (2004). Assessment tools: Eating disorder symptoms and self-harm behavior. In J. L. Levitt, R. A. Sansone, & L. Cohn (Eds.), *Self-harm behavior and eating disorders: Dynamics, assessment, and treatment* (pp. 93–104). New York: Brunner-Routledge.

Sansone, R. A., Wiederman, M. W., & Sansone, L. A. (1998). The Self-Harm Inventory: Development of a scale for identifying self-destructive behaviors and borderline personality disorder. *Journal of Clinical Psychology, 54,* 973–983.

Saxe, G. N., Chawla, N., & van der Kolk, B. (2002). Self-destructive behavior in patients with dissociative disorders. *Suicide and Life-Threatening Behavior, 32,* 313–320.

Saxe, G. N., Ellis, B. H., Folger, J., Hansen, S., & Sorkin, B. (2005). Comprehensive care for traumatized children. *Psychiatric Annals, 35,* 443–448.

Schore, A. N. (1994). *Affect regulation and the origin of the self: The neurobiology of emotional development.* Hillsdale, NJ: Erlbaum.

Schore, A. N. (2003a). *Affect dysregulation and disorders of the self.* New York: Norton.

Schore, A. N. (2003b). *Affect regulation and the repair of the self.* New York: Norton.

Schroeder, S. R., Rojahn, J., & Reese, R. M. (1997). Brief report: Reliability and validity of instruments for assessing psychotropic medication effects on self-injurious behavior in mental retardation. *Journal of Autism and Developmental Disorders, 27,* 89–103.

Searles, H. F. (1979). *Countertransference and related subjects.* Madison, CT: International Universities Press.

Selekman, M. D. (2006). *Working with self-harming adolescents: A collaborative strengths-based therapy approach.* New York: Norton.

Shapiro, D. (1999). *Psychotherapy of neurotic character.* New York: Basic Books.

Shepperd, C., & McAllister, M. (2003). CARE: A framework for responding thera-peutically to the client who self-harms. *Journal of Psychiatric and Mental Health Nursing, 10,* 442–447.

Simeon, D., & Favazza, A. R. (2001). Self-injurious behaviors: Phenomenology and assessment. In D. Simeon & E. Hollander (Eds.), *Self-injurious behaviors: Assessment and treatment* (pp. 1–28). Washington, DC: American Psychiatric Publishing.

Simpson, E., Zlotnik, C., Begin, A., Costello, E., & Pearlstein, T. (1994). *Self-injury survey.* Providence, RI: Author.

Skegg, K. (2005). Self-harm. *Lancet, 366,* 1471–1483.

Smetana, J. G., Campione-Barr, N., & Metzger, A. (2006). Adolescent development in interpersonal and social contexts. *Annual Review of Psychology, 57,* 255–284.

Smith, G., Cox, D., & Saradjian, J. (1999). *Women and self-harm: Understanding, coping, and healing from self-mutilation.* New York: Routledge.

Spinazzola, J., Ford, J. D., Zucker, M., van der Kolk, B. A., Silva, S., Smith, S. F., et al. (2005). Survey evaluates complex trauma exposure, outcome, and intervention among children and adolescents. *Psychiatric Annals, 35,* 433–439.

Stone, J. A., & Sias, S. M. (2003). Self-injurious behavior: A bi-modal treatment approach to working with adolescent females. *Journal of Mental Health Counseling, 25,* 112–125.

Straker, G., Watson, D., & Robinson, T. (2002). Trauma and disconnection: A trans-theoretical approach. *International Journal of Psychotherapy, 7,* 145–158.

Strong, M. (1998). *A bright red scream: Self-mutilation and the language of pain.* New York: Penguin Books.

Sue, D. W., & Sue, D. (2003). *Counseling the culturally diverse: Theory, research, and practice* (4th ed.). New York: Wiley.

Suyemoto, K. L. (1998). The functions of self-mutilation. *Clinical Psychology Review, 18,* 531–554.

Thoreau, H. D. (1906). *The writings of Henry David Thoreau* (Vol. 3). Boston: Houghton Mifflin.

Tillich, P. (1960). *Love, power, and justice.* London: Oxford University Press.

Turner, V. J. (2002). *Secret scars: Uncovering and understanding the addiction of self-injury.* Center City, MN: Hazeldon.

Turp, M. (2003). *Hidden self-harm: Narratives from psychotherapy.* London: Jessica Kingsley.

van der Kolk, B. (2003). The neurobiology of childhood trauma and abuse. *Child and Adolescent Psychiatric Clinics, 12,* 293–317.

van der Kolk, B. (2005). Developmental trauma disorder: Toward a rational diagnosis for children with complex trauma histories. *Psychiatric Annals, 35,* 401–408.

van der Kolk, B., Hostetler, A., Herron, N., & Fisler, R. E. (1994). Trauma and the development of borderline personality disorder. *Psychiatric Clinics of North America, 17,* 715–729.

van der Kolk, B., Perry, C., & Herman, J. (1991). Childhood origin of self-destructive behavior. *American Journal of Psychiatry, 148,* 1665–1671.

van der Kolk, B. A., Roth, S., Pelcovitz, D., Sunday, S., & Spinazzola, J. (2005). Disorders of extreme stress: The empirical foundation of complex trauma adaptation. *Journal of Traumatic Stress, 18,* 389–399.

Vanderlinden, J., & Vandereycken, W. (1997). *Trauma, dissociation, and impulse dyscontrol in eating disorders.* Philadelphia: Brunner/Mazel.

Walsh, B. (2006). *Treating self-injury: A practical guide.* New York: Guilford.

Walsh, B., & Rosen, P. (1988). *Self-mutilation: Theory, research and treatment.* New York: Guilford.

Warm, A., Murray, C., & Fox, J. (2003). Why do people self-harm? *Psychology, Health & Medicine, 8,* 71–79.

Weil, S. (2001). *Waiting for God.* New York: Perennial Classics. (Original work published 1951)

Weist, M. D., Ambrose, M. G., & Lewis, C. P. (2006). Expanded school mental health: A collaborative community–school example. *Children and Schools, 28,* 45–50.

Whitlock, J., Eckenrode, J., & Silverman, D. (2006). Self-injurious behavior in a college population. *Pediatrics, 117,* 1939–1948.

Whitlock, J., Powers, J., & Eckenrode, J. (2006). The virtual cutting edge: The internet and adolescent self-injury. *Developmental Psychology, 42,* 407–417.

Wolf, N. (2002). *The beauty myth.* New York: Harper Perennial.

Yates, T. M. (2004). The developmental psychopathology of self-injurious behavior: Compensatory regulation in posttraumatic adaptation. *Clinical Psychology Review, 24,* 35–74.

Young, J. E. (1999). *Cognitive therapy for personality disorders: A schema-focused approach* (3rd ed.). Sarasota, FL: Professional Resource Press.

Index

SPRINGER PUBLISHING COMPANY

Using Superheroes in Counseling and Play Therapy

Lawrence Rubin, PhD, RPT-S, Editor

"There is something democratic about a therapy that can respond empathically to the experiences that patients enjoy and feel that they understand emotionally."
—From the Foreword by **John Shelton Lawrence,** PhD
Morningside College, Emeritus

With an incisive historical foreword by John Shelton Lawrence and insight from contributors such as Michael Brody, Patty Scanlon, and Roger Kaufman, Lawrence Rubin takes us on a dynamic tour of the benefits of using these icons of popular culture and fantasy in counseling and play therapy. Not only can superheroes assist in clinical work with children, but Rubin demonstrates how they can facilitate growth and change with teens and adults. Early childhood memories of how we felt pretending to have the power to save the world or our families in the face of impending danger still resonate in our adult lives, making the use of superheroes attractive as well, to the creative counselor.

In presenting case studies and wisdom gleaned from practicing therapists' experience, the book shows how it is possible to uncover children's secret identities, assist treatment of adolescents with sexual behavior problems, and inspire the journey of individuation for gay and lesbian clients, all by paying attention to our intrinsic social need for superhero fantasy and play.

List of Contributors:

Leya Barrett	Harry Livesay	Karen Robertie
Michael Brody	William McNulty	Lawrence C. Rubin
Jan Burte	Cory A. Nelson	Jennifer Mendoza Sayers
George Enfield	Jeff Pickens	Patty Scanlon
Roger Kaufman	Robert Poole	Ryan Weidenbenner
John Shelton Lawrence	Robert. J. Porter	Carmela Wenger

2006 · 384pp · 978-0-8261-0269-0 · hardcover

11 West 42nd Street, New York, NY 10036-8002 • **Fax: 212-941-7842**
Order Toll-Free: 877-687-7476 • **Order Online: www.springerpub.com**

Conduct Disorders

A Practitioner's Guide to Comparative Treatments

W. M. Nelson III, PhD, ABPP
A. J. Finch, Jr., PhD, ABPP
K. J. Hart, PhD, ABPP, Editors

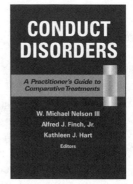

"In a word, Conduct Disorders *delivers. That is, it sets out to permit practicing clinicians from different theoretical orientations to describe what works best for conduct-disordered youth...organized and informative...an impressive collection of clinically informed and research knowledge that educates the graduate student and satisfies the experienced clinician."*

—Philip C. Kendall, PhD, ABPP
Professor, Director of Child and Adolescent Anxiety Disorders Clinic
Temple University

With a focus on the main population for which conduct disorder is a problem—children and adolescents—this book not only looks at the history of diagnosis in this population, but uses one case study to investigate several up-to-date treatments used by practicing clinicians from different theoretical orientations. A discussion of what these clinicians believe are the best treatments for this population is included.

Partial Contents:

The Case of "Michael" • The Psychoanalytic Approach to the Treatment of Conduct Disorder • Family Therapy • Cognitive-Developmental Treatment of Conduct Disorder • Behavioral Treatment for Youth with Conduct Disorder • Cognitive-Behavioral Psychotherapy for Conduct Disorder • Multisystemic Therapy in the Treatment of Adolescent Conduct Disorder • The Continuum of Residential Treatment Care for Conduct Disordered Youth • Pharmacologic Considerations in the Treatment of Conduct Disorder

2006 · 400pp · 978-0-8261-5615-0 · hard

11 West 42nd Street, New York, NY 10036-8002 • **Fax: 212-941-7842**
Order Toll-Free: 877-687-7476 • **Order Online: www.springerpub.com**